'By drawing on feminist IR work and critically engaging with notions of everyday peace, Helen Berents convincingly argues for widening our understandings of political engagement and questions narratives that situate young people as inevitably 'problems' rather than agential actors facing problems of conflict and violence alongside the wider community. This careful, ethnographically informed research offers rich, engaging details of the lived experiences of young people in the Colombian conflict and highlights how youth have navigated insecurity while demonstrating resilience and resistance.'

Lesley Pruitt, Monash University, Australia and author of *Youth Peacebuilding: Music, Gender & Change*

'Empirically rich and conceptually sophisticated, Helen Berents' latest contribution on young people's thoughtful and creative navigations of insecurity develops important insights into peacebuilding in the midst of conflict and violence. More broadly, it is exemplary not only of what can be brought to light by taking children and youth seriously as agents of change but also how to sustain affirmation of both their agency and relative powerlessness in ways that hold them productively in tension.'

J. Marshall Beier, Professor of Political Science, McMaster University

'*Young People and Everyday Peace* is a groundbreaking contribution to (re)populating IR that integrates ethnographic fieldwork with a focus on the meanings of peace constructed by people in their everyday lives. Berents listens carefully to the perspectives of young people on the margins of a complexly violent society. Drawing on feminist and embodiment theories, she centers young people's experience, knowledge, and aspirations, showing how they imagine and forge an "embodied-everyday-peace-amidst-violence." Berents' book is a must-read for anyone interested in how peacebuilding can be more genuinely inclusive, locally responsive, just and realistic. This book comes at just the right time for scholars and practitioners concerned about Colombia's peace process.'

Siobhan McEvoy-Levy, Professor, Butler University

Young People and Everyday Peace

Young People and Everyday Peace is grounded in the stories of young people who live in los Altos de Cazucá, an informal peri-urban community in Soacha, to the south of Colombia's capital Bogotá. The occupants of this community have fled the armed conflict and exist in a state of marginalisation and social exclusion amongst ongoing violences conducted by armed gangs and government forces. Young people negotiate these complexities and offer pointed critiques of national politics as well as grounded aspirations for the future. Colombia's protracted conflict and its effects on the population raise many questions about how we think about peacebuilding in and with communities of conflict-affected people.

Building on contemporary debates in international relations about post-liberal, everyday peace, Helen Berents draws on feminist international relations and embodiment theory to pay meaningful attention to those on the margins. She conceptualises a notion of embodied-everyday-peace-amidst-violence to recognise the presence and voice of young people as stakeholders in everyday efforts to respond to violence and insecurity. In doing so, Berents argues for and engages a more complex understanding of the everyday, stemming from the embodied experiences of those centrally present in conflicts. Taking young people's lives and narratives seriously recognises the difficulties of protracted conflict, but finds potential to build a notion of an embodied everyday amidst violence, where a complex and fraught peace can be found.

Young People and Everyday Peace will be of interest to scholars of Latin American studies, international relations, and peace and conflict studies.

Helen Berents is a lecturer in the School of Justice at Queensland University of Technology, Australia. Helen's research is centrally concerned with representations of youth in political events and engagement with the lived experiences of violence-affected young people, with a particular focus on Latin America. More broadly, she is interested in questions of how people are rendered insecure by institutions of authority and power, how young people are politicised but not seen as political, and how feminist methodologies open space to find 'the everyday' within these explorations. Her work has been published in journals including *International Feminist Journal of Politics*, *Peacebuilding*, *Critical Studies on Security*, and *Signs*.

Routledge Studies in Latin American Politics

14. Revolutionary Violence and the New Left
Transnational Perspectives
Edited by Alberto Martín Álvarez and Eduardo Rey Tristán

15. Business-State Relations in Brazil
Challenges of the Port Reform Lobby
Mahrukh Doctor

16. The Politics of Capitalist Transformation
Brazilian Informatics Policy, Regime Change, and State Autonomy
Jeff Seward

17. Negotiating Trade Liberalization in Argentina and Chile
When Policy creates Politics
Andrea C. Bianculli

18. Understanding Cuba as a Nation
From European Settlement to Global Revolutionary Mission
Rafael E. Tarragó

19. Challenging the U.S.-Led War on Drugs
Argentina in Comparative Perspective
Sebastián Antonino Cutrona

20. Manipulating Courts in New Democracies
Forcing Judges off the Bench in Argentina
Andrea Castagnola

21. Crime, Violence and Security in the Caribbean
M. Raymond Izarali

22. Young People and Everyday Peace
Exclusion, Insecurity, and Peacebuilding in Colombia
Helen Berents

For more information about this series, please visit:
https://www.routledge.com/Routledge-Studies-in-Latin-American-Politics/book-series/RSLAP

Young People and Everyday Peace

Exclusion, Insecurity, and Peacebuilding in Colombia

Helen Berents

NEW YORK AND LONDON

First published 2018
by Routledge
711 Third Avenue, New York, NY 10017

and by Routledge
2 Park Square, Milton Park, Abingdon, Oxon OX14 4RN

Routledge is an imprint of the Taylor & Francis Group, an informa business

© 2018 Taylor & Francis

The right of Helen Berents to be identified as author of this work has been asserted by her in accordance with sections 77 and 78 of the Copyright, Designs and Patents Act 1988.

All rights reserved. No part of this book may be reprinted or reproduced or utilised in any form or by any electronic, mechanical, or other means, now known or hereafter invented, including photocopying and recording, or in any information storage or retrieval system, without permission in writing from the publishers.

Trademark notice: Product or corporate names may be trademarks or registered trademarks, and are used only for identification and explanation without intent to infringe.

Library of Congress Cataloging in Publication Data
A catalog record for this title has been requested

ISBN: 978-1-138-55662-1 (hbk)
ISBN: 978-1-315-15021-5 (ebk)

Typeset in Times New Roman
by Taylor & Francis Books

Contents

List of figures		viii
Acknowledgements		ix
List of Abbreviations		xii
	Introduction	1
1	Embodied, Everyday Peace Amidst Violence	25
2	Half a Century of Struggles for Peace	48
3	Space, Power, and Terrains of Insecurity	80
4	Embodied Everyday Violences	104
5	Resilience and Resistance	128
6	Notions of Everyday Peace	149
	Conclusion	170
	Index	180

List of figures

2.1	Two views from the school *Minutos de Dios* over the community.	66
2.2		66
3.1	Aftermath of landslide.	81
5.1	The human rights forum at *Instituto Educativo Gabriel Garcia Marquez*.	129

Acknowledgements

Writing acknowledgements always reveals the absolute necessity and privilege of the connections of academic endeavour, and I am humbled by and grateful for the time and energy that so many people have contributed to this book. First and foremost, I owe an enormous debt of gratitude to the brilliant and inspiring young people of the community of los Altos de Cazucá. Your generosity in sharing your stories profoundly shaped this book, and I am so very thankful for your trust in me. It is a privilege to be have been welcomed into your lives and community, and I hope I have done justice to your stories here. I dream with you of a Colombia at peace, with opportunities and justice for everyone.

Also in Colombia, my thanks to all those working with Fundación Pies Descalzos. In los Altos de Cazucá, to the wonderful Ana Milena Martinez Gustin, Monica Portes, and Lola Velasquez, who assisted in myriad ways while working tirelessly on improving life for young people in the community, I give my sincere thanks. I am grateful also to Fundación Pies Descalzos's executive director, Patricia Sierra, for her generous time, as well as Fabian Mauricio Gerena, Andrea Torres, and all those in the *fundación*'s head office who assisted with my work in 2010 and 2016. I also truly appreciate the teachers at Instituto Educativo Gabriel Garcia Marquez and its connected site at Colegio Minutos de Dios. I am in awe of the work they do each day, and I am very grateful for their insights as well as their support of me in pursuing my research. I am deeply thankful to the many members of the community who, over months, welcomed me into their homes and lives and tolerated my presence and many questions. Conversations offered generously amongst the busyness of your everyday lives influenced my thinking on exclusion, insecurity, and peace enormously by allowing some insight into your experiences and beliefs. Thanks to the Departamento de Ciencias Politicas at the Universidad de los Andes for welcoming me as a visiting researcher during my time in Bogotá. Thanks also to Natalia Martinez Pardo at Fundación Restrepo Barco, Maria Tila Uribe and the team at CESTRA, and Andrea Cardona at Fundación Batuta for their assistance and contributions, in addition to all those from various NGOs and government offices I had informal conversations with during my time in the country. Mil gracias a mi 'familia

x   *Acknowledgements*

colombiana', Erika and Laura and their extended family who welcomed me and gave me a home-away-from-home. My time in Colombia was brightened enormously by the friendship and companionship of Sarah Todnem – ¡gracias chica! Thanks also to the many other friends that I made in Colombia for many adventures, including but definitely not limited to Maria Elena, Jorge, Dan, Irina, Gloria, Juan Manuel, Angelina, and Valeria.

This book started as my dissertation, and I want to recognise the invaluable guidance and support of my supervisor, Diane Zetlin, who encouraged and motivated me through the dissertation process and sharpened my analytical lens at every opportunity. I am lucky to have found community in many places during the development of this project, colleagues and friends who have enriched my intellectual experiences and generously provided their time and enormous brains on many occasions. I want to acknowledge the community of researchers of childhoods and youth from around the world whom I met at the 'Multiple Childhoods/Multidisciplinary Perspectives' Conference at Rutgers University in 2010. This community reminded me at a time I needed reminding of the validity and importance of studying and working with young people – thank you for your continuing engaging scholarship on children and youth that enhances my thinking all these years later. I am grateful to the witty and wise women of the University of Queensland POLSIS Postgraduate Feminist Reading Group who have provided encouragement, solidarity, and laughs, as well as a space to more critically interrogate the theories and ideas that came to inform this work in large and small ways: Constance Duncombe, Ellyse Fenton, Alissa Macoun, Danielle Miller, Lucie Newsome, Angela Setterlund, Rebecca Shaw, Elizabeth Strakosch, Erin O'Brien, and Lesley Pruitt. My thanks to the 'Northcote School' writing group during my time in Melbourne for valuable feedback at critical junctures: Mark Chou, David Duriesmith, Jean-Paul Gagnon, Sara Meger, Avery Poole, and Lesley Pruitt. The fortnightly writing group I have been a part of since joining the Faculty of Law at Queensland University of Technology in 2015 has helped get several chapters here over the line with much appreciated helpful insights: Cassandra Cross, Bridget Lewis, Fiona McDonald, and Carmel O'Sullivan. I am also grateful to all those who – as attendees, panellists, and discussants at various conferences over the years, or as anonymous reviewers of earlier work and this manuscript – have provided constructive feedback that has strengthened the arguments and ideas in this work.

In addition to those previously named, many thanks to those who read and provided valuable advice and critique for parts or all of this project at various stages: Ben Abraham, Timothy Aistrope, Leah Aylward, Matthew Ball, Naomi Barnbaum, Marshall Beier, Julie Berents, Roland Bleiker, Nicholas Casey, Angela Daly, Jess Gifkins, Jo Hatcher, Emma Hutchinson, Brendan Keogh, Roxani Krystalli, Kate Lee-Koo, Judith Merryweather, Siobhan McEvoy-Levy, Kelly Nightingale, Alexandra Phelan, Rebecca Shaw, Charlotte ten Have, Jessica West, Sophie Yates and any other excellent people I have no doubt missed here.

Acknowledgements xi

Initial fieldwork for this project was funded through the University of Queensland's School of Political Science and International Studies Research Funding. Fieldwork in 2016 was supported via a Queensland University of Technology Early Career Academic Recruitment and Development Grant. I am grateful for the opportunities provided by this funding. Small sections of Chapter One appeared in the journal *Peacebuilding* (3, no. 2: 115–125, 2015). My thanks to Taylor & Francis for permission to reprint these sections. I am also grateful for the willingness of Natalja Mortensen and Maria Landschoot at Routledge to answer the many questions I had during the publication process and for their keen eyes on my work.

I am deeply grateful for Naomi Barnbaum, Rebecca Shaw, and Jessica West, who have in all ways exceeded what might be expected of friendship, each offering endless encouragement, wisdom, and cake and wine when required. I cannot measure my gratitude for your friendships.

Last but not least, my thanks to my family, who have been a constant source of support, and who have weathered my absences and absentminded-ness at various stages of this work with tolerance and understanding. My sister, Alice, constantly inspires me with her intelligence, enthusiasm and determination; I remain her biggest fan. My parents, Julie and Harald, who decided when I was a child to take their young family to live in Latin Amer-ica, opened my eyes to the world and encouraged me to find my passion amongst all the possibilities; 'thank you' does not begin to encompass my appreciation. Finally, I don't have sufficient words for how grateful I am for the presence of my partner, Brendan Keogh, in my life. Without his constant love and his faith in my capacity, as well as his keen intelligence and will-ingness to read this work closely on multiple occasions, this book would genuinely be less in every way. This book is for him (and Harry).

List of Abbreviations

ACNUR/UNHCR	*El Alto Comisionado de las Naciones Unidas para los Refugiados*, United Nations High Commission for Refugees
AUC	*Autodefensas Unidas Colombianos*, Self Defence Forces Colombia
CESTRA-USIP	*Centro de Estudios e Investigaciones del Trabajo*, Center for Studies and Research of Work – United States Institute of Peace
ELN	*Ejército de Liberación Nacional*, National Liberation Army
FARC	*Fuerzas Armadas Revolucionarias de Colombia – Ejercito de Pueblo*, Revolutionary Armed Forces of Colombia
FDP	(the *fundación*) *Fundación Pies Descalzos*, Barefoot Foundation
HRW	Human Rights Watch
ICBF	*Instituto Colombiano de Bienestar Familiar*, Colombian Institute of Family Welfare
IDP	Internally Displaced Person/People
M-19	*Movimiento 19 de Abril*, 19th of April Movement
MSF	*Médecins Sans Frontiéres/Medicos Sin Fronteras*, Doctors Without Borders
Profamila	*Asociación Probienestar de la Familia Colombiana*, Association for Colombian Family Welfare (NGO)
RUV	*Registro Único de Víctimas*, The Victims Registry
UNCRC	United Nations Convention on the Rights of the Child (1989)

Introduction

> The most difficult thing about living here... is the insecurity... more than anything. Seriously. To be young.
> - Daniela, sixteen-year-old occupant of Los Altos de Cazucá[1]

The three students and I lean over the balcony that runs the length of the second story of the school. We are looking out up the hillside of the community of los Altos de Cazucá, part of the city of Soacha, just south of Bogotá's municipal border. The community here is predominantly made up of those who have been internally displaced by Colombia's half a century of conflict. The houses have been constructed with whatever materials are to hand; they are mostly 'illegal' in the eyes of the Soacha municipality, and cluster and stack precariously up the hill. As we watch the older men sitting on plastic chairs outside a tiny shop front just beyond the school's broken-glass-topped walls, seventeen-year-old Juliana says to our group that the community feels like a different place in the daytime. Her friends, fifteen-year-old Paola and seventeen-year-old Alejandro both nod. Last night there had been violence in the community; when I had arrived that morning a teacher told me it had been in-fighting among gang members. No one had been killed, but some houses had been damaged and these three students who lived near the street where it had happened had very little sleep.

This is the image of los Altos de Cazucá that those outside the community often see. On national television and in the newspapers, portrayals of this place are those of gang violence, late night semi-militarised police raids, young men standing in cuffs behind tables of drugs or guns with their heads bowed in brightly lit rooms for press conferences while uniformed men stand guard. The narratives of violence permeate and corrode stories of this community: it is a community of drug dealers, of gang members, of risk and violence to the broader city; people here are very poor and thus must be beggars or delinquents.

I am standing on the balcony with these three young people because we have been chatting for several weeks about their life in this community, how they understand the multiple forms of violence that impact their lives, and what they see for the future of their community and country. They've brought

2 Introduction

me up here to better explain their neighbourhood. Alejandro points to the soccer pitch, a dusty concrete expanse, and says it is a place his friends gather, a 'place for laughter'. Paola points to two different paths that zig-zag down the hill between houses and converge at the entrance to the school and explains how she sometimes takes one or the other depending on the 'news of the morning'; she's referring to the informal network of gossip and information sharing that everyone uses to avoid areas that are '*caliente*' ('hot', or risky). As we chat we watch two men trudge up the hill with buckets of soil and rocks and stop to tip them into an enormous deep rut in the dirt road up the hillside. Stomping it down with their boots, I'm relieved that my journey home will be slightly less of a rollercoaster in the small *buseta* (taxi bus) that jounces over these ruts made by torrential rain with nowhere else to go. Alejandro points the men out to me. We have been talking about the work the community does to sustain itself in the face of the absence of state support, and here is an example he says. Juliana tells me that when her mother isn't busy working she is part of a community committee that tries to get the municipal government to provide better services. Juliana has been to some meetings of the community committee and has told them that they need to include young people as well. Juliana has volunteered. The adults are considering it.

This is the los Altos de Cazucá that I have learned to see, one very different from that seen on the news. In conversations, through meetings, by playing games in the schoolyard, and eating meals with families, I watch how the young people of this community navigate multiple forms of violence wherever they can, and mourn the deaths and the injuries that befall friends and family. I see them actively negotiate their everyday lives to respond to insecurity, and learn the language and practice of resistance and resilience.

Such stories, both of violence and of resilience, form the basis of this book. That there are two such seemingly different 'Cazucás' illustrates the complexity of the environment explored in the following pages. These two visions of the community: one simply a dangerous place, where people seek refuge from the violence that has destroyed the homes they've fled; the other one a home in its own right, where they've grown up and a strong community looks after each other are deeply entwined. How then can we hold both these conceptions in focus at the same time, so that one doesn't get lost in the other? Liminal, peripheral spaces such as los Altos de Cazucá, are fraught. Such communities are often overlooked by traditional peacebuilding narratives which erase the presence of those whose lives are marginal to elite discourse. How then can the everyday politics of the margins be centred in considering peace? More than this however, I ask what does it mean to recognise young people as competent actors of their lives and contributory agents to their communities? Amidst violence, what does peace look like?

This book approaches these questions by paying attention to the lives and narratives of young people living in such situations. It explores what happens when the assumed 'non-place' and the 'non-adult' are made the centre of the inquiry. It argues that an understanding of peace that is embodied, everyday, and located amidst ongoing violence can enhance both efforts to theorise peacebuilding and concrete efforts of peace making. Through these explorations that centre the experiences of young people this book responds to and challenges the inadequacies of liberal peacebuilding narratives. Young people are profoundly affected by violence and act to respond in both mundane and radical ways. Forwarding a notion of everyday peace that is embodied and lived can open space to recognise their actions as meaningful and significant to broader discussion of peacebuilding.

Colombia has experienced decades of conflict fought not on sharply drawn battlegrounds, but in the spaces of, between, and through the lives of Colombians across the country: rural and urban, rich and poor, old and young. Violence and insecurity are daily features of life for marginalised communities, and occupants develop skilled way of navigating and responding to fear and violence. Young people play an important part in the negotiation of daily life in their communities but are rarely acknowledged. In extending Oliver Richmond's claim that the everyday is the 'essential zone of the political' (2011, 143), this book seeks an *embodied* everyday, which finds its purpose in the narratives and lives of those living in marginalised situations. Such an endeavour claims a space for young people's voices and experiences while arguing for a grounded approach to solutions to protracted conflict and violence that affects all members of a community. To recognise the existence of an everyday peace amidst a system of violence is to acknowledge the embodied beings *in* that environment, who move through it, negotiate it, and contribute to the ongoing *process* of building peace in such environments. Building from this grounded positioning this book outlines a notion of *embodied-everyday-peace-amidst-violence.*

Embodied understandings of everyday peace can complicate orthodox understandings of peacebuilding. Understanding how young people experience multiple forms of violence and how they build resilience and peace in their everyday lives helps in theorising a more representative understanding of peacebuilding that contributes to understanding ways of responding to conflict and violence in Colombia, as well as providing a framework for considering conflicts elsewhere in new ways. Intrastate conflict, particularly asymmetrical warfare, is an enduring feature of our international political landscape. Globally, young people disproportionately bear the brunt of the consequences of conflicts, yet are often absent in theorisations of how to build stable and lasting peace. Centring the margins, and bringing them into dialogue with the architecture of institutional peace making may offer new avenues to build a more peaceful world. This book conceptualises this notion of embodied-everyday-peace-amidst-violence in order to explore the space, presence, and voice of young people as stakeholders in a negotiation of what it means to live *cotidiano* (day-to-day) and build peace in the context of local and broader violence and marginalisation. It is crucial to pay attention to the everyday context of life, lived in the shadow of ongoing violence but shaped through resistances and resiliencies large and small.

4   *Introduction*

I argue through this book that the ways in which young people like Juliana, Paola, and Alejandro negotiate the consequences of conflict and violence, and pursue peaceful lives can shift how we understand the role of everyday contexts in peacebuilding. To pay attention to the ongoing consequences and the interconnected effects of living in situations of conflict, violence, and insecurity it is crucial to explore the narratives of the individuals who are affected, and who frequently are written out of the conversation, appearing as mere ciphers represented by statistics without the complex context of their everyday lives. It is here, on the margins, in the liminal spaces where people live, that this book begins. It takes seriously the experiences and knowledge of young people to argue for a *centring of the margins* to engage in a meaningful way with peacebuilding within the everyday even when that everyday is buffeted constantly by the lived realities of violence and insecurity.

Taking Young People Seriously: Theorising Capacity and Political Agency

To take young people seriously requires a theoretical and practical commitment to recognising their agency and capacities. Here I introduce briefly the conceptual underpinning of this book's position of young people as agential and competent contributors to their lives and communities. Such a position is embedded in an interdisciplinary scholarship concerning children and youth, which emerges out of sociological and anthropological endeavours and which has only recently been adopted to explore questions of relevance to international relations and peace and conflict studies.

Young people affected by conflict and in situations of exclusion, are barely visible as independent actors in discussions that so often both invoke and define them. Those who exist in conditions of marginality, from either the direct or indirect consequences of ongoing conflict and violence, are frequently defined only in relation to those who do not exist in such a condition. The places they inhabit, the violences they experience, and their resistances and struggles are seen as *other*. Young people are seen only as non-adult, as 'becomings' not beings (Qvortrup 1994), and as passive, resulting in their marginalisation in discussions of place, violence, and power. Yet these margins contain complex everyday lives and experiences. Taking the marginal as a central concern acts on Oliver Richmond's claim that the 'everyday' is the 'essential zone of politics' (2011, 143) and contests the dominant understandings that places such as los Altos de Cazucá are peripheral and that young people are marginal. In response to frameworks that see children and youth as passive and not worthy of consideration on their own terms, this book links understandings of young people as active agents with conceptions of everyday peace. Linking these distinct theoretical endeavours responds to the inadequacies of liberal (and even 'post-liberal') peacebuilding narratives and centres young people's contributions within the everyday lives they occupy. To recognise young people as competent commentators and observers of their world, and to acknowledge that their observations and narratives are intrinsically valuable, the site of young people's everyday experiences must be seen as significant and of value.

The word 'child' has particular meaning both through international and national norms and conventions and also through common use, as do the terms 'young people' and 'youth(s)'. The UN Convention on the Rights of the Child (UNCRC) (1989) defines children as anyone under the age of eighteen. However, the UN additionally defines 'youth' as people aged fifteen to twenty-four. In practice, the terms are often used interchangeably or dependent on the situation at hand. In the community of los Altos de Cazucá, young people would often refer to themselves as '*jovenes*' (youths) even while the teachers used '*niños*' (children) to describe them. 'Youth' is a contested category; in paying attention to the liminal through the book terms including youth (as well as violence, and peace) must be recognised as blurred and complex. I want to resist the need to make things sharp and rather pay attention to this liminality without necessarily resolving it. I am committed, through this book, to recognising the active contributions of people under the age of eighteen (as well as their contribution as they age into their late teens and early twenties), and thus grapple with the use of terminology. In attempting to find ways of meaningfully recognising experience, predefining the identity of the individual runs the risk of 'unconsciously already outlining in our minds what we expect from this social category' (Thomson 2007, 214). In this way then, while recognising the need to name (in some way) the group of interest here, overly semantic definitions of such a category can only damage the goals of recognising, hearing, and including their voices. Therefore, I use the term young people, rather than children, in recognition of the connotations of agency the word '*jovenes*' has for the young people involved.

Having said this, it is important to recognise that the very reason that young people are so often marginal and marginalised in discussions of peace and conflict is due to persistent and powerful social norms defining and framing understandings of childhood. Youth and children are also frequently subsumed into other categories of marginalisation which erase their presence *as* young people or children; such categories include being poor, of a particular racial or ethnic group, being female, being displaced or 'war affected', or suffering some form of disease or illness. Their difference is only highlighted when they become context-less, voiceless, visual ambassadors for the cause. In the worst cases of this, the silent, pleading child in advertising and charity appeals has been called 'disaster pornography' (Omar and de Waal 1993). Erica Burman argues such a term highlights the way children are silenced and spoken-for by 'experts' (2008, 246). While it is at its most 'gruesome' (Burman 2008, 246) in the context of aid appeals and related activities, it occurs also in academic and policy literature. In these literatures, in many cases, it is assumed that the adults who surround young people in everyday life – the parents, guardians, teachers, community elites, or intervening 'specialists' – know best and can speak on their behalf, in their best interests, *for* them.

6   *Introduction*

Yet there is a growing body of scholarship, with which this book aligns, that challenges this denial of agency of young people. Much of this work stems from the early contributions of sociologists Allison James, Chris Jenks and Alan Prout (1998; see also Wyness 2006; Lee 2001; Qvortrup 1994). These authors were foundational in arguing that childhood is a socially constructed concept, and more than this, that it is historically and geographically contingent, grounded in western philosophical and social traditions. Since this foundational work the importance of taking young people's voices seriously and engaging critically with their presence has increasingly been recognised across various disciplines including international relations.[2] Literature on young people's involvement in post-conflict and disaster environments, however, still often reproduces assumptions about young people's incapacity and passivity. Scholars concerned with recognising young people's capabilities argue that such approaches are often 'advocacy oriented research' (McEvoy-Levy 2006, 2) which suffers from a lack of detailed ethnographic studies and genuine engagement with the subjects of the research. Literature focused on protection and healing often neglects the actual experiences or desires of young people in these environments. Jo Boyden and Joanna de Berry go further in their condemnation, arguing that it tends to 'ignore the wider societal destruction that is associated with most conflicts' and has the effect of 'both pathologising the survivors of conflict and individualising a phenomenon that is in fact profoundly political' (2004, xiv). Work that is based in ethnographic research, grounded study, long term relationships with young people, and critical investigation into the norms and assumptions that operate in relation to young people in 'vulnerable' situations have challenged these constructions in significant ways.[3] It is in this critical, grounded sphere – which considers young people seriously, recognises the difficulties of such research, and engages in the context of the participants rather than pre-given assumptions – that this book finds its roots.

Research on young people's capacity to engage meaningfully in the world around them – particularly in situations of conflict, and in processes of peace – is increasingly being undertaken by academics within international relations (and the specific fields of peace studies and critical security studies).[4] Often this literature focuses on the particular sites of children's engagement (through specific programs, or in specific conflict-related roles) and these highlight the agency of young people. In Colombia there is excellent, detailed work being undertaken around the country by researchers who centre the experiences of young people.[5] While focused on Colombia, this book contributes to the expansion of a focus on young people and peace and broader questions of young people's role in peacebuilding. Through this, this book seeks to recognise such agency amongst the everyday lives of conflict-affected young people.

An Embodied Everyday Peace Amidst Violence

A commitment to recognising young people as having agency in their everyday lives also requires a more thorough theorisation of what the everyday

Introduction 7

looks like in contexts of building peace. While fully fleshed out in chapter one where I outline the idea of an *embodied-everyday-peace-amidst-violence*, the idea of an everyday peace that is experienced through bodies and within a risky insecure terrain is outlined here. The increasingly complex nature of conflicts requires a rethinking of how peace is conceived beyond the orthodox notions built on liberal institutionalism. Instead I take into account the agency and activity of those 'in the margins' and use these experiences as the basis for a more responsive way of understanding peace that builds from the sites of exclusion and marginality to contribute a more complete picture of insecurity and peace. This requires examining how 'the everyday' appears in situations of marginality in contexts of ongoing conflict to understand the violences that surround them are complicated, engaged, and meaningful.

An attention to the 'everyday' in peacebuilding has been proposed in response to the deficits of the dominant model of a 'liberal peace', arguing that a focus on the local and everyday involves concern for community, local needs, and everyday experience that the liberal peace misses (among others: Richmond 2011, 2012, 2013, 2015; Mac Ginty 2010, 2013; Mitchell 2011a, 2011b). An attention on the everyday would, Richmond argues, require a new focus on the agency of the population, on their everyday life. Rather than the existing focus on the state and institutions it would favour an 'aggregation' of local voices (2011, 141). These voices are those deemed the 'non-liberal other', the non-'best-suited' citizen, those marginal, and traditionally excluded. Reconceptualising and complicating a notion of 'everyday peace', as this book does, seeks to account for the people who live in these environments, particularly young people, and understands the practices, routines and radical events that shape their everyday lives and resistances that contribute to peacebuilding.

A focus on everyday politics and the possibilities offered by formulations of everyday peace would offer 'a *repopulation* of essentially "empty states"' and the problematic conceptions of peace that exist (Richmond 2011, 142, italics added).[6] Richmond provides a valuable focus point in discussing the complexities of peace and peacebuilding by proposing the everyday as a site of dynamic power relations and challenges. Through this book I argue for an expanded recognition of the potentialities inherent in such spaces; an understanding of everyday peace that takes seriously the idea that the everyday holds potential for action, is populated, is embodied. This requires two acknowledgements. First, a rejection of the dichotomisation inherent in the concept of a 'post-liberal' peace. Second, a recognition of the complexities of the 'local' which rarely exist in a pre-liberal vacuum, but rather are engaged in a process of adopting and rejecting liberal values and obligations in a variety of ways.

An attention to the everyday is located both within and on the bodies of young people and through the terrains they occupy. Feminist international relations (IR) scholars have long argued for a meaningful engagement with an 'everyday realm' (Sylvester 1994) of international relations that can help

8 *Introduction*

highlight the nature of inequality and hypocrisies of power. Extending existing notions of everyday peace, I argue that we must consider engagements with the *bodies* that populate states, on which the violence and insecurity of conflict is inscribed, and who move through spaces in modes of resilience and resistance to build peace. An attention to bodies offered by feminist embodiment scholars such as Weiss (1999), Sobchack (2004) and Haraway (1988) destabilises the assumptions of distance and impartiality that characterise much theorising of peace. Furthermore, attention to bodily engagement with people, space and time helps explore the actions of young people who are denied access to formal political spheres (see Colls and Hörschelmann 2009, Anderson and Smith 2001). Thus, to forward an understanding of everyday peace that is embodied is to recognise the effects of structural forces that affect people's lived experience, and the consequences of exclusion and insecurity on the bodies of young people affected by protracted conflict. Such a framing facilitates a theorisation of an embodied everyday peace that can account more fully for a multiplicity of marginal voices and people in complex conflict scenarios like that experienced in Colombia.

Peace, in this imagining, is not discrete, but built through everyday practices amidst violence. Violence runs unavoidably through the explorations of this book: violence as enacted physically upon bodies; violence which manifests as threat, psychological harm, and breakdown of communal relations; violence which is conceived of only in the abstract on the level of the state; violence which exists in memory, dis-placed from its origins. It is in the accounting of these multiple violences – and in finding forms of resistance, resilience, and negotiation amongst those who experience them – that an embodied account of everyday peace can begin to take shape. Such a recognition takes seriously the difficulties and complexities of protracted conflict, and argues that notions of peace exist and are sustained in spite of, and sometimes because of, the potentially violent, dangerous and precarious experiences of living amongst the consequences of conflict.

What, then, becomes visible when you make the non-place and the non-adult the centre of inquiry in explorations of violence, place, and power within the everyday? How can we more clearly see an 'everyday' which is usually only conceived of as a problem or as 'other' to the norm but which is a form of everyday life common to many who live with the consequences of conflict in Colombia and elsewhere? By committing to and recognizing the voices usually relegated to the margins, this book seeks ways of locating the stories and voices of young people as valid storytellers of their own experiences within and against the dominant narratives that shape their experiences and constrain their ability to participate and speak. I examine what it means to be political, particularly as a young person. Consequently, I challenge what can be conceived of *as* political in such contexts with the aim of broadening traditionally narrow, elite, institution-based concepts. The ways in which young people build peace within their everyday lives lies not only in perpetuating the rhythms of relationships and practices of day-to-day life, but is a complex response to institutional marginalization, a building of forms of existence that empower individuals without reliance on the distant, disinterested state.

Of particular interest is how these individuals – normally excluded from consideration – carry out these activities despite ongoing violence and social exclusion. In arguing for an *embodied-everyday-peace-amidst-violence*, I take as central the physical presence of young people who exist in the marginal positions of vulnerability and insecurity foisted upon them by circumstance. Recognising possibilities within both the routines and radical potential of the everyday requires astute attention to the ways in which particular modes of belonging, or conversely the denial of presence, affect the conception of self and community. By accounting for the people that exist in places of insecurity and marginality this book recognises struggles for peace as grounded, embodied, and moreover, as struggles for everyday existence.

Living with Violence and Peace in Colombia

This book locates these questions, and an exploration of the idea of an embodied-everyday-peace-amidst-violence within a specific context. Doing this reveals not only new theoretical insights about everyday peace that have relevance beyond the specific geographic context, but demonstrate grounded ways of engaging with and thinking about violence, insecurity, and exclusion in Colombia. Colombia's half century of internal conflict has taken a devastating toll on the country. Initially launched in the 1960s as an ideological struggle waged by leftist guerrillas – the *Fuerzas Armadas Revolucionarias de Colombia* (Revolutionary Armed Forces of Colombia, known by the Spanish acronym FARC) – against the state, the conflict has involved multiple groups. At different times, various leftist groups (including the FARC as well as the ELN, M-19, among others), right-wing paramilitary organisations, the state, and criminal organisations have been involved. The evolution of the conflict has seen the growth and influence of large illegal economies of arms and drug trafficking and lucrative kidnappings. The conflict has been further complicated by the nature of fighting, which has been characterised by irregular fighting and contested on difficult terrain. The conflict has also directly impacted the lives of those who live in rural and remote regions, as well as cities across the country.

This protracted, complex conflict has resulted in multiple forms of violence experienced by marginalised communities, and broader consequences for the nation as a whole. Between 1958 and 2012 the conflict caused the deaths of almost 220,000 people and the forced disappearances of over 25,000 people according to a significant report by the *Centro Nacional de Memoria Historica* (National Historical Memory Centre) (GMH 2013). Armed groups have kidnapped and murdered prominent figures including politicians, judges, human rights workers, union leaders and leaders of other marginalised groups including the displaced, afro-Colombians, and indigenous people (Human

10 *Introduction*

Rights Watch 2010, 2011; IDMC 2009). In 2016, according to Colombian NGO Indepaz at least 117 human rights defenders were killed (Gonzalez Perafán, 2016). The Colombian government's *Registro Único de Víctimas*, (RUV, the Victims Registry) which recognises people that have had their human rights violated and aims to realise their rights to reparations (see Rivas 2016) is constantly growing as more individuals come forward. By mid-2017 there were over eight million registered victims, and this number will no doubt continue rising.[7] By the start of 2017 there were over seven million people internally displaced by the conflict (UNHCR 2017) with 360,000 refugees crossing neighbouring borders or in other ways leaving the country (UNHCR 2016). These figures mean Colombia has one of the world's highest populations of internally displaced persons (IDPs), accounting for approximately thirteen per cent of the population (UNHCR 2016). Forced displacement in Colombia is overwhelmingly rural-to-urban (approximately ninety per cent) and this, along with economic migration over many decades, means Colombia has one of Latin America's most urbanised populations, with approximately seventy per cent of Colombians living in 'urban' areas (CODHES 2010). Such trends are not recent but linked to historic migration processes. Historical tension over access to land between landowners and peasants was reflected in political contests, and has fed into the armed conflict and violence. Sebastián Albuja and Marcela Ceballos (2010) note that for these reasons economic pressures are intimately connected with both the broader conflict, and the individual reasons for forced displacements. In Colombia over fifty percent of those living either displaced from their home community or below the poverty line are under eighteen years old (CODHES 2010). Young people in these communities are disproportionately affected by poverty, the complex consequences of conflict, and lack of access to basic support systems and resources making young people central to considerations of challenges in these communities.

Over the past decades the government and various armed groups have engaged in periods of more intense fighting as well as attempts to reach negotiated solutions. While several other groups have previously demobilised, previous attempts at peace talks with the FARC have fallen apart. However, the process started by President Juan Manuel Santos in 2012 with FARC guerrillas had success. After being narrowly defeated in a plebiscite in September 2016 it was reworked, signed by both sides, passed by both houses of parliament in late 2016 and put into effect. The signing of the peace agreement in 2016 brings a formal end to the conflict between FARC and the government; however, has not ended the insecurity and violence experienced by many Colombians. Since the signing of the peace agreement, attacks against human rights defenders have increased, and violent contests for power have emerged in zones vacated by the FARC and not yet appropriately reclaimed by the state. Society, affected by decades of conflict, is divided about the FARC peace agreement, and there is a lack of trust amongst some in all sides. Peace talks with the other enduring left-wing guerrilla group, the

Introduction 11

ELN (*Ejército de Liberación Nacional*, National Liberation Army) commenced in February 2017. Direct violence, social fracture, and suspicion of institutions will be ongoing challenges for Colombia; despite these challenges civil society organisations, communities and individuals across the country are working to build peace that draws legitimacy from the formal talks, but is created within everyday contexts.

To contribute to an ongoing exploration of how to engage with local peacebuilding, and how to conceptualise a discourse of the 'politics of the everyday' is both a theoretical and empirical task, and as such this discussion is grounded in and draws upon the stories and experiences of young people in los Altos de Cazucá. These young people are understood by this project to be crucial stakeholders in a negotiation of what it means to live *cotidiano* (day-to-day) amidst ongoing violence and amongst the consequences of social exclusion. Colombia's protracted conflict and its effects on the large population displaced and affected daily by the surrounding violences raises many questions for how we think about peacebuilding in and with communities of conflict-affected people.

Los Altos de Cazucá

The existence of 'informal' peripheral communities like los Altos de Cazucá is one of the highly visible features of Colombia's half a century of conflict. Los Altos de Cazucá (often referred to simply as Cazucá by occupants, and referred to throughout this book by its shortened name) is part of Comuna 4 (the 4th 'region') of the municipality of Soacha in the Department of Cundanimarca. The Comuna is one of the poorest in Colombia, and its poverty and segregation is immediately visible in its lack of paved roads, the ad-hoc construction of houses, tangles of electricity lines, and limited curated public space. Soacha is one of the highest recipient-communities of internally displaced people in Colombia, a trend that has persisted for several decades (Picón, Arciniegas and Becerra 2006; Human Rights Watch 2011). The community of Cazucá is not unique in Colombia however, as there are similar places that skirt all of the country's cities. In Soacha people have been arriving to *la loma* (literally 'the hillside') since the 1970s, when the political violence throughout the country caused a massive surge in rural-urban migration. While death threats and fear of violence have been identified in a Human Rights Watch report as the top two reasons why people leave their home communities in Colombia (2005), such problems are not left behind, but persist as a lived reality in communities like Cazucá itself. In this environment there is low job opportunity, high poverty, and lack of access to services. Young people risk recruitment by gangs, there are high levels of teen pregnancy, and violent assault – including sexual assault – occurs frequently. Families arriving in the community on occasion have to leave again because they are put for various reasons on '*listas negras*' (black lists) that mark people for death by the armed groups that control the territory (see also:

12   *Introduction*

Renfigo Castillo 2005; Pinzon Ochoa 2001, Villamizar and Zamora 2005). The occupants of Cazucá also face social exclusion and inadequate government provision of services including water, sanitation, health and education.[8]

Discussions about the complexities and consequences of protracted violence often focus on the statistics of communities like los Altos de Cazucá, inadvertently rendering those who comprise the statistics passive and invisible. The occupants of marginal and marginalised *barrio* communities like los Altos de Cazucá become lost in a conception of a *place* as violent, dangerous, and miserable, and this conception folds back on the people who inhabit such spaces, rendering *them* violent, dangerous, and miserable. Young people frequently are portrayed as delinquents, or as having 'lost' their childhood. In defiance of such characterisations, young people of the *barrio* contest such readings and locate themselves as active agents in their own lives and the lives of their communities. Amidst the challenges of the environment life doesn't stop, young people make meaning of their lives and plan for the future. They seek out education, they care for and continue to support their family, and they form friendships and build community. Young people often exercise high levels of responsibility despite their contributions not being recognised beyond their family and community; they claim a space in public discourse and participate in the life of their community. They are participating as citizens in the broad understanding of the term, both engaging with public life and demanding those things due to them including respect, rights and participation.

It is the tensions that exist between the insecurity and violence, and the potential for resilience and change in these young people's lives that underlies this book. Grounding this book in a specific, *local* geographic area allows a consideration of how the dominant structures and wide-ranging consequences of protracted conflict manifest in and are constituted through the everyday lives of these most excluded citizens.

Finding the Everyday: Methodological Notes

An attention to the margins is the theoretical and methodological basis of this project. Cynthia Enloe introduced the phrase 'womenandchildren' in an attempt to 'capture' a totalising notion of a naturalised link between 'women and children as the non-political bodies – innocent, voiceless, passive – on which political violence is inflicted' (1990, 32). Relegated to the 'private' sphere, women and children's concerns are seen of less import, and their contributions and voices are generally not heard. Denaturalising this assumption of passivity and non-participation is an intrinsic task broadly of feminist theory, and a key task of this project in relation to the young people of Cazucá. Centring a commitment to the margins recognises the agency and voice of young people within spaces they are normally silenced.

An ethnographic approach to fieldwork requires not only a reflection on the data, but also on the presence and presentation of self in the field. As Ruth Emond argues, 'with specific regard to children, it requires us to suspend our

Introduction 13

sense of 'superior' knowledge and to learn the practices and perspectives of those under study' (2005, 136–137). Reflexive research recognises that the researcher is part of the social world under study (see Gouldner 1971) and that as such my own history and relationship with the field constructs the 'lens' through which I view the research. For this reason, I have attempted to make myself 'present' in this discussion of the methods and processes of fieldwork, and to acknowledge some of the dilemmas, interactions, and decisions that were made, as well as to provide context, highlight ambiguities and silences and reflect on how I use the stories and information I collected. If we create meaning out of the intersubjective relations between each other, then the meaning created through my research must be taken into account in following chapters of analysis of data and theory that make up this project.

Legitimising young people's experience requires finding ways of taking them seriously, recognising and respecting their experiences, understandings, and views in a discipline where there is limited attention to doing so. Such inquiry leads to questions of how to create space to account for that experience in the first place. To respond to such a question, this project draws on narrative based research; understanding narratives as experience-centered and meaning-making (see Wibben 2011). Marginal narratives can contribute to broader political thinking and life precisely because they are 'experience-rooted but creatively reproduced narrative texts' which gain significance through interpretation by particular groups (Stone-Mediatore 2003, 5). As humans, argues Annick Wibben, we are more than '*homo significans* (meaning makers)', we are also '*homo fabulans*', a concept that recognises we also 'interpret and tell stories about our experiences, about who we are or want to be and what we believe' (2010, 43, original italics). It is the inherent partiality, but concomitant flexibility and legitimacy of narratives, which lend narrative research particular strength in work with marginal groups. As this book seeks to question the silencing and absenting of young people from broader recognition in peacebuilding efforts, engaging in a process that recognises, allows, and legitimises voice is a logical and insightful process.

My approach to these questions is informed by ethnographic research methods. This research wasn't true ethnography in the anthropological sense – I did not live constantly among those I was studying, nor did I seek to spend sufficient time there to conduct true longitudinal ethnographic work, although I did maintain relationships virtually, and returned in 2016, which allow some reflections of this nature. However, the research takes as its primary methods core aspects of ethnographic fieldwork in spending periods of time amongst the everyday lives of the community members, using participant observation and interviewing, being involved 'in people's daily lives for an extended period of time, watching what happens, listening to what is said, asking questions' (Hammersley and Atkinson 2007, 1). It also holds a commitment to the aims of ethnographic work, namely a desire to understand the cultural and social environment in which I am gathering information and a constant reflexivity in relation to my experience and data (Walsh 2004). Such an

14 Introduction

approach is gaining recognition within the field of international relations, as the value of close, detailed work with those affected by conflict and violence is recognised.[9]

This project is grounded in fieldwork[10] conducted with young people and various adults who surround them in this community. From September to December 2010, I spent on average four days per week in the community of Cazucá. Access to the community was gained through the organization *Fundación Pies Descalzos* (the *fundación*, known in English as the Barefoot Foundation) whose objective is to provide and support education initiatives to 'vulnerable' children across Colombia (Fundación Pies Descalzos 2010; 2011). Via the *fundación* I entered one of the local schools, *Instituto Educativo Gabriel Garcia Marzquez*, and its connected second site, *Colegio Minutos de Dios* located further up the hillside of the community. The school serves approximately one thousand children, with classes containing thirty-five to forty students. Resources in the school are basic, and access is granted by a security guard at both sites. There are approximately twenty teachers across the two sites, and a variety of non-teaching support staff. *Garcia Marquez* is built around a central concrete yard and also contains a *comedor* (cafeteria), cramped teachers' room and principal's office. *Colegio Minutos* has similar facilities but is built on two levels with small concrete play areas in front of classrooms. I also spent time at the *fundación's casita* ('little house'), that served as their office and space for organised activities in the community.

The stories and experiences presented in this book are drawn from notes from the days I spent with the young people and their community; as well as recorded interviews with twenty-eight young people between the ages of ten and seventeen from a local school supported by the *fundación*, as well as interviews with various teachers, parents and guardians, and employees of the *fundación*. I also spoke with people associated with other NGOs involved in children's rights and child services while in Colombia[11]. In 2016 I returned to Colombia and spoke with several of the young people (now in their 20's) and representatives of the *fundación*. Combined with ongoing friendships online with people who had been involved in the research in Colombia, these two trips allow me to draw out some observations about changes over time through this book. All research was conducted in Spanish, which I speak with fluency.

Interviews were conducted in the final weeks of my time with the community. In the preceding months I made notes of conversations and observations during days at the school or with the foundation. Permissions for interviews were sought from parents and the school as well as seeking informed consent from the young people themselves before interviews. Some young people spoke to me individually, while others preferred to speak in pairs or groups of three or four. I let the young people decide how they wanted to speak with me in order to do all I could to ensure their comfort and confidence during the interview. While authors highlight the importance of conducting interviews in a quiet, private space (see Freeman and Mathison 2009; Hart and Tyrer 2006) the reality was in many situations this was not possible. Interviews generally

Introduction 15

occurred in empty classrooms during break time, one in the *comedor*, and one in the playground during class time and on one occasion we used a disused storage space. Sometimes they were interrupted by other students or teachers, or in one case by classmates thinking it was amusing to bang loudly on the metal door from outside. Recognising this and ensuring participants were as comfortable as possible was a key priority when conducting the recorded interviews. Ethical considerations of research with young people intimately shaped this research and its focus on young people's own narratives; from being open about my presence when participating in daily life, to considerations in the interview process including the right of the young people to consent to participate and chose to withdraw or opt out of answering at any point, and the use of pseudonyms to enable recognition of individual contributions but ensure the young people's anonymity and security.[12]

Outline of this Book

This book argues for a more grounded approach to understanding and addressing protracted conflict and violence that make a sincere commitment to a notion of embodied everyday peace as its obligation and goal. This requires recognition of the fact that everyday life manifests not only in radical ways but in the resilience and routines of the everyday lives of young people and, as a result, this book demonstrates the value of considering a notion of an embodied everyday peace which exists amidst violence. It asks: what is missing when such voices are absent, how might these marginalised communities be made more visible in peacebuilding discourse, and how can the contributions of the marginalised people who live in them – in particular, young people – be recognised? Taking young people's accounts of lived experience seriously as a starting point reverses the usual top-down framing of concern for marginal populations. Moving beyond sole consideration of the usual actors considered in peacebuilding raises new possibilities for theorising peace. The potential of a conception of peace as everyday, embodied, and built amidst violence, can be recognised by bringing the margins to the centre of concern.

This book proceeds in three steps. It first considers the contextual and theoretical framework in Chapters One and Two respectively, outlining the notion of an embodied-everyday-peace-amidst-violence, and situating this analysis within the Colombian context. It then builds an argument for this notion of peace. Chapters Three and Four consider the implications of violence and insecurity in everyday life, before Chapters Five and Six outline the resilience and capacity of young people in conceiving of peace in contexts of violence. Together it demonstrates the potential of an embodied everyday peace that exists amidst and despite multiple violences and exclusions experienced by conflict-affected young people – evident in this specific Colombian context, but relevant to theorising and engaging peacebuilding more broadly.

The first two chapters seek to reorientate the everyday in theoretical and practical ways. Chapter One expands on the theoretical argument of the book

16   *Introduction*

as outlined above, proposing a more complex understanding of 'everyday peace' and its embodied potential. This emerges from a feminist commitment to recognising the voices and silences of the margins which also informs my consideration of the agential potential of young people that is so frequently elided in international relations and peace and conflict discourse. It recognises that everyday life of those profoundly affected by conflict and social exclusion challenges us to think in different ways about notions of peace beyond the statist liberal peace. It asks how an 'everyday' can be revealed as a productive site of analysis, building on and extending existing work done by Oliver Richmond and others. Finally it embraces ideas of embodiment, pushing both the critique of liberal peace and feminist critiques of IR by arguing for a centring of the physical presence of those who exist in the margins. Against a distant liberal peace, the everyday repopulates our conception of peace. Together these strands lay out a notion not just of everyday peace but *embodied-everyday-peace-amidst-violence*. Chapter Two provides a brief account of Colombia's protracted conflict with a focus on its impacts on marginal populations and the role of young people both in war and peace. It also describes the community of Cazucá and the key challenges of the environment for the occupants to contextualise the material that follows. Through these discussions this chapter presents a way of reading the conflict that begins with the people who endure and respond to violences, insecurity and risk.

Chapters Three and Four highlight the everyday violences that present fraught and complex challenges to young people and their communities. Using the narratives and experiences of young people and the adults in their lives, Chapter Three explores the terrains of insecurity of life in Cazucá, framing this exploration via a concern for spatiality and the politics of constructing places against practices of exclusion that exacerbate insecurity. Places like Cazucá, constructed as beyond the concern of broader society, can be conceived of as 'non-places' (Nordstrom 2004). In understanding the implications of such a configuration, this chapter centres young people's accounts of movements through the community, experiences of insecurity and risk. In speaking *from* the 'non-place' young people's accounts prompt a questioning of what a politics of space might mean and how young people's negotiations of their insecure terrains reconfigures the 'non-place' into a claimed, populated 'place'. Building from this spatialised insecurity, Chapter Four analyses how the violences that move through this insecure terrain are experienced through and upon the bodies of young people in everyday ways. Through the words of young people themselves, this chapter explores the physical violence enacted by the armed actors of the community, the more hidden violences of sexual assault, the risks and insecurities of intimate relationships and the consequences of ruptures in family relationships. This attention to the *everyday*, and profoundly *embodied* encounters with violence highlight how insecurities and interruptions to everyday bonds emerge through and against the bodies of young people.

Chapters Five and Six respond to the violence and insecurity outlined in the previous chapters and ask how forms of everyday peace are conceived amongst these violences. Again, through the narratives of young people they highlight the limits of current theorisation of everyday peace. Chapter Five explores notions of resilience and resistance that respond to uncritical narratives that locate problems within the bodies of the occupants of the community and the spaces they occupy. Instead, young people argue against these totalising narratives and reclaim agency within their everyday lives. While it is disingenuous to suggest such practices of resistance and resilience are sufficient to cancel out the insecurity of daily life, by identifying and validating these sites and relationships, young people in communities such as Cazucá can be legitimised as actors playing active roles in fostering peacebuilding at the everyday level. Chapter Six directly considers what is meant by 'peace' in these environments. It argues for a reconceptualisation of peace as a notion of everyday-peace-amidst-violence drawing from the ways in which young people talk about and understand peace in their daily lives. The radical potential of a notion of everyday peace is its ability to recognise individual's attempts to negotiate violence, address material needs, and find sites of resistance and solidarity. Forwarding a concept of everyday-peace-amidst-violence requires not only exploring the manifestations and negotiations of multiple violences as described in previous chapters, but must also take into account how young people understand the notion of peace both abstractly and as a functional (or dysfunctional) concept in their everyday lives

Travelling home after speaking with Juliana, Paola, and Alejandro the day of our conversation, I am struck that their stories of daily life contain direct experiences of violence such as gunfire through the night as well as community actions such as those of the men we observed filling in potholes; a community constrained by danger, and a place where people live and strive. These stories are not contradictory but rather are important to hold simultaneously to understand young people's complex and meaningful understandings of peace. Life for these young people does not stop due to the broader conflict and localised violences but it does affect their everyday experiences. The radical potential of a notion of everyday peace is its ability to recognise individuals' attempts to negotiate violence, address material needs, and find sites of solidarity. An attention to everyday and profoundly embodied encounters with insecurity and violence suggests a starting point for inclusive, constructive and responsive understandings of peace that centre the lives of young people who are so often invoked as touchstones of peacebuilding, but whose experience is rarely placed at its centre.

Notes

1 Names of all young people who participated in this research are pseudonyms. All quotes from interviews and fieldwork are translated from Spanish by the author.

18 *Introduction*

Unless indicated otherwise (such as from field notes, or a 2016 date), all quotes are taken from interviews conducted during the 2010 period of fieldwork.

2 'Childhood Studies' is not a uniformly conceived discipline, and even some of those included in this citation might not associate themselves with such an endeavour. However, it is readily apparent that since the early 1990s children and young people have been recognised across disciplines as being worthy of study and uniquely situated to critique dominant ideologies. Here I include a brief and very much incomplete list of some of those writing on children and childhoods: Some of those cited as 'foundational', particularly but not exclusively from sociology, include James, Jenks and Prout 1998; Lee 2001; Qvortrup, Bardy, Sgritta and Wintersberger (eds) 1994; Alderson 2003; Wyness, 2006; Jenks 2005; Mayall 2002. On the anthropology of childhood, particularly in conflict or disaster situations, and often through detailed ethnographic work: Boyden 1994, 2004, 2006; Boyden and de Berry 2004; Hart 2006; Hart and Tyrer 2006; Arnaut 2008; Riaño-Alcala 2010; Honwana 2006; Denov 2010; Nordstrom 2006; Scheper-Hughes and Sargent 1998; Wessells 2006; Utas 2004, 2005. On thinking of children in a global context, particularly in relation to globalization, development and inequality both within academic pursuits and in policy and practice: Katz 2004; Holloway and Valentine 2000; Ackerman, Feeny, Hart and Newman, 2003; Aitken, 2001; Burman 1994, 2008.

3 Of particular note is work by Boyden and de Berry (2004) and McEvoy-Levy (2006) as cited in this paragraph; along with Honwana 2006, Denov 2010, Scheper-Hughes and Sargent 1998, and Wessells 2006, Riaño-Alcala 2010 among others

4 See in particular: Beier (ed) 2011, Beier 2015; Brocklehurst 2004, 2006, 2015; Carpenter, 2006, (ed) 2007; Lee-Koo 2011; McEvoy-Levy 2006, 2007, 2014; Pruitt 2011, 2013, 2015; Watson 2006, 2008, 2009; Huynh, d'Costa and Lee-Koo 2015; Jacob 2016; and Mollica 2017.

5 See illustratively, among many others, the excellent work by Riaño-Alcala 2008, 2010, Baird 2012, 2015, 2017; Butti 2016.

6 On Richmond's conceptualization of the everyday see particularly 2011, 2012, 2013, 2015.

7 Numerical indicators such as the number of 'victims' registered with the government are both a challenge to include in academic work as they will no doubt be out of date as soon as they are included; and are a fraught way of measuring the impacts of conflict and violence. The numbers kept and reported by the Registro Único de Víctimas (RUV, the Victim's Registry) are contested, and critics note that the criteria for inclusion is partial, as well as the reality that many people do not self-identify and thus are not included in such counts. Such an observation is true of most, if not all, statistical indicators included in this book, and they are included with recognition that they are imperfect but provide some insight into the scope of issues.

8 More detailed exploration of the difficulties and challenges facing the community of Cazucá are explored in Chapter Two, and also emerge through the narratives of the young people themselves in later chapters.

9 See Eckl and Vrasti for initial considerations of the importance of ethnographic methods. The fabulous contributions to the edited volume on *Political Ethnography* by Schatz (2009a), provide conceptual and theoretical frameworks for engaging in ethnographic work that are valuable for considerations of conducting ethnographic work in international relations. Schatz, in the introduction recognises the methodological bases, but also argues for an understanding of ethnography as *sensibility*: 'It is an approach that cares-with the possible emotional engagement that implies-to glean the meanings that the people under study attribute to their social and political reality' (2009b, 5). Arias argues compellingly for the value of ethnography in the context of Latin America in particular (2009).

Introduction 19

10 Ethical approval for the project was obtained from the University of Queensland's Behavioural and Social Science Review Board on the 1st September 2010. Ethical approval for subsequent research at the beginning of 2016 was obtained from the Queensland University of Technology's Human Research Ethics Committee on the 18th December 2015. At relevant stages during fieldwork, approval for this research was acquired from the head office of *Fundación Pies Descalzos,* and the principal of the school through which I worked.

11 These included recorded interviews with Natalia Martinez Pardo, the Program and Cooperation Monitor for *Fundación Antonio Restrepo Barco*, with Maria Tila Uribe, the Director of CESTRA-USIP, and un-taped meetings with Adriana Cardona, the Social Management Coordinator at *Fundación Batuta*, as well as conversations and meetings with representatives of *Accion Social* in Soacha, the Department of Education, Soacha´s municipal government, and several conversations with Colombian academics working on related topics.

12 The use of pseudonyms was discussed with young people at the time, making it clear they would not be identifiable and I would use a name that was not theirs when writing about our conversations. All young people's name are pseudonyms. Names of teachers and representatives of various NGOs are actual names, used with permission.

References

Ackermann, Lisanne, Thomas Feeny, Jason Hart, and Jesse Newman. 2003. *Understanding and Evaluating Children's Participation: A review of contemporary literature.* London: Plan UK / Plan International.

Aitken, Stuart C. 2001. *Geographies of Young People: The Morally Contested Spaces of Identity.* New York: Routledge.

Albuja, Sebastián, and Marcela Ceballos. 2010. "Urban displacement and migration in Colombia." *Forced Migration Review* 34:10–11.

Alderson, Priscilla. 1995. *Listening to Children: Children, Ethics and Social Research.* London: Barnardos.

Anderson, Kay, and Susan Smith. 2001. "Emotional geographies." *Transactions of the Institute of British Geographers* 26:7–10.

Arias, Enrique Desmond. 2009. "Ethnography and the Study of Latin American Politics: An Agenda for Research." In *Political Ethnography: What Immersion Contributes to the Study of Power*, edited by Edward Schatz, 239–254. Chicago, IL: University of Chicago Press.

Arnaut, Karel. 2008. "Marching the nation: an essay on the mobility of belonging among militant youngsters in Cote d'Ivoire." *Afrika Focus* 21(2):89–105.

Baird, Adam. 2012. "Negotiating Pathways to Manhood: Rejecting Gangs and Violence in Medellín's Periphery." *Journal of Conflictology* 3(1):30–41.

Baird, Adam 2015. "Duros and Gangland Girlfriends: Male Identity, Gang Socialisation and Rape in Medellín." In *Violence at the Urban Margins in the Americas*, edited by J. Auyero, Philippe Bourgois and Nancy Scheper-Hughes. Oxford: Oxford University Press.

Baird, Adam 2017. "Becoming the 'Baddest': Masculine Trajectories of Gang Violence in Medellín." *Journal of Latin American Studies* online first. doi:10.1017/S0022216X17000761

Beier, J. Marshall, ed. 2011. *The Militarization of Childhood: Thinking Beyond the Global South*. New York: Palgrave Macmillan.

20 Introduction

Beier, J. Marshall, ed. 2015. "Shifting the burden: childhoods, resilience, subjecthood." *Critical Studies on Security* 3(3):237–252.

Boyden, Jo. 1994. "Children's Experience of Conflict Related Emergencies: Some Implications for Relief Policy and Practice." *Disasters* 18(3):254–267.

Boyden, Jo. 2004. "Anthropology under Fire: Ethics, Researchers and Children in War." In *Children and Youth on the Front Line: Ethnography, Armed Conflict and Displacement*, edited by Jo Boyden and Jo De Berry. New York: Berghahn Books.

Boyden, Jo. 2006. "Children, War and World Disorder in the 21st Century: A Review of the Theories and the Literature on Children's Contributions to Armed Violence." In *QEH Working Paper Series*. Oxford: Queen Elizabeth House (QEH), University of Oxford.

Boyden, Jo, and Joanna de Berry, eds. 2004. *Children and Youth on the Front Line: Ethnography, Armed Conflict and Displacement*. Edited by Stephen Castles and Dawn Chatty, *Studies in Forced Migration*. New York: Berghahn Books.

Brocklehurst, Helen. 2004. "Kids 'R' Us? Children as Political Bodies." In *Ethical Theory in the Study of International Politics*, edited by Mark Evans, 89–102. New York: Nova Science Publishers, Inc.

Brocklehurst, Helen. 2006. *Who's Afraid of Children?: Children, Conflict and International Relations*. Aldershot: Ashgate.

Burman, Erica. 1994. "Innocents Abroad: Western Fantasies of Childhood and the Iconography of Emergencies." *Disasters* 18(3):238–253.

Burman, Erica. 2008. "Beyond 'Women vs. Children' or 'WomenandChildren': Engendering Childhood and Reformulating Motherhood." *International Journal of Children's Rights* 16:177–194.

Carpenter, R. Charli. 2006. *'Innocent Women and Children': Gender, Norms and the Protection of Civilians*. Edited by Jane Parpart, Pauline Gardiner Barber and Marianne H. Marchand, *Gender in a Global/Local World*. Aldershot: Ashgate.

Carpenter, R. ed. 2007. *Born of War: Protecting Children of Sexual Violence Survivors in Conflict Zones*. Bloomfield, CT: Kumarian Press.

CODHES (Consultoria para los Derechos Humanos y el Desplazamiento). 2010. *Número de personas desplazadas por Departamento de Llegada*. Bogotá, Colombia: CODHES.

Colls, Rachel, and Kathrin Hörschelmann. 2009. "The geographies of children's and young people's bodies." *Children's Geographies* 7:1.

Denov, Myriam. 2010. *Child Soldiers: Sierra Leone's Revolutionary United Front*. Cambridge: Cambridge University Press.

Emond, Ruth. 2005. "Ethnographic Research Methods with Children and Young People." In *Researching Children's Experience: Approaches and Methods*, edited by Sheila Greene and Diane Hogan. London: SAGE Publications Ltd.

Enloe, Cynthia. 1990. "Womenandchildren: Making Feminist Sense of the Persian Gulf Crisis." *Village Voice*.

Freeman, Melissa, and Sandra Mathison. 2009. *Researching Children's Experiences*. New York and London: Guildford Press.

Fundación Pies Descalzos. 2010. Fundación Pies Descalzos: Voluntariado. Bogotá: Fundación Pies Descalzos.

Fundación Pies Descalzos. 2011. "Proyectos: Los Altos de Cazucá." accessed 12 March, 2011. www.fundacionpiesdescalzos.com/es/programas/los-colegios/altos-de-cazuca.html.

Gouldner, Alvin. 1971. *The Coming Crisis of Western Sociology*. London: Heinemann.

Introduction 21

Grupo de Memoria Historica (GMH). 2013. ¡Basta Ya! Colombia: Memorias de Guerra y Dignidad. Bogotá: Centro Nacional de Memoria Histórica.

Hammersley, Martyn, and Paul Atkinson. 2007. *Ethnography: Principles in Practice 3rd Edition*. New York: Routledge.

Haraway, Donna. 1988. "Situated Knowledges: The Science Question in Feminism and the Privilege of Partial Perspective." *Feminist Studies* 14(3):575–599.

Hart, Jason. 2006. "Putting Children in the Picture." *Forced Migration Review*. Special Supplement: Education and Conflict, 9–10.

Hart, Jason, and Bex Tyrer. 2006. Research with Children Living in Situations of Armed Conflict: Concepts, Ethics & Methods. In *RSC Working Paper Series*. Oxford: Refugee Studies Centre (RSC), Department of International Development, University of Oxford.

Holloway, Sarah L, and Gill Valentine. 2000. "Spatiality and the new social studies of childhood." *Sociology* 34:763–783.

Honwana, Alcinda Manuel. 2006. *Child Soldiers in Africa*. Philadelphia: University of Pennsylvania Press.

Human Rights Watch. 2005. Colombia: Displaced and Discarded: The Plight of Internally Displaced Persons in Bogotá and Cartagena. New York: Human Right Watch.

Human Rights Watch 2010. Paramilitaries' Heirs: The New Face of Violence in Colombia. New York: Human Rights Watch.

Human Rights Watch 2011. "Chapter: Colombia." In *World Report 2011*. New York: Human Rights Watch.

Huynh, Kim, Bina d'Costa, and Katrina Lee-Koo. 2015. *Children and Global Conflict*. Cambridge: Cambridge University Press.

Internal Displacement Monitoring Centre (IDMC). 2009. Colombia: New displacement continues, response still ineffective. Geneva: Norwegian Refugee Council.

Internal Displacement Monitoring Centre (IDMC). 2016. Global Report on Internal Displacement (GRID 2016). Geneva, Switzerland: IDMC.

Jacob, Cecilia. 2016. *Child Security in Asia: The Impact of Armed Conflict in Cambodia and Myanmar*. London: Routledge.

James, Allison, Chris Jenks, and Alan Prout. 1998. *Theorizing Childhood*. New York: Teachers College Press, Teachers College, Columbia University.

Jenks, Chris. 2005. *Childhood* (2nd edition). London: Routledge.

Katz, Cindi. 2004. *Growing Up Global: Economic Restructuring and Children's Everyday Lives*. Minnesota: University of Minnesota Press.

Lee, Nick. 2001. *Childhood and society: growing up in an age of uncertainty*. Buckingham: Open University Press.

Lee-Koo, Katrina. 2011. "Horror and hope: (re)presenting militarised children in global North-South relations." *Third World Quarterly* 32(4):725–742.

Lowicki, Jane, and Matthew Emry. January, 2005. *Youth Speak Out: New Voices on the Protection and Participation of Young People Affected by Armed Conflict*. New York: Women's Commission for Refugee Women and Children.

Mac Ginty, Roger. 2010. "Hybrid peace: The interaction between top-down and bottom-up peace." *Security Dialogue* 41(4):391–412.

Mac Ginty, Roger 2013. "Indicators+: A proposal for everyday peace indicators." *Evaluation and Program Planning* 36(1):56–63.

Mayall, Berry. 2002. *Towards a Sociology of Childhood*. Buckingham: Open University Press.

22   Introduction

McEvoy-Levy, Siobhán. 2006. "Introduction: Youth and the Post-Accord Environment." In *Troublemakers or Peacekeepers?: Youth and Post-Accord Peace Building*, edited by Siobhán McEvoy-Levy, 1–26. Notre Dame, IN: University of Notre Dame Press.

McEvoy-Levy, Siobhán. 2007. "Human Rights Culture and Children Born of Wartime Rape." In *Born of War: Protecting Children of Sexual Violence Survivors in Conflict Zones*. Bloomfield, CT: Kumarian Press.

McEvoy-Levy, Siobhán. 2014. "Stuck in circulation: children, 'waithood', and the conflict narratives of Israelis and Palestinians." *Children's Geographies* 12(3):312–326.

Mitchell, Audra. 2011a. *Lost in Transformation: Violent Peace and Peaceful Conflict in Northern Ireland*. Basingstoke: Palgrave.

Mitchell, Audra. 2011b. "Quality/control: international peace interventions and 'the everyday'." *Review of International Studies* 37:1623–1645.

Mollica, Caitlin. 2017. "The diversity of identity: youth participation at the Solomon Islands Truth and Reconciliation Commission." *Australian Journal of International Affairs* 71(4):371–388.

Nordstrom, Carolyn. 2006. "The Jagged Edge of Peace: The Creation of Culture and War Orphans in Angola." In *Troublemakers or Peacemakers?: Youth and Post-Accord Peace Building*, edited by Siobhán McEvoy-Levy. Notre Dame, IN: University of Notre Dame Press.

Omar, R., and A. de Waal. 1993. "Disaster Pornography from Somalia." *Media and Values* (Winter).

Picon, Yuri Romero, Liliana Arciniegas, and Javier Jimenez Becerra. 2006. "Desplazamiento y reconstruccion de tejido social en el barrio Altos de la Florida." *Revista Tendencia & Retos* 11:11–23.

Pinzon Ochoa, Nelson M. 2007. "Los jovenes de 'la loma': Altos de Cazucá y el paramilitarismo en la periferia de Bogotá." *maguare* 21:271–295.

Pruitt, Lesley. 2011. "Creating a Musical Dialogue for Peace." *International Journal of Peace Studies* 16(2).

Pruitt, Lesley 2013. *She Danced, He Sang, and They all Caused a Sea Change? The Use of Music in Youth Peacebuilding*. New York: SUNY Press.

Pruitt, Lesley. 2015. "Gendering the Study of Children and Youth in Peacebuilding." *Peacebuilding* 3(2):157–170.

Qvortrup, Jens. 1994. "Childhood Matters: An Introduction." In *Childhood Matters: Social Theory, Practice and Politics*, edited by Jens Qvortrup, Marjatta Bardy, Giovanni Sgritta and Helmut Wintersberger, 1–23. Hants: Avebury.

Qvortrup, Jens, Marjatta Bardy, Giovanni Sgritta, and Helmut Wintersberger. 1994. *Childhood Matters: Social Theory, Practice and Politics*. Hants: Avebury.

Rengifo Castillo, Carmen. 2005. "Balance comparativo: Conflictos por territorio, conflictos por participacion politica y jovenes en las comunas 7 de Barrancabermeja, 13 de Medellin, 15 de Cali y Cazucá (Soacha) y la Estancia (Ciudad Bolivar-Bogotá)." In *Jovenes, Conflictos Urbanos y Alternativas de Inclusion*, edited by Viviana Sabogal Ruiz. Bogotá, Colombia: Plataforma Conflicto Urbano y Jovenes, CIVIS Suecia & ASDI.

Riaño-Alcalá, Pilar. 2010. *Dwellers of Memory: Youth and Violence in Medellín, Colombia*. New Brunswick, NJ: Transaction Publishers.

Richmond, Oliver. 2011a. *A Post-liberal Peace*. London: Routledge.

Richmond, Oliver. 2011b. "De-romanticising the local, de-mystifying the international: hybridity in Timor Leste and the Solomon Islands." *The Pacific Review* 24 (1):115–136.

Richmond, Oliver. 2012. "A Pedagogy of Peacebuilding: Infrapolitics, Resistance, and Liberation." *International Political Sociology* 6:115–131.

Richmond, Oliver. 2013. "Peace formation and local infrastructures for peace." *Alternatives: Global, Local, Political* 38(4):271–287.

Richmond, Oliver. 2015. "The dilemmas of a hybrid peace: Negative or positive?" *Cooperation and Conflict* 50(1):50–68.

Rivas, Jairo. 2016. "Official Victim's Registries: A tool for the recognition of human rights violations." *Journal of Human Rights Practice* 1(1):116–127.

Schatz, Edward, ed. 2009a. *Political Ethnography: What Immersion Contributes to the Study of Power*. Chicago, IL: The University of Chicago Press.

Schatz, Edward. 2009b. "Introduction: Ethnographic Immersion and the Study of Politics." In Political Ethnography: *What Immersion Contributes to the Study of Power*, edited by Edward Schatz, 1–22. Chicago, IL: University of Chicago Press.

Scheper-Hughes, Nancy, and Carolyn Sargent, eds. 1998. *Small Wars: The Cultural Politics of Childhood*. Berkeley: University of California Press.

Sobchack, Vivian. 2004. *Carnal Thoughts: Embodiment and Moving Image Culture*. Berkeley: University of California Press.

Stone-Mediatore, Shari. 2003. *Reading across Borders: Storytelling and Knowledges of Resistance*. New York: Palgrave Macmillan.

Sylvester, Christine. 1994a. "Empathetic Co-operation: A Feminist Method for IR." *Millennium: Journal of International Studies* 23(3):315–334.

Thomson, Fionagh. 2007. "Are Methodologies for Children keeping them in their Place?" *Children's Geographies* 5(3):207–218.

UNHCR. 2015. "UNHCR Global Trends: Forced Displacement in 2015." www.unhcr.org/576408cd7.pdf

UNHCR2017. "Forced displacement growing in Colombia despite peace agreement." UNHCR, Last Modified 10 March. www.unhcr.org/en-au/news/briefing/2017/3/58c26e114/forced-displacement-growing-colombia-despite-peace-agreement.html.

United Nations. 1989. *The United Nations Convention on the Rights of the Child*. New York: The United Nations.

Utas, Mats. 2004. "Fluid Research Fields: Studying Excombatant Youth in the Aftermath of the Liberian Civil War." In *Children and Youth on the Front Line: Ethnography, Armed Conflict and Displacement*, edited by Jo Boyden and Jo De Berry. New York: Berghahn Books.

Utas, Mats. 2005. "Victimcy, girlfriending, soldiering: Tactic agency in a young woman's social navigation of the Liberian war zone." *Anthropological Quarterly* 78 (2):403–430.

Villamizar Rojas, Rosa, and Sara Zamora Vasquez. 2005. "Vivir juvenil en medios de conflictos urbanos: una aproximacion en la zona colindante entre Bogotá y Soacha." In *Jovenes, Conflictos Urbanos y Alternativas de Inclusion*, edited by Viviana Sabogal Ruiz. Bogotá, Colombia: Plataforma Conflicto Urbano y Jovenes, CIVIS Suecia & ASDI.

Walsh, David. 2004. "Doing Ethnography." In *Researching Society and Culture: Second Edition*, edited by Clive Seale. London: SAGE Publications Ltd. .

Watson, Alison M. S. 2006. "Children and International Relations: a new site of knowledge?" *Review of International Studies* 32:237–250.

Watson, Alison M. S. 2008. "Can there be a "Kindered" Peace?" *Ethics and International Affairs* 22(1):35–42.

24 *Introduction*

Watson, Alison M. S. 2009. *The Child in International Political Economy: A Place at the Table* Abingdon: Routledge.

Weiss, Gail. 1999. *Body Images: Embodiment as Intercorpororeality.* New York: Routledge.

Wessells, Michael. 2006. "A living wage: The importance of livelihood in reintegrating former child soldiers." In *A World Turned Upside Down: Social Ecological Approaches to Children in War Zones*, edited by Neil Boothby, Alison Strang and Michael Wessells. Bloomfield, CT: Kumarian Press Inc.

Wibben, Annick T. R. 2011. *Feminist Security Studies: A Narrative Approach.* London: Routledge.

Wyness, Michael. 2006. *Children and Society: An Introduction to the Sociology of Childhood.* Houndsmills: Palgrave Macmillan.

1 Embodied, Everyday Peace Amidst Violence

> War cannot be fully apprehended unless it is studied up from people's physical, emotional, and social experiences, not only down from 'high politics' places that sweep blood, tears, and laughter away, or assign those things to some other field.
> - Christine Sylvester, *War as Experience*, 2013, 2

This chapter lays out an idea of an embodied-everyday-peace-amidst-violence that serves as the theoretical underpinning for this book. The notion of the everyday is useful because it poses a challenge to think about how we might recognise local voices (in this case young people) and acknowledge the space of the everyday as a site of political engagement. It situates its exploration within the diverse and complex scholarly field that critiques the liberal peace and seeks to find more meaningful and responsive ways of understanding how peace and resilience are lived, not in the absence of violence, but despite its persistence.

At the heart of recognising and legitimating the voices of young people affected by conflict is the question of why, at present, they are barely visible in the discussions that revolve around and define them. Bina d'Costa argues that marginalisation, while a contested topic, is associated with 'economic and political weakness or powerlessness', and exemplifies her statement by recognising that 'women and children remain socially, politically, and economically marginal' because of their gender or their age (2006, 130). Refugees, religious minorities, or other people based on their class, wealth, or geographic location are also frequently marginalised. All such processes of marginalisation rely on an understanding of an assumed or presupposed centre – centring some people is a form of social and political organisation that benefits some at the expense of others, and is an active process. Women and children are frequently marginalised both in academic analyses, and the processes of peace-making and state-building. Cynthia Enloe introduced the term 'womenandchildren' in an attempt to 'capture the totalising nature of international relations which naturalises a link between women and children as the non-political bodies – innocent, voiceless, passive – on which political violence is inflicted' (1990, 29–32). Following Enloe, many researchers have challenged the naturalisation of such a configuration. Erica Burman argues that

26 *Embodied, Everyday Peace Amidst Violence*

'womenandchildren' constructs both women *and* children as 'objects of social manipulation ... embodying untapped, future economic potential, and as emotional touchstones of both tradition and futurity' (2008, 181). While this project is supported by feminist commitments to the recognition of agency and the reclaiming of voice against a disciplinary silencing, it does not take gender as its primary unit of analysis (although it does recognise and respond to variously gendered issues encountered in fieldwork). Rather, it takes feminist critiques of these spaces and marginalisation as a starting point to build recognition of young people's engagement with their everyday experience of violence and of peace.

Similarly, an attention to the margins and a critique of that which is uncritically centred motivate this chapter's discussion of the limits of the liberal peace and the promise of a notion of local, everyday peace. This chapter seeks to outline an understanding of an 'everyday peace', which is built on the contributions of key theorists – in particular, Oliver Richmond – but which endeavours to complicate such understandings in the context of ongoing conflict and continued marginalisation. This theoretical exploration proposes that notions of politics fail to resonate with people's lived experience if they are understood to occur only in a disembodied space of reason. Rather, such an exploration acknowledges that even the level of the everyday recognised by theorists engaged in conversations about 'post-liberal' peace is still structured in institutional ways, and the everyday constituted by the meanings given to daily practice have significance for understanding a notion of peace that starts in the complex, fraught everyday.

This chapter proceeds in two parts. It firstly traces a more complex notion of 'everyday peace'. To do this, I outline an understanding of the liberal peace and its critiques before focusing in particular on the work of Oliver Richmond, who takes us some way to a conception of everyday peace through his discussion of a post-liberal, local peace. This configuration is important and useful; however, it has limits. These limits are explored and the notion is rendered more complex through a consideration of the effects of social exclusion and daily survival in situations of insecurity and ongoing violence. This is the foundation of an understanding of everyday peace that exists *amidst-violence*. The chapter then turns to feminist engagements with peace and everyday life to understand an everyday peace as experienced and enacted, simultaneously, in mundane and radical ways. What is missing in many accounts of post-liberal, local, or hybrid peace is an attention to the bodies that move through these spaces and interact with the structures and processes of peacebuilding. Hence, having drawn on feminist international relations (IR), this chapter also incorporates an understanding of embodiment theory to, literally, flesh out the subject of analysis. In doing this, I ask what more is required to understand the everyday as *embodied*, and what an embodied politics of the everyday looks like. Thus, through these movements, this chapter builds an understanding of how taking presence and voice seriously can help build a theory of an *embodied-everyday-peace-amidst-violence*, which starts within and at the bodies and lives of young people living in situations of conflict and exclusion. These steps illuminate the presence of young people as meaningful experiencers and narrators of their lives and the events that impact them. Young people challenge ideas of 'best suited' citizens; yet, their bodies remain centrally located in negotiations of securing the state and the (in)security of the state's citizens. Thinking about what an everyday peace looks like allows room for more than just the orthodox peace's 'best suited' actors so that those on the margins, and those within the fluid, shifting borders, can be heard and can contribute to a multiple, everyday peace.

The Liberal Peace and its Limits

Exploring the way in which the everyday can be conceptualised as a useful site to challenge the distance of politics, and locating embodied accounts of those who live within violent contexts, supports feminist critiques of the depopulated states of international relations and the imbalances of power. Against a distant politics of liberal peacemaking, conceptions of the everyday offer a site for a repopulation of local peace and a site in which an embodied politics of the everyday can be found. Authors including Oliver Richmond (2009a, 2009b, 2009c, 2011, 2012), Audra Mitchell (2010, 2011a, 2011b), Philip Darby (2009), Roger Mac Ginty (2008, 2012), and David Roberts (2011a, 2011b) voice concerns about the totalising narrative of liberal peacebuilding endeavours and have, in various ways, attempted to describe and engage with a concept of 'the local' or 'the everyday'. I draw on the work of these authors in particular, as well as feminist IR's contributions discussed below, to forward an understanding of the everyday in the context of Colombia's protracted conflict and to point to the theoretical ways in which this understanding could provide space to expand the engagement with young people who are generally entirely written out of orthodox discourses of making peace.

Over the past several decades, the notion of the liberal peace has become a powerful theoretical framework that has been promoted as the aspirational model for countries affected by inter-state and, increasingly, intra-state conflict and for post-conflict peacebuilding efforts. Built on the post-World War II experience of the group of mostly Western, developed states, which have largely avoided conflict with each other, it is underpinned by theories of the liberal social contract that informs the commitment to notions of liberal-institutionalism, and concomitant attention to rights, institutions, markets, and international trade (Ramsbotham, Woodhouse, and Miall 2011, 129–130; see also Doyle 2005). The notion of a liberal peace rose to prominence in response to what was seen to be the changing nature of wars globally, where civilians increasingly bore the brunt of the violence, and in which lack of democracy and the inherent illiberalism of the state(s) in conflict was understood to have *caused* the violence. The logic of the liberal peace framework dictates that liberalisation of the state is the solution (Pugh 2010, 268). Roland Paris (1997, 2004) argues that the current understanding of

28 *Embodied, Everyday Peace Amidst Violence*

peacebuilding was built on the assumption that a 'liberal domestic polity and a market-oriented economy' are the most reliable foundations for peace, and that peacebuilding attempts to transplant the requirements for these foundations into conflict-affected states – in Paris' words, 'pacification through political and economic liberalization' (1997, 56).

Richmond understands the liberal peace as multi-stranded, including the 'victor's peace', 'institutional peace', 'constitutional peace', and 'civil peace' (2008). Each contributes to different aspects of the model, including institutions, security, governance, human rights, economic development, marketisation, as well as civil society. Having said this, the liberal peace is not hegemonic or uniform. Rather, these different 'aspects' of liberal peace can be seen to represent different forms of engagement with different foci and objectives. The first three are more concerned with security and institutional reform, framed by attention to the state and the market as well as ostensibly (at least rhetorically) a particular notion of individual freedom. The idea of the civil peace offers a 'grounded legitimacy', as it is based in direct action by citizens; although, in reality, such action is often coordinated and directed by an INGO or NGO. Similarly Doyle (2005) argues that liberal democratic peace relies on a tripartite approach of representative government. The first part of this approach entails building a relationship between those in power and their constituents on a national level. The second is a commitment to (liberal notions of) human rights where such a commitment not only involves ensuring the rights of those within the polity but also forms the basis for mutual respect and trust internationally. Finally, international economic ties that create incentives for states to promote peace so as to be able to benefit from participation in an open market form the third 'pillar' of liberal democratic peace.

The adequacy of the liberal peace model has been increasingly questioned within the field of peace studies, particularly with the emergence of 'new wars', protracted conflicts, and interventionist behaviours. Broadly, the liberal peace has been criticised for perpetuation of inequality and the resecuritisation of the state where politics is seen to stem from institutions and structures of security rather than civil society and attention to human rights, justice, and local peace, as well as for pursuing a model of state-building that fails to be responsive to local realities (Duffield 2007; Richmond 2011a; Barnett and Zuercher 2008; Pugh 2005, 2010; Mac Ginty 2008). Various authors have both labelled as problematic certain aspects of liberal peace frameworks and proposed theoretical and empirical changes. Exploring the criticisms of the liberal peace here highlights my concern that such frameworks do not adequately consider those most affected and most marginalised by the conflict.

Traditional, orthodox approaches to peacebuilding find legitimacy externally in internationally endorsed frameworks for 'correct' intervention; however, it is dubious just how effective such practices are, or whether, in many cases, the priorities of such approaches have relevance to local societies. For Roland Paris and Timothy Sisk, liberal intervention and peacebuilding should

Embodied, Everyday Peace Amidst Violence 29

not be abandoned despite critiques of particular cases as they have done 'more good than harm'; yet 'serious doubts persist' about their ability to create sustainable peace (2009, 11). Mark Duffield (2007) refers to the orthodox peace as a 'liberal imperialism' in which the structures and functions come to dominate the environment in which peacebuilding occurs. The focus on assuring institutions, economic entities, and elections in many cases forms nothing more than a 'virtual peace' consisting of empty states that are distant from everyday life (2008a, 440). Richmond (2011a, 13) highlights that this is due to the fact that liberal peacebuilding is, at its heart, an institutional framework 'derived from the logic of stabilising the Westphalian system and its positivist ontologies of security and strategy'. The assumption of statehood as the foundation of peace, in Richmond's opinion, 'automatically disempowers most local voices which do not use, or aspire to this [institutional] language' (2009b, 331). However, even as international relations scholars have problematised the state and notions of sovereignty, liberal state-building has remained the dominant form of engagement in peacebuilding endeavours.

Theoretical and methodological practices that emerge from the liberal peace often end up sacrificing concern for community, local needs, and everyday experience because of an assumption that the basic tenets of the liberal peace are inherently rational and universally applicable (Brown 2013, 135–136). The process lacks a mechanism of dialogue to make participation and inclusion sufficiently meaningful to legitimate the approach on a local level (Roberts 2011b, 2011a, 411). Other critiques of the liberal orthodoxy challenge the underlying methodological assumptions (Roberts 2011a), others recognise the reduction in space for 'the local' in liberal peacebuilding (Mac Ginty, 2008), and others have argued that the dominant model is inflexible and limited (Richmond 2006, 2009b, 2011b). Chandler (2006) critiques the increasing conflation of peacebuilding with state-building, and Duffield (2007) argues that development and security agendas inherent in orthodox peacebuilding exert bio-political control over all aspects of human life. In addition to Duffield's critique of liberal peace as an 'imperial peace', mentioned previously, Vivienne Jabri (2007) argues that the language and policy framing of peacebuilding functions to identify non-Western societies as fundamentally lacking compared with Western knowledge-systems and that universalising practices of intervention have replaced subjugation by conflict.

Questions of power, representation, and control, as well as recognition, participation, and agency, form the central pillars of most critiques of the liberal peace. Richmond argues that the liberal peace functions to 'represent the ways donors, governments and institutions *produce political subjects or citizens best suited* to fulfil their policies, agendas, interests and ideologies' (2011a, 12, italics added) rather than paying attention to the reality on the ground. In the process of producing 'best suited' political subjects, large groups of people become hidden. The liberal peace creates and perpetuates a conception of a *non-liberal other* – those for whom it infers a lesser status. Such people are not necessarily 'non-liberal' in that they may still aspire to

30 *Embodied, Everyday Peace Amidst Violence*

the perceived benefits of a liberal system, and desire to participate, but fall outside of the framework of recognition inherent in the liberal peace.

A Local, Everyday Peace

To move away from a preoccupation with institutions and the mirage of 'best suited' subjects means focussing on those actors who are marginalised and silenced in dominant discourses. It requires recognition of the fact that formal political processes and intimate, personal life are neither distinct nor distinguishable, but that each inform the other. In recognising this, it demands we ask whether and how those who are not elite can be represented. The importance of stepping away from analyses that adhere too closely to liberal peace models in the context of Colombia is significant, as models built on notions of an end to formal conflict and the commencement of steps towards sustainable peace are complicated by the presence of ongoing violence. In the context of protracted conflicts such as Colombia's, the boundaries of 'peace' and 'conflict' become blurred, as do those people inhabiting the local spaces in which conflict plays out. Internally displaced people (IDPs) and young people confound notions of 'best suited' citizens, but the bodies of both are centrally located in negotiations of securing the state and the (in)security of its citizens.

Ideas of peace that are rooted in the local have proliferated in recent years. Understandings of peace as 'hybrid' (Mac Ginty 2010, 2011; Wilén 2012; Albrecht and Wuiff Moe 2015; Boege 2012; Boege et al. 2009) focus on those situations where local life is intertwined with liberal peacebuilding. Van Leeuwen et al. (2012) argue for 'peacebuilding heterotopias' that are varied and create real alternatives to a singular narrative of liberal peace, while notions of 'emancipatory peace' (Richmond and MacGinty 2015) or 'popular peace' (Roberts 2011b) have also been explored. Work within the 'local turn' that pays attention to local context, agency, and ownership, often based in country or context-specific case studies, has proliferated in the last decades.[1] These diverse approaches and responses to the liberal peace indicate that a complex, important debate is occurring in this space. I explore an idea of 'the everyday' in recognition that not all peacebuilding occurs post-conflict or within organised frameworks (or in resistance to organised liberal frameworks). To centre the margins, the everyday is a useful lens.

Recognising the potential of the everyday allows people to move from 'subjects' of political orders to 'active citizens'. I start by considering Richmond's definition of the everyday,

> a space in which local individuals and communities live and develop political strategies in their local environment, towards the state and towards international models of order. It is not civil society, often a Western-induced artifice, but it is representative of the deeper local-local. It is often transversal and transnational, engaging with needs, rights,

Embodied, Everyday Peace Amidst Violence 31

custom, individual, community, agency and mobilisation in political terms. Yet, these are often hidden or deemed marginal by mainstream approaches.

(2010, 670)

The everyday can be seen as a 'juxtaposition to the conservative politics that preserve existing power relations … or liberal politics which focuses on institutional structures of governance that preserve state frameworks' (Richmond 2010, 676). In this reading, the everyday is a form of resistance against 'institutionalism and elitism' when they have 'lost touch with a social contract' according to their citizens (Richmond 2010, 676). An attention to the everyday, a focus on everyday politics, and the possibilities offered by formulations of everyday peace would offer 'a *repopulation* of essentially "empty states"' and the problematic conceptions of peace that exist (Richmond 2011a, 142, italics added). Rejecting structural attempts of coercion and dominance allows the everyday to become a site of politics in its own right.

Richmond argues that a liberal peace can be contrasted against an empathetic and emancipatory peace, which argues that both 'agents and recipients of the liberal peace' can find ways of relating and engaging 'on an everyday, human level, rather than merely through problem-solving institutional frameworks that dictate or negate lived experience' (2011a, 9). To achieve this relational, dialogical 'hybrid' conception of peace requires a step away from the rationalist logic of liberal peace to encompass a'concern for the deeper issues of political agency … in its everyday and empathetic sense', which allows the recognition of rights and needs (Richmond 2009b, 339). Such an understanding of peace remains largely abstract, although there has been some exploration of what a 'hybrid, everyday peace' might look like in particular environments (Richmond 2011a, 2011b, 2012). In seeking to understand peace formation in the context of conflict, Richmond notes that the everyday is an important subaltern site of peace formation in which 'everyday agency maintains basic needs and order in the absence of assistance from the state or internationals but also makes clear demands on both' (2016, 70–71). Richmond's thinking on the liberal peace and responses to it, as well as the engagements of many other scholars with Richmond and these themes, more broadly facilitates and permits the beginnings of an understanding of an *everyday* peace that can account more fully for a multiplicity of voices and people in complex conflict and post-conflict scenarios.

Conceptualising 'the everyday' in this manner supports an argument that the everyday has potential to hear more varied voices than liberal peace frameworks, and can account for the conditions of protracted conflict amongst liberal development, as it exists in Colombia. Richmond himself is preoccupied with renegotiating the framework for theorising and engaging with peacebuilding beyond a liberal peace; however, this task also asks how research might start with the everyday and what that might mean for dominant interpretations of international relations. Richmond hypothesises that

32 *Embodied, Everyday Peace Amidst Violence*

this means a break with the discipline's traditional focus of 'the interests of a 'security establishment', or the West, the developed or enlightened in general' and rather focus alternatively on the multiple conditions of the everyday and the 'emancipatory and transformative projects that are elucidated in these contexts' (2011a, 15). In Richmond's conceptualisation, the everyday becomes a place from which to critique the established liberal peace and to propose new ways of engaging in peacebuilding in conflict-affected situations.

Richmond has not been alone in the recent past in conceptualising and discussing notions of the everyday in the context of conflict and peacebuilding; however, having positioned himself as central in discussions of post-liberal and everyday peace, it is Richmond's engagement that this book uses to locate current theorising of the everyday. While Richmond's discussion of an everyday peace is a useful conceptual tool, his analysis tends to reify the concept and removes it from the *embodied* world of those who experience violence, conflict, and marginalisation on a daily basis. With a focus on the theoretical challenges posed by conceiving of an everyday peace, there is a lack of exploration of how the discursive relationships between the local and other actors that are central to his everyday (or post-liberal) peace actually function. Randozzo argues that the emancipatory drive of the everyday (evident in Richmond 2009a; Richmond and Mac Ginty 2015) is engaged with 'at the rhetorical and nominal level only' and limits engagement with the complexities of multiple forms of agency in the everyday (2016, 1358). Megoran bluntly argues that while Richmond provides an important conceptual frame, his notion of hybrid peacebuilding is essentially 'local peace as long as at its heart it enshrines Western concepts of human rights and democracy' (2011, 180). This presents a definition of peace that moves people in one 'direction' – participation at the elite level. Alternatively, Richmond sees those who do not participate in liberal peacebuilding, or who challenge models of the liberal peace, as fundamentally in resistance: those who engage solely by rejecting the liberal peace and positing other forms of peace. Such dichotomisation may not be intentional, yet runs the risk of rhetorically emancipating those people located at 'the everyday' level, while empirically and theoretically defining them into particular forms of engagement, which they themselves may not see as appropriate.

In many ways, there is a lack of precision in defining the everyday. While Richmond invokes de Certeau (1984) and a range of other academics working on broad conceptions of the everyday, his discussion of everyday peace is actually often centred on the actions of formal organisations of civil society or efforts by local NGOs. As a result, those who question the liberal peace demand more from it, or simply do not fit within its framing, and are seen as in resistance. Inherent in this configuration is a simplification of the notion of resistance, which does not account for situations in which individuals are not rejecting (or even engaging with) the tenets of liberal peace itself, but rather are rejecting and challenging the way in which they have been marginalised in this discourse. Richmond himself notes that

Embodied, Everyday Peace Amidst Violence 33

liberalism ... is less likely to recognise the local, the contextual and customary order. Liberalism is more likely to actively marginalize the local than the local is to marginalise the liberal. This is partly due to the power-relations between liberalism and the local which inevitably favour liberal political orders.

(2010, 689)

While Richmond argues that his notion of post-liberal peace, or everyday peace, is an attempt to 'highlight the evolving relations' (2010, 689) between the local and the liberal, his focus on theoretical claims of hybridity and resistance elide the actual bodies present in such interactions.

Richmond and others have proposed the everyday as a site of dynamic power relations and challenges and this is a valuable perspective, yet exploring the potentialities inherent in such a space requires further action. Firstly, this requires a rejection of the dichotomisation inherent in the concept of a 'post-liberal' peace.[2] Secondly, it is necessary to recognise the complexities of the 'local' that rarely exist in a pre-liberal vacuum, but rather are engaged in a process of adopting and rejecting liberal values and obligations in a variety of ways. However, David Roberts draws attention to Roland Paris' critique of the limits of critical peacebuilding discourse (which includes, but is not limited to, Richmond) (Paris, 2010). While, as described previously, orthodox peacebuilding has been disinterested in the everyday, critical peacebuilding has been 'willing but unable to advance working alternatives ... (as opposed to abstract thinking)' (Roberts, 2011a, 415). I argue here that this notion of the everyday should be extended to form the basis of a grounded reexamination of what it means to discuss a politics of the everyday in situations like Colombia where peace and conflict are not distinct, but persist side by side.

Insecurity, Exclusion, and a More Complex Everyday Peace

Here I focus on how 'the everyday' or notions of 'everyday life' might be conceived to find the people missing in dominant discussions of institutional peacebuilding. Michel de Certeau – perhaps the best-known theorist of the everyday – argues that everyday life consists of practices that are repetitive and distinctive. Against the structural attempts at organising life – what de Certeau calls the 'techniques of sociocultural organization' (1984, 14) – the practices of everyday life reappropriate the space. People, in this way, are able to adapt and take ownership over structures and institutions (whether local or global). This practice, according to de Certeau, is a 'surreptitious reorganization of power' (1984, 14). Institutions and states have the ability to act in a strategic manner, controlling resources and establishing a dominant functional order. In response, individuals use what de Certeau terms 'tactical agency', which is malleable and resourceful, responding in the context of their daily lives. For theoretical frameworks more concerned with forms of power and institutional state-building,

34 *Embodied, Everyday Peace Amidst Violence*

examples of tactical agency can be invisible. Individuals or communities attempt to make space for their own activities, reappropriating spaces, while navigating, negotiating, or negating structures of power. Recognising these behaviours as tactical agency acknowledges that while such people are not in positions of structural power, they are able to deploy their agency in local contexts. While de Certeau is primarily concerned with notions of the everyday practice of life in Western societies, the concept's potential is greater than this initial engagement.

Mitchell (2011a) uses the term 'world-building' to describe the practices through which groups of people create, affect, and move through worlds, and how, through both radical and mundane practices, they constitute and perpetuate everyday life. This is not to sketch a notion of the everyday that is connected to a specific place, but rather opens potential for exploring what Richmond termed 'local-local' relations. Local-local relations situate themselves within existing networks of relationships that are less accounted for in systems of power and control than the hierarchical modes of engagement dominant in orthodox peacebuilding efforts. The everyday can be conceived as the origin of 'plural forms of personality which gives rise to communities composed of unique and varied individuals' (Mitchell 2011b, 1627). Knowledge created by practices of everyday life is not instrumentalised, but rather is derived from 'the experience of building, maintaining and interacting within a community' (Mitchell 2011b, 1627).

Thinking about what a practical engagement with the everyday might look like requires a more nuanced notion of the everyday. Stemming from de Certeau's notion of 'surreptitious reorganization of power', the everyday can be seen as 'the myriad socially sanctioned ways in which, to secure their being, people outsmart their environmental limitations and manage the gaps between constraints and aspirations in the face of inadequate, disinterested and incompetent authority and power' (Roberts 2011a, 412). In conflict- and violence-affected contexts, this holds particular potential. Roberts posits a notion of the everyday in conflict-affected spaces as a 'reaction to chronic personal insecurity, as well as to a range of other contingencies' (2011a, 412). Duffield (2007) recognises that the idea of 'self-securing', which is contrasted against a notion of the state as the provider of security, might prompt a more productive notion of peacebuilding. Such an idea of security is also distinct from that present in dominant conceptions of peace that are focused on institutions. While personal spaces might sometimes be 'partly secured' from violence by security sector reform, the most pervasive threats to everyday life are the effects of poverty; ill health; displacement from familiar surroundings; and lack of sufficient food, water, and sanitation. Such people, in attempting to secure their everyday lives, will prioritise solutions to these everyday threats, rather than care about institutions of a distant, uncaring state. While Roberts is more concerned with whether the everyday can be more usefully conceived of in dominant forms of peacebuilding, he is accurate in noting the consequences of the adherence to liberal institutionalism for those located within the everyday:

Embodied, Everyday Peace Amidst Violence 35

The impact of local and global political economy priorities is routinely experienced in everyday life as ongoing poverty, vulnerability and the persistent sense that the state is disinterested in the population's immediate and most pressing priorities. This translates into a lack of relevance and legitimacy of the institutions prioritised in state-building.

(2011a, 416)

To successfully engage in an exploration of a notion of an embodied everyday peace requires the firm recognition of the structural forces that affect the lives of people in an everyday context – in particular, the hypocrisies of power and the challenges of insecurity. To begin to recognise an everyday *peace* is to recognise the possibility of individual presence and community coherence, both of which are destroyed, crippled, or perverted by conflict and endemic violence. Nordstrom (2004, 184) notes that peace cannot work at an elite level if the base is not present to build on, yet elites broker peace 'as if' they were the true font of peace, and thus of power, and 'take authorship' of the institutions and links built at the ground level by those who suffer most in the course of violence. Violence here is taken to mean more than formal actions on a battlefield, or even the inchoate actions of disparate armed groups across variable terrains (rural, urban, formalised, disaggregated). It consists of physical action and psychological injury, as well as damage to social fabric. To describe a concept of peace that stems from the local and the everyday is to recognise that the local terrain is not unified and peaceful, but rather that insecurity and violence often dominate.

These conditions are not endemic or native to marginalised communities, but are caused by a variety of factors. One of the most enduring and damaging is persistent social exclusion. Poverty, exclusion, and informal means of livelihood are not necessarily linked to violence; however, such conditions, combined with an absent state, can allow the manifestation of violence. Those communities most exposed to such violences become stigmatised despite the fact that most residents attempt to continue around and through such conflict. The result of such stigma is a marginalisation and rejection of these communities, forcing them to or beyond the edges of 'civilised' life, and perpetuating the problems of poverty, unemployment, and illegal activity.

Understanding the notion of social exclusion is important in considering the limits of applicability of concepts of everyday peace. Such communities are often defined by violence; yet, they are at a most crucial juncture in creating peace. It is exactly here that a conception of everyday peace, concerned with more than the preoccupations of state-building and institutions, allows for the reality of the consequences of social exclusion, hypocrisies of the power of elites, and the embodied experience of those who live in such environments, as well as their ability to ameliorate and negotiate embedded violences. The concept of social exclusion has been used to discuss situations in which opportunities are denied to one group based on particular criteria (e.g., race, gender, or geographic location, amongst others). Kees Koonings and

36 *Embodied, Everyday Peace Amidst Violence*

Dirk Kruijt (2007, 2) note that violence 'through notions of vulnerability and insecurity' has become part of analyses and conceptions of poverty and social exclusion (considering this from another vantage point, Elaine Scarry has argued that violence is a way of excluding people from the space of exchange [1985]). Furthermore, the deeply embedded nature of insecurity, violence, and fear in many urban environments in Colombia has required residents to find new ways of coping with violence and insecurity in everyday life. Daniel Pécaut describes Colombia's violence as banal, recognising that with the proliferation of various armed groups and the prevalence of insecurity, such violence has become 'normalized' (2000, 91) both as a functional (if incredibly problematic) part of society, and something to be negotiated and managed. Such violence and insecurity is not extra-ordinary, but part of everyday life. The everyday isn't absent amidst violence, but instead it is where violence is resisted, navigated, responded to, and where peace is built.

The everyday, then, is the site within which people affected by conflict and insecurity engage with ongoing difficulties and challenges of building and sustaining routines in the face of institutionalised marginalisation and disregard, and which has the potential for small (but potentially radical) change while perpetuating everyday rhythms of relationships, practices, and roles. Defining the everyday in this way also responds to a conviction that much of the literature on peacebuilding and politics in conflict-affected zones is inherently 'distant' from those living that conflict. In this approach, the voices of those who are overlooked or marginalised can be recognised.

Individuals affected by conflict and excluded from broader political community continue to explore ways of building peace despite ongoing violence. Often, such efforts are 'small', and fundamentally located at an intimate level (see Nordstrom 2004; Boege 2011; Koopman 2011). In this insecure and complex everyday, conceptions of what is political differ radically from institutional understandings. Peace can be understood as everyday practices of working, relating, and collectively imagining and working towards a future. Elise Boulding calls such actions 'cultures of peace' (2000), while John Paul Lederach draws on 'everyday understandings' to influence the nature of conflict (1995, 27). In these understandings of peace there is a closeness of social distance. 'Elicitive' peace (Lederach 1997) prioritises local knowledge and expertise – a relational, embodied encounter in the plurality of the everyday. Stuart Kent and Jon Barnett (2012) contribute to this understanding by arguing that in the same way we talk of violence having causes, peace too has causes and is not only reactive. Such an understanding of peace, built and sustained in the routines and practices of everyday life, offers a rich foundation for conceiving of a notion of peace that emerges from, and is dependent on, relationships and community.

In these contexts, made insecure by elite and structural forces, it is the interrelationships *between* people that hold communities together. As described previously, the everyday is not merely limited to de Certeau's descriptors of 'repetitive' or 'unconscious', but rather holds the potential for solidarity, resistance, and creativity. One way of understanding the responses of communities affected by violence and insecurity, living with fear, is through a notion of their capacity to 'navigate' violence in their everyday lives, finding ways of responding tactically and drawing on knowledge and experience to become 'skilled navigators' who negotiate ways of living amidst violence (see Berents and ten Have 2017). Such proactive readings of the space of the everyday are not static, but rather find their origin and performance in the physical presence of people. Connectivity is crucially important to discussions of the everyday, where meta-narratives of orthodox peacebuilding fail to account for lived experience, and sites of exclusion and marginality are silenced in broader discourse (see also Scarry 1985). Yet, these marginalised people are present as objects about which others speak, and, accordingly, they have already been politicised. Allen Feldman (1991) argues that those affected by violence *are* able to speak, that a space exists conceptually 'because this agent is already the recipient of narratives in which he or she has been inserted as a political subject … because [they] already been written and subjected to powerful inscriptions' (1991, 13). Such a theorisation echoes the move from subject to active citizen inherent in notions of the everyday already discussed, and presents an opportunity to question traditional exclusion mechanisms, as well as challenge traditional forms of knowledge creation through speaking from and through everyday practices and experience.

Engaging with the concept of social exclusion provides a way of recognising the difficult and fraught nature of communities such as Cazucá, and open up paths to discuss an embodied everyday peace in such environments. Such an everyday peace, building on the definition above, not only preserves the rhythms of relationships and practices of day-to-day life but is also a complex response to institutional marginalisation and a building of forms of existence that empower individuals without reliance on the distant, disinterested state. Particularly, however, everyday peace is the carrying out of all these activities despite ongoing violence and social exclusion. It is thus conceived of through this book as a conceptualisation of *everyday-peace-amidst-violence.*

Margins and Embodiment: Feminist Approaches to the Everyday

Notions of the everyday are not isolated but are connected in multiple ways; they both strengthen and frustrate elite forms of power. In locating research in *embodied* ways, the idea of an everyday both forms a powerful analytic tool as well as a more accountable notion of what action might look like. Building a notion of everyday peace allows space for us to acknowledge the ways in which those who experience violence and exclusion make meaning in the spaces and routines of the everyday. Closing off the conceptual space of peacemaking – in a practical sense by excluding marginal populations from full participation, and theoretically through sense-making that takes no account of the bodies within a state, relying at the same time on economic and formal political power of 'virtual states' – isolates individuals from the

38 *Embodied, Everyday Peace Amidst Violence*

broader relationships of a polity. The state also becomes isolated from its source of effective legitimacy. Without being able to reinforce political community, the state may be stable but is not deeply rooted (this is part of the challenges and limits experienced by the Colombian government). Questioning not only how people are marginalised or silenced but also how they respond requires a commitment to the everyday in which politics find its origins.

If the criticism here – both in relation to children and young people, and in relation to the theories of peacebuilding in the discipline of international relations – is of marginalisation, dismissal, and misrecognition, then the key task is to find a way of addressing these fundamental concerns. It is here that feminist approaches to violence, peace, and marginalisation provide a useful lens. Feminist interventions in peace and conflict studies in international relations (IR) provide rich language and tools to speak of the everyday, while feminist interventions into theorising embodiment provide a framework to recognise the lived, everyday existence of individuals and the collective presence of those on the margins.

The exploration of feminist IR in the space of global conflict and the pursuit of peace bring explicit attention to everyday lives and the interactions between structural forces and the nature of power over those lives. Swati Parashar argues that much of IR theory attempts to 'offer a normative framework that can help make sense of global events', and yet she notes that 'missing from these kinds of macro-analyses are a variety of people and their complex emotional and bodily experiences' (2011, 624). Attention to 'micro-narratives', argues Parashar, can help us better account for complexity in our knowledge about the consequences of conflict. Macro-narratives that rely on simplistic framings of women and children as victims and men as perpetrators limit our ability to understand not only the conduct of violence but also efforts to build peace. Cynthia Enloe importantly argues that 'womenandchildren' are conflated and located in the private homes that support masculine, public 'citizensandstates' (1990, 29–32). As Enloe notes, this dominating configuration is a theoretical and practical fallacy that merely makes marginalised groups *invisible*, but not *nonexistent*. It is here a concept of the everyday is crucial. Christine Sylvester argues for a practice of 'empathetic cooperation', a

> process of positional slippage that occurs when one listens seriously to the concerns, fears, and agendas of those one is unaccustomed to heeding when building social theory, taking on board rather than dismissing, finding in the concerns of others borderlands of one's own concerns and fears.
>
> (1994, 317)

Sylvester's notion of empathetic cooperation is important for recognition of the significance of questioning not only the way in which people are marginalised or silenced, but also how those people understand and articulate the experience of marginalisation and silencing. The sphere of the conceptually marginal everyday is not distinct to that of our own as researchers, nor

Embodied, Everyday Peace Amidst Violence 39

distinct from that of the endeavours of the state. We must recognise that concerns, fears, and agendas meet and overlap in 'borderlands' which are often seen as impenetrable, but rather have potential to breach preconceived notions of where significant agendas and connectivity might be located.

There is, in Sylvester's words, an 'everyday realm' to international relations and empathetic engagement can help highlight the hypocrisies of power, the nature of inequality (both including and beyond gender), and the negotiation of identity and belonging (1994; see also 1996). This focus *beyond* the state and international systems is indebted to critical feminist endeavours in international relations.[3] While feminist international relations has explicitly focused on gendered critiques, these explorations open space for other forms identities who are marginalised by the dynamics of violent conflict and liberal statebuilding and excluded from the concept of 'citizensandstates'. In the space opened up by considering Sylvester's empathetic engagement with Enloe's 'womenandchildren' obscured by the public, liberal state, we can build a conception of the everyday that starts in the space where local individuals live and engage with political strategy.

It is crucial to recognise the contributions of local people as valid and despite, or because of, the nature of exclusion, which presupposes silence and disenfranchisement. The accounts of young people's explanations of violence and notions of peace, which forms the core of this book, ask myself as a researcher and the reader of this book to recognise that these explanations are located, embedded, lived, and embodied. In exploring a concept of an everyday peace I argue such a concept is necessarily *located*, not only within and on the bodies of the young people, but in and through the terrains they occupy. Accordingly, we must recognise that theories of peace, just like theories of war, in international relations, often seem devoid of actual people and work to acknowledge and engage them.

Even where IR theories 'show eyes peeking through the cracks in the analysis', they quickly return to abstract actors (Sylvester 2013, 2). There is an imperative to take lived experience more seriously if we are to fully understand how conflict and violence are understood and experienced, and how individuals and communities respond to threats and fears. However, there can still be a tendency to affect a degree of impartiality or distance on the subject. Attending to bodies and embodied practice can function to destabilise these assumptions. Lived experience is embodied, and within daily experience these embodied encounters complicate simplistic notions of everyday spaces and actions that conform to expectations.

This argument for paying attention to bodies stems from feminist political and phenomenological work who have given us a vocabulary and critical lens to locate and recognise the necessity of embodied thinking. Gail Weiss challenges the historic 'impartiality' of classic political thinkers such as Rawls or Kant by drawing attention to the particularities 'of my own body and the bodies of others' (1999, 158); while Elizabeth Grosz (1994), seeking to theorise a 'sexed corporeality' critiques a 'mind/body opposition' that underpins

40 *Embodied, Everyday Peace Amidst Violence*

much Western philosophical thinking, and subordinates body to mind, and also creates other oppositional pairs (including 'reason and passion, sense and sensibility, outside and inside'). Feminist thinkers also encourage us to consider how our bodies interact with other bodies and other things in the world. Vivian Sobchack (2004, 4) argues that 'however direct it may seem, our experience is not only always mediated by the lived bodies that we are, but our lived bodies (and our experiences of them) is always also mediated and qualified by our engagements with other bodies and things'. For Weiss, 'to be embodied is both a necessary and sufficient condition for the generation of a bodily imperative', an imperative that is the ethical demand for attention that bodies require of each other when occupying space together (1999, 162). The lifeworlds of individuals – those varied component parts of how they experience the world subjectively – in relation with others, centres the bodily experience. Thinking phenomenologically is to recognise embodiment as the 'radically material condition of human being that necessarily entails both the body and consciousness, objectivity and subjectivity in an *irreducible ensemble*' (Sobchack 2004, 4, italics original; see also Haraway 1988). It is also to recognise that bodies exist within and constitute spaces; Henri Lefebvre argues that individuals position themselves at the centre, but are also positioned within spaces (see 1991, 182–183); our flesh is immanent 'thrown 'here' and 'now' into a space–time occupied by other immanent things and beings in dynamically material combinations and consequences that we may often think but cannot begin to imagine' (Sobchack 2004, 86). Lifeworlds are sense-making in spatialised ways, and violences and insecurities can penetrate, distort, and reshape these ways of making meaning of self as embodied and imbricated in relationships. Thus, this requirement to begin at the bodies and bodily experience of individuals and communities emerges.

This bodily imperative is evident in the work of many feminist IR scholars. Sylvester urges scholars to recognise that 'the body is a biopolitical fact of war and we must not train ourselves any longer to avoid studying, or get so confused about that we cannot study 'it'' (2013, 5). Lauren Wilcox centres the body in her analysis of the securing structures of international politics, arguing that bodies central to the violence of concern to international relations are 'deeply political bodies' (2015, 11) and that theorising violence without attention to bodies is incomplete. Wilcox argues for taking bodies seriously as political, as they

> serve an explanatory role in thinking about how subjects are constituted and how violent practices are enabled in IR but also becomes a critical project for opening up space for thinking about politics and resistance in ways previously overlooked.
>
> (2015, 5)

Veena Das, a feminist anthropologist and post-colonial theorist, asks for a 'descent into the ordinary' (2006), seeking agency and bodies' experiences of violence and conflict within the everyday. As the epigraph to this chapter notes, we cannot fully understand war – and I would add, peace and resistance – unless we 'study up', and begin at the bodies, and through the lives, of those most often written out of theorisations of peace. Attending to bodily engagements is a crucially useful tool for uncovering the actions and experiences of young people who are written out of, and denied access to, formal political spheres (whether liberal, local, or hybrid). It is by taking seriously the exhortations of feminist theorists who seek to locate the everyday, and those who seek to centre the bodies within it, that this book argues for an everyday peace that is embodied; finally here then the threads come together to forward an *embodied-everyday-peace-amidst-violence*.

Conclusions

In building a notion of a more inclusive complex notion of everyday peace, this book focuses on those who are marginalised in dominant discourses, an interest in experience as definitively meaningful in its own right, and a belief in the importance of inclusive and participatory notions of politics. This book is underpinned by a feminist ethic of attention to the margins, and questions why young people affected by conflict, in situations of exclusion, are barely visible as independent actors in discussions that so frequently invoke and define them. To recognise young people as competent commentators and observers of their world, and to acknowledge that their observations and narratives hold value, we must move beyond dominant understandings of both peacebuilding frameworks and 'childhood', and instead open up conceptual space at the site of young people's lived experience. Notions of an everyday peace, as a response to the failings of orthodox peacebuilding, provide a useful theoretical site to base this work. But further than that, this project extends the concept of an everyday peace beyond institutions and structures into the daily violence of protracted conflict to use as an exploratory scaffolding to uncover an everyday peace that starts at the bodies and through the experiences of those who live in these insecure everydays. Such people are regularly seen as peripheral, as mere 'receivers' of peacebuilding. Literature and policy often confines these people to categories that are erased by the rhetoric of state-building and liberal peace, which cannot account for them even as they continue to exist.

In arguing for an *embodied* politics of the everyday, I take as central the physical presence of those who exist in the marginal positions of vulnerability and insecurity foisted upon them by circumstance and consequence. This is the first crucial step towards recognition of the embodied politics that exist between and through those who occupy the margins. But more than this, such a recognition requires attention to the ways in which particular modes of belonging, or their denial, affect our conception of self as they become 'deeply embedded in our spatial, temporal and embodied ontologies' and more so contributing to 'how we perceive the context in which we act politically and the authority we have for doing so' (McNevin 2009, 164). An

42 *Embodied, Everyday Peace Amidst Violence*

account of people that begins in these places of insecurity and marginality recognises struggles for peace as grounded, as embodied, as struggles for everyday existence. If lived experience can be recognised as meaningful, experience can be a legitimising practice, allowing the recognition of young people's experience. In this way, children and young people can be conceived of as part of those communities often excluded from participation in top-down peacebuilding, as actors who are able to engage with the world around them, negotiating violence and insecurity, and contributing to a creation of an embodied-everyday-peace-amidst-violence.

If the everyday is the site of *potential* participation and peace, speaking and being heard is crucial, because it builds and strengthens everyday relationships and helps provide coherence and comprehensibility to what can seem fragmented and disparate experiences of pain, violence, and exclusion. De Certeau's everyday – characterised as mundane and repetitive – seems very different from the insecurity and violence in Cazucá. Yet without minimising the consequences of the violences that shapes everyday experiences, there is also an everyday where young people live, play, work, and attend school. Accordingly, recognising that life continues despite the social exclusion, structural violence, and stereotyping by broader society is key to foster a more grounded, responsive, and respectful notion of an everyday peace that needs to be reconceptualised to account for the tension of a life of peace-amidst-violence. Widening the sphere of the political to recognise the agency of those located in the excluded or marginal zones is a commitment to the specifics of the everyday, recounted through action and voice, written into discussions of peace because the bodies of those speaking *already* figure as objects in political discourse. This is an extension of Richmond's claims for the everyday that is more meaningfully able to account for embodied experience. The strength of notions of embodied everyday peace not only attribute action and presence to those traditionally marginal but also liberate young people from their conceptualised passivity and allow their experience to be recognised as meaningful in conceiving of peace.

Notes

1 Some of these pay attention to formal structures of peacebuilding and their interaction at local levels. Among many others, see: Brinkerhoff 2011; Bland 2007; Jackson 2013; Donais 2012; Bjorkdahl and Gusic 2013; Tadjbakhsh 2011; van Leeuwen 2009. Some pay attention to the local as a potential emancipatory site for peacebuilding. Among many others, see: Paffenholz 2010; Kent and Barnett 2012; Autesserre 2010 (for important work on the local context of UN missions, see Autesserre's *Peaceland,* 2014); Richmond 2009a, 2010, 2011a, 2015; Boege 2012; Mac Ginty 2010, 2011; Roberts 2011a; de Coning 2013. Leonardsson and Rudd's (2015) review of the 'local turn' provides a good overview of some of these developments and tensions. Randazzo's critique of the 'paradoxes of the 'everyday'' (2016) is also an excellent critical assessment of the field.
2 This critique isn't to say that some of these authors have not engaged with the dichotomisation. Richmond 2012 and Richmond and Mac Ginty 2015, as well as

Embodied, Everyday Peace Amidst Violence 43

Mitchell 2011b, have all attempted to engage the challenges here and work to resist the easy liberal-local framing.
3 This includes, in particular, but not exhaustively, the foundational work of Sylvester (1994, 2013), Enloe (1990, 2000, 2004, 2010), and Gilligan 1982, and an attention on 'nontraditional' aspects of peace and war through varied lenses such as d'Costa (2006, 2011), Wibben (2011, 2014, 2016), Parashar (2011, 2013), Shepherd (2010, 2013), Cuomo (1996), Sjoberg (2013, 2016) and Sjoberg and Gentry (2007, 2015).

References

Albrecht, Peter, and Louise Wuiff Moe. 2015. "The Simultaneity of Authority in Hybrid Orders." *Peacebuilding* 3(1):1–16.

Autesserre, Severine. 2010. *The Trouble with the Congo: Local Violence and the Failure of International Peacebuilding*. Cambridge: Cambridge University Press.

Autesserre, Severine. 2014. *Peaceland: Conflict Resolution and Everyday Politics*. Cambridge: Cambridge University Press.

Barnett, Michael, and Christopher Zuercher. 2008. "Peacebuilder's Contract: How External Peacebuilding Reinforces Weak Statehood." In *The Dilemmas of Statebuilding*, edited by Roland Paris and Timothy Sisk. London: Routledge.

Berents, Helen, and Charlotte ten Have. 2017. "Navigating Violence: Fear and Everyday Life in Colombia and Mexico." *International Journal for Crime, Justice and Social Democracy* 6(1):103–117.

Bjorkdahl, Annika, and Ivan Gusic. 2013. "The Divided City – A Space for Frictional Peacebuilding." *Peacebuilding* 1(3):317–333.

Bland, Gary. 2007. "Decentralization, Local Governance and Conflict Mitigation in Latin America." In *Governance in Post-Conflict Societies: Rebuilding Fragile States*, edited by Derick W. Brinkerhoff. Abingdon: Routledge.

Boege, Volker. 2011. "Hybrid Forms of Peace and Order on a South Sea Island: Experiences from Bougainville (Papua New Guinea)." In *Hybrid Forms of Peace: From Everyday Agency to Post-Liberalism*, edited by Oliver Richmond and Audra Mitchell. Basingstoke: Palgrave Macmillan.

Boege, Volker. 2012. "Hybrid Forms of Peace and Order on a South Sea Island: Experiences from Bougainville (Papua New Guinea)." In *Hybrid Forms of Peace: From Everyday Agency to Post-Liberalism*, edited by Audra Mitchell and Oliver Richmond, 88–106. Basingstoke: Palgrave Macmillan.

Boege, Volker, Anne Brown, Kevin Clements, and Anna Nolan. 2009. "Building Peace and Political Community in Hybrid Political Orders." *International Peacekeeping* 16 (5):599–615.

Boulding, Elise. 2000. *Cultures of Peace: The Hidden Side of History*. Syracuse, NY: Syracuse University Press.

Brinkerhoff, Derick W. 2011. "State Fragility and Governance: Conflict Mitigation and Subnational Perspectives." *Development Policy Review* 29(2):131–153.

Brown, M. Anne. 2013. "Anthropology and Peacebuilding." In *The Routledge Handbook of Peacebuilding*, edited by Roger MacGinty, 132–146. Abingdon: Routledge.

Burman, Erica. 2008. "Beyond 'Women vs. Children' or 'WomenandChildren': Engendering Childhood and Reformulating Motherhood." *International Journal of Children's Rights* 16:177–194.

44 *Embodied, Everyday Peace Amidst Violence*

Chandler, David. 2006. *Empire in Denial: The Politics of State-Building.* London: Pluto.

Cuomo, Chris J. 1996. "War Is Not Just an Event: Reflections on the Significance of Everyday Violence." *Hypatia* 11(4):30–45.

d'Costa, Bina. 2006. "Marginalized Identity: New Frontiers of Research for IR?" In *Feminist Methodologies for International Relations,* edited by Brooke A. Ackerly, Maria Stern and Jacqui True, 129–152. Cambridge: Cambridge University Press.

d'Costa, Bina. 2011. *Nationbuilding, Gender and War Crimes in South Asia.* New York: Routledge.

Darby, Philip. 2009. "Rolling Back the Frontiers of Empire: Practicing the Postcolonial." *International Peacekeeping* 16(5):700.

Das, Veena. 2006. *Life and Words: Violence and the Descent into the Ordinary.* Berkeley, CA: University of California Press.

de Certeau, Michel. 1984. *The Practice of Everyday Life.* Berkeley, CA: University of California Press.

de Conig, Cedric. 2013. "Understanding Peacebuilding as Essentially Local." *Stability* 2(1):1–6.

Donais, Timothy. 2012. *Peacebuiding and Local Ownership: Post-Conflict and Consensus-Building.* New York: Routledge.

Doyle, Michael W. 2005. "Three Pillars of the Liberal Peace." *American Political Science Review* 99(3):463–466.

Duffield, Mark. 2007. *Development, Security and Unending War: Governing the World of Peoples.* Cambridge: Polity Press.

Enloe, Cynthia. 1990. "Womenandchildren: Making Feminist Sense of the Persian Gulf Crisis." *Village Voice,* 25 September.

Enloe, Cynthia. 2000. *Bananas, Beaches and Bases: Making Feminist Sense of International Politics.* Berkeley, CA: University of California Press.

Enloe, Cynthia. 2004. *The Curious Feminist: Searching for Women in a New Age of Empire.* Berkeley, CA: University of California Press.

Enloe, Cynthia. 2010. *Nimo's War, Emma's War: Making Feminist Sense of the Iraq War.* Berkeley, CA: University of California Press.

Feldman, Allen. 1991. *Formations of Violence: The Narrative of the Body and Political Terror in Northern Ireland.* Chicago, IL: University of Chicago Press.

Giligan, Carol. 1982. *In a Different Voice.* Boston, MA: Harvard University Press.

Grosz, Elizabeth. 1994. *Volatile Bodies: Toward a Corporeal Feminism.* Bloomington, IN: Indiana University Press.

Haraway, Donna. 1988. "Situated Knowledges: The Science Question in Feminism and the Privilege of Partial Perspective." *Feminist Studies* 14(3):575–599.

Jabri, Vivienne. 2007. *War and the Transformation of Global Politics.* Basingstoke, England: Palgrave.

Jackson, David. 2013. "Who Won and Why Lost?: The Role of Local Governments in Post-Conflict Recovery." In *The Imperative of Good Local Governance,* edited by J. Ojendal and A. Dellnas. Tokyo: United Nations University Press.

Kent, Stuart, and Jon Barnett. 2012. "Localising Peace: The Young Men of Bougainville's 'Crisis generation.'" *Political Geography* 31(1):34–43.

Koonings, Kees, and Dirk Kruijt. 2007. "Introduction." In *Fractured Cities: Social Exclusion, Urban Violence and Contested Spaces in Latin America,* edited by Kees Koonings and Dirk Kruijt. London: Zed Books.

Embodied, Everyday Peace Amidst Violence   45

Koopman, Sara. 2011. "Alter-Geopolitics: Other Securities Are Happening." *Geoforum* 42:274–284.

Lederach, John Paul. 1995. *Preparing for Peace: Conflict Transformation Across Cultures.* Syracuse, NY: Syracuse University Press.

Lederach, John Paul. 1997. *Building Peace: Sustainable Reconciliation in Divided Societies.* Tokyo: United Nations University Press.

Lefebvre, Henri. 1991. *The Production of Space.* Translated by Donald Nicholson-Smith. Hoboken, NJ: Wiley-Blackwell.

Leonardsson, Hanna, and Gustav Rudd. 2015. "The 'Local Turn' in Peacebuilding: A Literature Review of Effective and Emancipatory Local Peacebuilding." *Third World Quarterly* 36(5):825–839.

Mac Ginty, Roger. 2008. "Indigenous Peace-Making Versus the Liberal Peace." *Cooperation and Conflict* 43:139–163.

Mac Ginty, Roger. 2010. "Hybrid Peace: The Interaction Between Top-down and Bottom-up Peace." *Security Dialogue* 41(4):391–412.

Mac Ginty, Roger. 2011. *International Peacebuilding and Local Resistance: Hybrid Forms of Peace.* Basingstoke: Palgrave Macmillan.

Mac Ginty, Roger. 2012. "Between Resistance and Compliance: Non-participation and the Liberal Peace." *Journal of Intervention and Statebuilding* 6(2):167–187.

McNevin, Anne. 2009. "Contesting Citizenship: Irregular Migrants and Strategic Possibilities for Political Belonging." *New Political Science* 31(2):163–181.

Megoran, Nick. 2011. "War and Peace? An Agenda for Peace Research and Practice in Geography." *Political Geography* 30:178–189.

Mitchell, Audra. 2010. "Peace Beyond Process?" *Millennium: Journal of International Studies* 38(3):641–665.

Mitchell, Audra. 2011a. *Lost in Transformation: Violent Peace and Peaceful Conflict in Northern Ireland.* Basingstoke: Palgrave.

Mitchell, Audra. 2011b. "Quality/Control: International Peace Interventions and 'the Everyday.'" *Review of International Studies* 37:1623–1645.

Nordstrom, Carolyn. 2004. *Shadows of War: Violence, Power and International Profiteering in the Twenty-First Century.* Berkeley, CA: University of California Press.

Paffenholz, Thania. 2010. *Civil Society and Peacebuilding: A Critical Assessment.* Boulder, CO: Lynne Reinner.

Parashar, Swati. 2011. "Embodied 'Otherness' and Negotiations of Difference: A Critical Self-Reflection on the Politics of Emotion in Researching Militant Women." *International Studies Review* 13(4):687–708.

Parashar, Swati. 2013. "What Wars and 'War Bodies' Know About International Relations." *Cambridge Review of International Affairs* 26(4):615–630.

Paris, Roland. 1997. "Peacebuilding and the Limits of Liberal Internationalism." *International Security* 22(2):54–89.

Paris, Roland. 2004. *At War's End: Building Peace after Civil Conflict.* Cambridge: Cambridge Unversity Press.

Paris, Roland. 2010. "Saving Liberal Peacebuilding." *Review of International Studies* 36(2):337–365.

Paris, Roland, and Timothy Sisk. 2009. *The Dilemmas of Statebuilding: Confronting the Contradictions of Postwar Peace Operations.* Abingdon: Routledge.

Pecaut, Daniel. 2000. "The Loss of Rights, the Meaning of Experiences, and Social Connection: A Consideration of the Internally Displaced in Colombia." *International Journal of Politics, Culture, and Society* 14(1):89–105.

46 *Embodied, Everyday Peace Amidst Violence*

Pugh, Michael. 2005. "The Political Economy of Peacebuilding: A Critical Theory Perspective." *International Journal of Peace Studies* 10(2):23–42.

Pugh, Michael. 2010. "Welfare in War-Torn Societies: Nemesis of the Liberal Peace?" In *Palgrave Advances in Peacebuilding: Critical Developments and Approaches*, edited by Oliver Richmond. London: Palgrave Macmillan.

Ramsbotham, Oliver, Tom Woodhouse, and Hugh Miall. 2011. *Contemporary Conflict Resolution: The Prevention, Management and Transformation of Deadly Conflicts*, 3rd ed. Cambridge: Polity.

Randazzo, Elisa. 2016. "The Paradoxes of the 'Everyday': Scrutinising the Local Turn in Peace Building." *Third World Quarterly* 37(8):1351–1370.

Richmond, Oliver. 2008. *Peace in International Relations*. New York: Routledge.

Richmond, Oliver. 2009a. "A Post-Liberal Peace: Eirenism and the Everyday." *Review of International Studies* 35(3):557–580.

Richmond, Oliver. 2009b. "Becoming Liberal, Unbecoming Liberalism: Liberal-Local Hybridity via the Everyday as a Response to the Paradoxes of Liberal Peacebuilding." *Journal of Intervention and Statebuilding* 3(3):324–344.

Richmond, Oliver. 2009c. "The Romanticisation of the Local: Welfare, Culture and Peacebuilding." *The International Spectator* 44(1):149–169.

Richmond, Oliver. 2010. "Resistance and the Post-Liberal Peace." *Millennium: Journal of International Studies* 38(3):665–692.

Richmond, Oliver. 2011a. *A Post-Liberal Peace*. London: Routledge.

Richmond, Oliver. 2011b. "De-romanticising the Local, De-mystifying the International: Hybridity in Timor Leste and the Solomon Islands." *The Pacific Review* 24 (1):115–136.

Richmond, Oliver. 2012. "A Pedagogy of Peacebuilding: Infrapolitics, Resistance, and Liberation." *International Political Sociology* 6:115–131.

Richmond, Oliver. 2015. "The Dilemmas of a Hybrid Peace: Negative or Positive?" *Cooperation and Conflict* 50(1):50–68.

Richmond, Oliver. 2016. *Peace Formation and Political Order in Conflict Affected Societies*. Oxford: Oxford University Press.

Richmond, Oliver, and Roger Mac Ginty. 2015. "Where Now for the Critique of the Liberal Peace?" *Cooperation and Conflict* 50(2):171–189.

Roberts, David. 2011a. "Post-Conflict Peacebuilding, Liberal Irrelevance and the Locus of Legitimacy." *International Peacekeeping* 18(4):410–424.

Roberts, David. 2011b. *Liberal Peacebuilding and Global Governance: Beyond the Metropolis*. Abingdon: Routledge.

Scarry, Elaine. 1985. *The Body in Pain: The Making and Unmaking of the World*. Oxford: Oxford University Press.

Shepard, Laura J. 2010. *Gender Matters in Global Politics: A Feminist Introduction to International Relations*. London: Routledge.

Shepard, Laura J. 2013. "The State of Feminist Security Studies: Continuing the Conversation." *International Studies Perspectives* 14(4):436–439.

Sjoberg, Laura. 2013. *Gendering Global Conflict: Toward a Feminist Theory of War*. New York: Columbia University Press.

Sjoberg, Laura. 2016. "Centering Security Studies Around Felt, Gendered Insecurities." *Journal of Global Security Studies* 1(1):51–63.

Sjoberg, Laura, and Carol Gentry. 2007. *Mothers, Monsters, Whores: Women's Violence in Global Politics*. London: Zed Books.

Sjoberg, Laura, and Carol Gentry. 2015. "Introduction: Gender and Everyday/Intimate Terrorism." *Critical Studies on Terrorism* 8(3):358–361.

Sobchack, Vivian. 2004. *Carnal Thoughts: Embodiment and Moving Image Culture.* Berkeley, CA: University of California Press.

Sylvester, Christine. 1994. "Empathetic Co-operation: A Feminist Method for IR." *Millennium: Journal of International Studies* 23(3):315–334.

Sylvester, Christine. 1996. "The Contributions of Feminist Theory to International Relations." In *International Theory: Positivism and Beyond*, edited by Steve Smith, Ken Booth and Marysia Zalewski. Cambridge: Cambridge University Press.

Sylvester, Christine. 2013. *War as Experience: Contributions from International Relations and Feminist Analysis.* London: Routledge.

Tadjbakhsh, Shahrbanou, ed. 2011. *Rethinking the Liberal Peace: External Models and Local Alternatives.* London: Routledge.

van Leeuwen, Mathijs. 2009. *Partners in Peace: Discourses and Practices of Civil-society Peacebuilding.* Farnham, England: Ashgate.

van Leeuwen, Mathijs, Willemijn Verkoren, and Freerk Boedeltje. 2012. "Thinking Beyond the Liberal Peace: From Utopia to Heterotopias." *Acta Politica* 47(3): 292–316.

Weiss, Gail. 1999. *Body Images: Embodiment as Intercorporeality.* New York: Routledge.

Wibben, Annick T. R. 2011. *Feminist Security Studies: A Narrative Approach.* London: Routledge.

Wibben, Annick T. R. 2014. "Researching Feminist Security Studies." *Australian Journal of Political Science* 49(4):743–755.

Wibben, Annick T. R., ed. 2016. *Researching War: Feminist Methods, Ethics and Politics.* London: Routledge.

Wilcox, Lauren B. 2015. *Bodies of Violence: Theorizing Embodied Subjects in International Relations.* Oxford: Oxford University Press.

Wilén, Nina. 2012. "A Hybrid Peace Through Locally Owned and Externally Funded SSR-DDR in Rwanda." *Third World Quarterly* 33(7):1323–1336.

2 Half a Century of Struggles for Peace

The difficulties of protracted conflict, both in the absence of a peace agreement, or in places attempting to implement formal peace agreements, are not unique to Colombia. Such places have prompted a range of scholars to consider the complexities of liberal peacebuilding and establishing last peace that has legitimacy among the population. This book takes an understanding of an embodied-everyday-peace-amidst-violence and applies it to the Colombian context, however, there is value in considering what such an understanding might offer other contexts also. Colombia has long been in a situation of protracted conflict and is only taking the first steps towards a state of post-conflict. The efforts of the Colombian government in addressing the internal conflict have been supported by various international groups. Largely, the hallmarks of a liberal democracy are present; however, the benefits of this state of affairs are limited, with much of the country continuing to suffer the effects of protracted conflict. Faced with a long absence of meaningful elite-level peace endeavours organisations, communities, and individuals have attempted to build peace within their everyday lives. Recognising these activities, as well as the ongoing day-to-day lives of those profoundly affected by conflict, challenges scholars to think about how we might talk in different ways about notions of peace beyond the statist, liberal peace that prevails in conflict resolution and peacebuilding literature, and how we might talk in different ways about an everyday that contains political engagement when traditionally the everyday has been separated from the sphere of politics. Moreover, it asks how such an 'everyday' can be discussed to reveal the sites and ways resistance is built and expressed in response to the violences that surround people in these difficult situations.

This chapter provides context and background to the everyday lives of the young people of Cazucá in order to contextualise later explorations; it provides detail of the context and complexity of the conflict, but is not a detailed history. It firstly describes a general history of violence in Colombia to the present day. After this summary it outlines the significant consequences of this conflict including violence and insecurity in conflict-affected areas, forced displacement, and disruption of political and civic processes. It also highlights some particular kinds of peace-making efforts in Colombia that young people

Half a Century of Struggles for Peace   49

have involved themselves within. Finally, having provided a general overview of the conflict, its effects, and the young people's efforts towards peace, this chapter describes the community of los Altos de Cazucá. The history of Colombia's violence, the complex consequences as well as self-organised responses to conflict, and the particular reality of Cazucá show the limits of constructions of peace that do not account for everyday experience, and the potential contribution of an understanding of peace that is located in the everyday, amidst violence.

Brief History of Colombia's Violence

The conflict in Colombia can be viewed as a series of historical events that have resulted in a political institution that legitimises violence. Violence as a response to social and civil disagreement has, through a process of limiting broad participation and legitimating various violent actors, penetrated all aspects of Colombian life. Conflict in Colombia has its origins in disputes between the Liberal Party and Conservative Party stretching back to the mid 1800s. While violence and disputes were common for more than a hundred years, it was fierce political debate over land reform in the early to mid 1940s – the culmination of a process of repression by the incumbent Conservative government of Mariano Ospina Perez against Liberal Party supporters in the countryside – that can be argued to have initiated the current conflict. By the middle of the 1940s, Jorge Eliécer Gaitán had emerged as a populist figure, uniting people across party lines (although eventually assuming the leadership of the Liberal Party) through calls for reformist measures of economic redistribution, participation, and a rejection of the dual domination of the Liberals and Conservatives. Favoured to win the 1950 election, he was seen as a revolutionary challenge to Colombia's historically elitist and closed political establishment. On April 9 1948 Gaitán was assassinated on the streets of Bogotá. His assassination prompted a week of riots, protest, and looting in the capital, commonly referred to as *La Bogatoza* (usually translated as the Bogotá Riots), and a broader and longer lasting conflict between partisans of the two parties, known as *La Violencia* (The Violence). Fought mainly in rural areas and exacerbated by local politics from region to region, the conflict initially was characterised by conflict between partisans with peasant workers aligning with their employees, however shifted to a class conflict with landowners and peasant farmers at odds with each other. By 1958 the conflict had resulted in over 200,000 deaths (Meertens and Sánchez 2001).

After various, and at times violent political posturing, in 1958 the National Front was established – a mutually agreed upon arrangement between the Liberal and Conservative parties in which the presidency would rotate on four year terms between them. Rather than a popular uprising springing from Gaitán's death, which had the potential to radically address the economic and political roots of much inequality and oligarchic control over resources, the consequences of *La Violencia* was instead a realignment of existing

50   *Half a Century of Struggles for Peace*

institutions and a continuation of previous methods of control. Nazih Richani notes that the

> National Front unwittingly inaugurated a new phase in the institutional history of the country by allowing two institutions (violence and restricted democracy) and two political modalities (election and excessive repression) to interact and coexist within the framework of the same socio-economic political system. ... [P]olitical exclusion ... propelled the institution of violence, particularly when an armed opposition emerged.
>
> (2002, 26)

By limiting true democratic elections, the National Front excluded potential challengers, who instead turned to violent protest and armed rebellion.

While the creation of the National Front is cited as the end of *La Violencia*, it heralded the subsequent fifty years of complex conflict and violence. Motivated by political exclusion several guerrilla movements emerged across Colombia, turning to armed revolution. The best known of these is the FARC-EP, or more commonly just the FARC (*Fuerzas Armadas Revolucionarias de Colombia – Ejército del Pueblo*, Revolutionary Armed Forces of Colombia – People's Army), founded in 1964. Further, the ELN (*Ejército de Liberación Nacional*, National Liberation Army) formed in 1965, inspired by events in Cuba. One of the other significant armed groups was the M-19 (*Movimiento 19 de Abril*, 19th of April Movement), founded in 1973, and was distinct from the FARC and the ELN through its urban roots (Palacios, 2006, 188). The most infamous action by the M-19 was the seizure of the *Palacio de Justicia* (Palace of Justice, Colombia's Supreme Court) in Bogotá in November 1985, in which they held the entire Supreme Court hostage. The situation was resolved – albeit violently and tragically – when the building was stormed by the military, causing the deaths of half of the judges and most of the M-19 leadership (Bushnell 1993, 254). In 1989, the remaining M-19 leaders signed an agreement with the government and abandoned armed struggle in favour of political participation. While the M-19 renounced violence, both the FARC and the ELN continued in their armed struggle for political recognition (as well as participation in illegal activities and terrorist actions).

By the 1960s, large landowners were creating self-defence groups to respond to the FARC's actions in regional areas. These groups were then legalised through Decree 3398 – a move intended to 'organise the national defence' of citizens against communism (cited in Garcia-Godos and Lid 2010, 492). As well as fighting the guerrillas these paramilitary forces attacked those suspected of assisting the guerrillas, exacerbating and complicating the violence. In the late 1980s, responding to data which showed paramilitaries had been responsible for more deaths and violence than the leftist guerrillas, various degrees were passed, culminating in Decree 1194 which made such groups illegal. This did not stop their presence however, and with ties between some members of the military and government such groups continued their

Half a Century of Struggles for Peace   51

violent campaigns and illegal activities, terrorising local populations, extorting leaders, and raiding areas controlled by guerrillas as well as involvement in drugs and arms trafficking. Some of these militia groups formalised in 1997 through the creation of the umbrella of the AUC (*Autodefensas Unidas Colombianos* – United Self-Defence Forces Colombia), with each group responding to local conditions and attacking left-wing groups in their areas. By 1997, Colombia had 132 guerrilla groups (mainly with allegiance to either the FARC or the ELN) and approximately 100 paramilitary organisations (Moser and McIllwaine 2004). Through this time the FARC and ELN also continued campaigns of terror, particularly through rural areas where they consolidated control through constant presence in civilian populations, as well as specific instances of targeted attack, kidnap and destruction of property.

In the intervening years since the 1950s, all illegal armed groups in Colombia have become complicit in various illegal trades, from kidnapping to drug production, arms dealing to recruitment of children. Between 1958 and 2012, at least 220,000 violent deaths occurred, 80 per cent of which were civilians (GMH 2013, 15), and uncountable others were victims of torture, abduction, forced disappearance, landmines, sexual violence and forced recruitment. As the 2000s began the violence in Colombia was some of the worst in the country's modern history; a failed peace process with the FARC, and failure to get the ELN to the table, under the Pastrana government, prompted increased violence and the election of Alvaro Uribe in 2002. Elected on the promise of military action and with no further dialogue with the FARC, these promises became his policy of *seguridad democratica* (democratic security), which weakened the FARC but also created significant human rights violations by the army including the false positives scandal and insecurity prompted by retaliatory actions by the FARC and ELN in rural and urban areas. The 2012–2016 peace process between the government of Juan Manuel Santos and the FARC resulted in a peace agreement, signed in late 2016 (discussed further below). In February 2017 the ELN and the government commenced peace talks also. These moves to the negotiating table have shifted the framework of violence in Colombia and raised new possibilities of peace.

Through the 1990s, right-wing paramilitary groups, which frequently enjoyed tacit support of the army and local politicians despite the official position, came to effectively control a large portion of the drugs trade of the area (often then becoming a problem rather than an ally for the government forces in the region). Garcia-Godos and Lid (2010) note that military expansion by the paramilitaries was accompanied by forays into politics. By controlling local constituencies they increased their access to national politics. In 2002, the paramilitary organisations claimed to control over a third of the national Congress and a third of Colombia's municipal governments. This claim, verified by researchers, became known as the *parapolítica* scandal (Romero 2007). Between 2003 and 2006, the government began a demobilisation process with the AUC via access to reintegration programs, incentives,

52 *Half a Century of Struggles for Peace*

and reduced sentences if AUC members admitted culpability and did not reengage in combat. Government figures indicate more than 30,000 adults were involved in the program; however, although the government claimed broad success, strong critiques have been made concerning the actual success of demobilisation efforts (Ball et al. 2008; Garcia-Godos and Lid 2010, 494). Despite challenges and critiques, many combatants did demobilise, and in 2006 new reforms led to the creation of the *Alta Consejería para la Reintegración* (High Council for Reintegration), prompting new expectations of further, and more successful, demobilisations.

The combined effects of the disbanding of the AUC and the military offensive against the various guerrilla groups effectively reduced murder and violent crime rates – at least according to government figures – between 2002 and 2007 (Garcia-Godos and Lid 2010, 494; Derks, Rouw, and Briscoe 2011, 8). In many places, however, formally demobilising paramilitaries resulted in the emergence of new non-state armed groups, known in many cases as *bandas criminale*s (neo-paramilitary criminal groups, known popularly by the term *bacrims*). They have adopted many of the strategies of the former paramilitary groups (or are run or populated by former AUC members), and now dominate illegal activity across the country (see Human Rights Watch 2010 for detailed analysis on successor groups to the AUC groups). The Colombian National Defence Ministry describes these non-state actors as

> nationally disjointed criminal structures, with high corrupting, intimidating and armed power that have combined the production and sale of drugs with the violent infringement of civil rights and liberties in certain rural zones and the periphery of some urban centres.
>
> (Ministerio de Defensa Nacional 2011, 17)

In 2011 the head of the Colombian National Police identified the non-state armed groups as the 'biggest threat to national security'. As Watchlist (2012, 12) notes, the emergence of these groups not only contributes to ongoing violence but also makes it more difficult to distinguish politically motivated violence from criminal violence (Bushnell 1993 and Richani 2002 have previously made similar observations).

Colombia's conflict is not an insulated conflict. Rather its internal violences have had regional effects including the displacement of over 400,000 refugees into neighbouring countries (UNHCR 2012); but also through the drug trade, which sees Colombian-produced cocaine reaching global destinations including Europe and the United States. As a result there have been various external efforts and support to end the conflict. Possibly the most significant of these interventions is the creation and deployment of Plan Colombia in 2000, a US government-supported endeavour that focused on military support for targeting drug production (particularly through aerial fumigation), as well as improving the rule of law, promoting social and economic justice, and fostering development (Mejía 2010; Pizarro and Gaitán 2006; Chernick 2001; Jones 2009).

Half a Century of Struggles for Peace   53

Initially Plan Colombia was linked to the – ultimately unsuccessful – peace negotiations of then-president Pastrana with the FARC from 1999 into the early 2000s. However, the political fallout of the September 11 attacks in the US meant that as the Plan was implemented its focus became increasingly linked to the US's broader aims of counterterrorism and counter-drug policies (Pizarro and Gaitán 2006, 53). Between 2000 and 2005 the US spent $2.8 billion (USD) on assistance to Colombia; three quarters of which went to military aspects of the war on drugs (including training, equipment, and helicopters) (Mejía 2010, 143). Cocaine production did not decrease despite this spending (Mejía and Restrepo 2008; Mejía 2010). Since the signing of the peace accord with the FARC, the US has promised to continue aid to Colombia, through a range of support including 'Peace Colombia' (White House 2016). The participation and pressures of outside forces – in particular the US which remains Colombia's strong ally – has further complicated an already complex conflict. The complexities of a long running conflict, with multiple attempts at negotiating peace, and imperfect demobilisation and reintegration processes, alongside the reality of the protracted nature of the conflict has resulted in endemic corruption, profitable illegal endeavours and entrenched violence all contributing to make Colombia's conflict deeply entwined in the daily life of all Colombians. Nazih Richani argues that

> since the turn of the 20th century, violence in Colombia can be explained partly in terms of failure of the state … to adjudicate and resolve social conflicts, particularly in the distribution of income and resources.
>
> (2002, 12)

The contemporary conflict in Colombia has been a complex conflict that deeply affects particularly the rural and urban poor, as well as all Colombians generally.[1]

Effects of Conflict and Violence

It was not until 2010 when Juan Manuel Santos won the presidency that the government formally recognised the existence of an armed conflict in Colombia. Statistics go some way to revealing the depth and breadth of the violence in Colombia. The US Department of State reports more than 90 per cent of heroin and cocaine consumed in the US has its origins in Colombia (US Department of State 2006). There were over six million people internally displaced by the conflict at the end of 2015 (IDMC 2016) with almost 350,000 refugees crossing neighbouring borders or in other ways leaving the country (UNHCR 2015). Furthermore, over 50 per cent of Colombia's IDPs are under eighteen years old. In 2009, the most recent year for which a comprehensive study is available, Colombia had the second highest number of landmine victims in the world, a statistic that impacts young people disproportionately as they are more likely to be playing or moving across unsafe

54 *Half a Century of Struggles for Peace*

terrain (Landmine Monitor 2011). In 2015, joint mine-clearing exercises were commenced by the FARC and government as a confidence building measure as part of the peace process (Presidencia Republica de Colombia and FARC 2015). The conflict has seen the kidnap and murder of prominent figures including politicians, judges, human rights workers, union leaders, leaders of other marginalised groups including the displaced, afro-Colombians, and indigenous people (Tate 2007; Human Rights Watch 2011; Watchlist 2012, 12). Various laws have since been enacted to assist with the consequences of the conflict. Both the sociocultural consequences of the conflict and the political and legal responses are briefly discussed, with a particular focus on young people.

Violence in Conflict-Affected Areas

The changing nature of the conflict, where narco-trafficking has long played a large role in the activities and behaviours of armed groups, means ongoing insecurity for civilians as most of the non-state armed groups, in securing their drug trade, rely on instilling fear in local communities, corrupting municipal politicians and carrying out acts of violence. The forms of threat and physical violence that lead people to flee their homes are diverse. People are often threatened with assassination unless they leave their land; Donny Meertens and Margarita Zambrano argue that such threats are made in order to appropriate arable, or otherwise desirable land (2010). People are also 'disappeared' sometimes following a threat, but at other times with no apparent warning or cause. From 1985 to 2016, there were 46,970 cases of 'enforced disappearances' recorded by the government's *Registro Único de Víctimas* (Register of Victims, RUV) (Red Nacional de Información 2017) Additionally, rape and sexual violence are regularly used as a tool of war against women and girls – a report on sexual violence across Colombia found that between 2001 and 2009 almost half a million women were victims of sexual violence (Amparo et al. 2011), and very rarely are cases successfully prosecuted or even brought to court, contributing to an environment of impunity with regard to the violation of the bodies of women and girls (Amparo et al. 2011; Meertens 2010; Alzate 2007; Amnesty International 2004).

For young people one of the largest threats is the potential recruitment to armed groups. In 2003, the Colombian government and the UN estimate the number of children recruited to range anywhere between 5,000 and 14,000 (Watchlist 2012), but there are no reliable statistics on the numbers of young people under the age of eighteen recruited by armed forces or groups in Colombia. In February 2017, as part of the ongoing peace process, minors left the FARC ranks and entered demobilisation programs (Domínguez Loeda 2017). The Office of the High Commissioner for Human Rights in Colombia notes that the average age of recruitment decreased from 13.8 years in 2002 to 11.8 in 2009 (Watchlist 2012). While the Colombian army does not recruit children as combatants, they have been criticised for using children as spies and informants to gather information about armed groups (United Nations 2011, para. 156). All other parties to the conflict have been responsible for the recruitment of young people. The FARC has been listed on the UN Secretary-General's annual report as one of the most 'persistent perpetrators' of child recruitment since 2003 (United Nations 2012, 2016). The ELN, as well as successor groups to the AUC and other criminal gangs also recruit young people. Such recruitment is often facilitated by the constant presence of these groups in the communities where these children live. There is an Early Warning System in place through the country, which does receive reports of those at risk of recruitment and provides assistance; however, the reality is that large numbers of families are forced to leave their homes to prevent recruitment, a phenomenon that is not captured in statistics.[2]

Forced Displacement and its Consequences

With more than seven million people displaced by the effects of the conflict, forced displacement is a significant issue, and it is a significant number of people who face the consequences of inadequate support once forced to flee their homes. Forced displacement disproportionately affects young people: according to the RUV almost half those displaced by the conflict since 1958 are age twenty-eight or younger (Red Nacional de Información 2017). Forced displacement in Colombia is overwhelmingly rural-to-urban (Hanson 2012, 2). Such a trend is not recent, but rather linked to historic migration processes. Historical tension over access to land between landowners and peasants was reflected in the politics over time, and has fed into the armed conflict and violence that continues today. Sebastián Albuja and Marcela Ceballos (2010) note that for these reasons economic pressures are intimately connected with both the broader conflict, and the individual reasons for forced displacements. Further, Ana Maria Ibáñes and Pablo Querubín (2004, 8) argue that displacement in Colombia is connected particularly to the intensification of conflict due to land interest, territorial disputes between armed groups and the cultivation and trade of illicit drugs. The government's ongoing use of military violence as a strategy of the government, principally through the launch of then President Alvaro Uribe's 2002 'Democratic Security' Policy which was a military operation aimed against armed groups with the aim of reclaiming territory, has resulted in continuing waves of displacement throughout Colombia. Colombia consequently has one of Latin America's most urbanised populations, with approximately 75 per cent of Colombians living in 'urban' areas.

That Colombia's conflict is not fought on one front but is rather entwined in the daily lives of almost all Colombians complicates processes of displacement and of building peace. Those who are displaced face ongoing violence and discrimination in their community of arrival (Chaowasangrat 2011). Police and security apparatus in communities where illegal armed groups operate are often weak, or worse, in collusion with the armed groups

56 *Half a Century of Struggles for Peace*

(International Crisis Group 2012, 5), and resultantly do not offer protection or assurance to those living in these communities. The other effect of formal demobilisation is less obvious, but also significant. Once demobilized, many of those formally associated with armed groups often have to integrate back into communities that they were just recently threatening and attacking. Angelika Rettberg and Juan Diego Prieto (2010) found that many victims interviewed in a nationwide survey in 2008 said the person responsible for their victimisation lived in their community, and more generally victims living near to perpetrators of the crime are less trusting of both judicial process and of eventual peace in the country. This is made more complex since, as Prieto (2012) argues, individuals can move from being a victim to a bystander to a perpetrator at different points in their life, complicating processes of reconciliation and 'peaceful coexistence'.

While Colombia is the fourth largest economy in Latin America, wealth distribution is drastically uneven and almost forty per cent of Colombians live below the poverty line. Such structural inequality contributes to the vulnerability of many Colombians. The difficulties of navigating the bureaucratic process associated with being poor, marginalised, and often displaced, exacerbate such inequality. Juan Esteban Zea (2010, 111) notes that such people 'continue to live in social structures that reinforce discrimination and mask their past experiences and histories'. Such practices reinforce inequalities. Furthermore, on a national level, there have been convictions of politicians at all levels of politics in connection to various armed actors and illegal activities of the conflict and politics more broadly (for examples see Pearce 1990; CNN Español 2017; Robles 2017). These elite-level convictions demonstrate the manner in which the conflict and its consequences affect and influence all levels of society and facilitate the reinscription of vulnerability and inequality.

There is a range of challenges facing people affected by the conflict. Some of these inequalities, economic challenges, and security risks are present as a direct consequence of the conflict itself – fighting, forcible appropriation of land, death threats, and forced displacement. The landmark report by the *Centro Nacional de Memoria Historica* (National Historical Memory Centre) in 2013, *¡Basta Ya!* (Enough!) details the extent and depths of violence and suffering experienced by civilians throughout the conflict (GMH 2013). The *¡Basta Ya!* report noted the wide repertoires of violence used by paramilitary groups and guerrilla groups including massacres, assassinations, forced disappearances, terrorist attacks, and destruction of property, while state forces engaged in arbitrary detention, forced disappearances torture and assassinations (GMH 2013; see also GMH 2010, 2011, 2012). Other consequences are more the result of under-development perpetuated by of the conflict, but may not be a result of direct fighting – such as the absence of sufficient services, transport, job opportunities, and similar. These are forms of the explicitly everyday nature of violence discussed in the previous chapter. Due to ongoing military actions, the restrictions to movement of people, and the fumigating of coca crops people are often unable to return to their community of origin. The destruction of food crops through aerial fumigation of coca, alongside the consequences of displacement means that many Colombians struggle to find a way of making a livelihood (O'Shaughnessy and Branford 2005). For those who flee to urban communities such as Cazucá, the opportunities for employment are scarce, and many find 'informal' work through recycling materials or street vending, or insecure domestic service. In 2015 the OECD noted that informal employment accounted for over half of total employment (OECD 2015), a trend that has been consistent for years. In 2009, approximately forty per cent of the Colombian workforce was employed in the informal sector (Aysa-Lastra 2011, 278). Young people often find it necessary to work around (or sometimes, instead of) attending school, or carry the burden of domestic duties and care for young siblings in the daily absence of parents who have to seek work. Research demonstrates that women who have children are more likely to end up working in the informal sector, as it allows more flexibility to look after children; however, its uncertain nature provokes other problems of securing reliable income (Ribeiro 2003).

There are a variety of protection mechanisms and laws dealing with displacement and those who have been displaced in Colombia (for a comprehensive account of the laws and mechanisms dealing with IDPs see Chaowasangrat 2011; Guerrero 2008, 56–58; Zea 2010). In 1997 Law No 387 established an Advisory Board to the President, and additionally specified the responsibility of the government to create policies and proactively assist victims of displacement (Guerrero 2008, 57). This law recognised the legal legitimacy of internally displaced people and affirmed their right to housing, education, health, security, and socioeconomic assistance in addition to humanitarian emergency attention, as well as recognising the government's obligation to provide this assistance (Profamilia 2011, 12). The success of this law has been very mixed. In 2003, the UNHCR noted that despite the government policy and laws for displaced people, NGOs provide approximately eighty per cent of the assistance for families arriving in Bogotá (ACNUR [UNHCR] 2003).[3]

Since 2004 the Colombian Constitutional Court has paid increased attention to the IDP population. In 2004 it found the conditions displaced Colombians lived in amounted to an 'unconstitutional state of affairs'. In response to this finding, the government formulated Decree 250, entitled '*Plan Nacional de Atención Integral a la Población Desplazada por la Violencia*' ('Comprehensive National Plan for Assistance to the Population Displaced by Violence'), with the aim of strengthening local response mechanisms and providing additional support to vulnerable populations. In October of 2008, the Constitutional Court found that displaced children and young people's rights were not being respected. The Court ordered the government to adopt a 'differentiated policy' for the protection of displaced youth, which focused on prevention of risk and increased support for critical areas of need (Corte Constitucional Auto No. 251 2008). Additionally, it

58 *Half a Century of Struggles for Peace*

noted that displaced children faced particular risk to physical security (including recruitment and trafficking), hunger, preventable heath issues, lack of access to education and psychological trauma (Corte Constitucional Auto No. 251 2008). While there has been some documented success and the government has been responsive in addressing the issues raised (see SNAIPD 2010), in 2010 the Constitutional Court again found the response in dealing with displaced children inadequate. Furthermore, the *Comisión de Seguimiento de la Sociedad Civil* (Civil Society Monitoring Commission) – a group created to support the Constitutional Court's oversight of the government's response to internal displacement – still reports that despite specific systems and provisions having been developed there are significant oversights and problems remain in the deployment and execution of government programs (IDMC 2009; CODHES 2010). In 2015, the Centro Nacional de Memoria Histórica noted that there is statistical evidence of disproportionate impact of forced displacement on minors; particularly noting that 'displacement also creates an obstacle for children and adolescents to develop their capacities and participate politically and socially' and the impact of 'growing up in houses that transmit a sensation of danger and threat' (2015, 416). The effects of Colombia's conflict are multiple and interrelated. Violence and insecurity has impacted Colombians across all aspects of daily life.

Legal and Political Moves to Address the Conflict and Its Victims

The Colombian Constitution, which was rewritten and approved in 1991, notes that the rights of children 'have priority over the rights of others'.[4] It also recognises that the pursuit of peace in Colombian society is a constitutional obligation (Constitucion Politica de Colombia 1991).[5] Beyond the Constitution itself, and in addition to various laws and policies described above dealing with displaced people's rights, there are a suite of laws implemented by the Colombian government at various points to address the conflict, the search for peace, and the rights of victims. Three key moves are the 2005 Justice and Peace Law, the 2011 Victim's Law, and the constitutional amendment in 2012 known as the Legal Framework for Peace. While all three have had successes, they have been critiqued for their limited scope or capacity.

The *Ley de Justicia y Paz* (Justice and Peace Law [Law 975]) of 2005 aimed to advance the progress towards peace by demobilising 'illegal armed groups', mainly AUC (for critiques of its function, see International Crisis Group 2008). In a move to respond to the needs of those civilians who have suffered during the conflict in 2011, the government passed the *Ley de las Victimas* (Victims Law [Law 1448]) in order to provide reparation for victims. It is retroactive to incorporate violence since 1985 and is without a finishing date. Although this is both appropriate and generous, it is increasingly unsustainable, as the number of victims continues to rise. As a result, there is both an ever-increasing caseload and an ever-increasing financial cost. In June 2012, the Colombian Congress approved an amendment to the

Half a Century of Struggles for Peace   59

constitution, called the *Marco Juridico para la Paz,* 'Legal Framework for Peace', which is designed to facilitate a negotiated peace process by allowing only those 'most responsible' to face criminal proceedings, and granting amnesty to combatants who disarm through a government process. Critics say it grants impunity for serious crimes, and for negating care and justice for victims (Human Rights Watch 2012; El Tiempo 2012; Colombia Reports 2012b).

Peace talks between the Santos government and the FARC (discussed below), running for four years from August 2012 to their eventual signing in November 2016, have contributed much more to the legal and political framework for addressing the conflict and victims. Of particular note is the creation of the *Jurisdicción Especial para la Paz* (Special Jurisdiction for Peace), which will constitute the justice component of a *Sistema Integral de Verdad, Justicia, Reparación y no Repetición* (Comprehensive System of Truth, Justice, Reparation, and Non-Repetition) and will allow victims an avenue to find the truth, and receive reparations (Oficina del Alto Comisionado para la Paz 2017). Debate around what justice would look like within the peace agreement and in practice was fierce throughout the negotiations and those who opposed the peace talks leveraged concerns of impunity. As discussed previously, the agenda and resultant peace plan are ambitious documents that are still being put into effect by various branches of government. All these efforts have been met with mixed reception, but underlie the attempts by the state to respond to the conflict itself as well as the very human consequences. These overarching efforts, combined with individual laws and decrees at the both federal and district levels, impact on the lives of those who have fled the conflict and those who exist in situations of social marginality.

Peace Process and 2016 Agreement

On the 24 November 2016, President Juan Manuel Santos and FARC leader Rodrigo Londoño, known as Timochenko, signed a peace agreement, bringing a formal end to fifty-three years of conflict. Although all of the research for this book was conducted before the peace process was finalised (it had yet to be commenced during my time in Colombia in 2010, and was the subject of fierce debate in 2016 when I returned), I include a brief discussion of the peace process here for context of what the formal elements of the peace agreement between the Colombian government and the FARC includes.

Juan Manuel Santos had been the defence minister in President Uribe's second term in office. When elected it was assumed he'd continue the policies of his predecessor. However, he left the door open for negotiations in his 2010 inauguration speech (Presidencia de la República de Colombia 2010). Following secret exploratory meetings between the government and the FARC in 2011, facilitated and guaranteed by Cuba and Norway and 'accompanied' by Chile and Venezuela, Santos announced in September 2012 a 'general agreement' (*Acuerdo General para la Terminación del Conflicto y la Construcción de Una Paz Estable y Duradera*, A General Agreement for the Termination of the Conflict and the Construction of a Stable and Lasting Peace) setting out the agenda and guiding rules for peace talks. The talks, held in Cuba, included six areas of negotiation: rural integral development, political participation, solution to the problem of illicit drugs, end of the conflict, victims, and ratification and implementation (Gobierno de Colombia and FARC 2012). Both parties committed to the talks, under the arrangement that 'nothing is agreed until everything is agreed'. Agreements were progressively reached on each area of negotiation. This process is also notable for including several unique features. A subcommission on gender was set up with the task to consider each aspect of the agreement from a gender perspective, providing feedback to the main negotiating table (see Bouvier 2014). The two parties to the talks received delegations of victims of the conflict: individuals and representatives of communities who had suffered at the hands of all parties. These delegations presented their stories to lead negotiators and other members of both sides, a novel and important inclusion in the process (Bouvier 2014). The peace process also established a Technical Subcommission, which carried out important, detailed work on established processes and considering implications for implementing an eventual accord including terms for the bilateral ceasefire and the eventual setting aside of arms (Presidencia de la República de Colombia 2014). Additionally, regional roundtables were organised to discuss the issues of relevance to the peace process, and delegations of victims from all sides of the conflict travelled to Havana and shared their stories and experiences with representatives from both sides.

The peace negotiations were often fraught, with political events and incidences of violence in Colombia threatening to derail the process. Vocal opposition from former president Alvaro Uribe and allies both draw on and exacerbated concerns and suspicions within the Colombian community about the talks. Despite this, an agreement was reached on August 24 2016. The agreement was submitted to a plebiscite for approval on October 2 2016. It failed by the narrowest of margins: 50.2 per cent against, and 49.8 per cent in favour. Only 37.4 per cent of the population voted. The failure of the plebiscite was a serious threat to the peace process; however, both parties once again sat down, listening to the concerns of those who had led the 'No' campaign for the plebiscite, and revised the agreement, signing a new document on 24 November 2016 (Acuerdo Final 2016). The revised agreement was sent to Colombia's Congress where it was approved. Since November 2016 the FARC have been in a process of transitioning from an armed insurgency to a political party. There have been significant delays, and the shifting power balance in some regions has led to increased insecurity, as the government has not secured lands vacated by the FARC. The government also commenced peace talks with the ELN in February 2017, opening the possibility of an end to that low intensity conflict also. Formal peace does not mean lived peace for all Colombians and many serious challenges still remain, however, it can be hoped going forward, the peace and security of Colombia increases.

Peace Movements and Young People

In the face of protracted violence, Colombians have long organised and acted for peace and in resistance to the violence and danger that impacts their lives. These actions have often come at very high costs, with human rights activists, union organisers, and community leaders targeted for death by armed actors opposed to their efforts to build peace amidst ongoing conflict. In this section I briefly highlight some moments and movements within Colombian peace activism. This is necessarily partial and incomplete and focused to draw attention to the involvement of children and youth in peace making in Colombia. This includes attention on various forms of protest, peace communities in rural regions of Colombia, specific movements by children and youth, and the mobilisations in support of peace in the context of the peace agreement in 2016. Consideration of efforts by civil society to build peace is crucial as they demonstrate the continue struggle by those who live with the effects of violence to respond through their daily lives to construct peace.

Women's peace activism has been particularly strong in Colombia. Following the failure of the Pastrana-led peace talks in 2002, women continued to organise and advocate for a political solution (Bouvier 2015). In regional areas, movements such as the *Ruta Pacifica de la Mujer* (Pacific Route of Women) negotiated local ceasefires that held for several months (Ramírez 2013). The *Ruta Pacifica de la Mujer* was later involved in organising 'regional encounters for peace' alongside other advocacy organisations associated with the 2012–2016 peace talks (Aguirre 2014). Throughout the peace process women's groups, alongside other civil society actors were instrumental in maintaining pressure on the parties to remain at the table and negotiate a comprehensive agreement. This is just the most recent, in a long history of activism. Such groups have been active at local, regional, national and international levels; negotiating with armed groups, advocating for recognition of the consequences of conflict, and campaigning to attract international attention to the conflict.

Indigenous and afro-descendent communities in Colombia have long fought for peace, and often been some of the most insistent voices against violence in regions around Colombia. Indigenous and Afro-Colombian people have been significantly affected by the conflict, and their activism often comes at great personal risk. Indigenous people have campaigned for recognition at formal political levels for decades (see Benavides-Vanegas 2009; Troyan 2008). In the context of the peace process indigenous and Afro-Colombian communities advocated strongly for inclusion and for their specific rights and needs to be recognised in the final accord. Peak organisations, combining regional organisations, including the Afro-Colombian National Peace Council, the ONIC (National Indigenous Organization of Colombia), and *Autoridades Tradicionales Indigenas de Colombia Gobierno Mayor* (Traditional Indigenous Authorities of Colombia Higher Government) advocated strongly for inclusive language in the peace accord (see Gruner 2017).

62 *Half a Century of Struggles for Peace*

Young people have also worked and advocated for their rights and safety within the ongoing conflict. For example, young people have been involved in the creation of 'peace communities' in the middle of the war zone in which approximately 12,000 peasants negotiated a return to their land on which they live out their politics of non-violence and advocate for a peaceful resolution to the conflict (Sanford 2006, 52–53). Sanford argues that in this, they 'represent a new kind of political power grounded in community integrity and moral courage' (2006, 53). Alongside other activists and leaders in the peace communities young people have organised to actively resist recruitment, spoken out against the armed groups and campaigned for peace. These actions are not without risk. In 2002, two representatives of children and youth in the peace communities were assassinated (UN News Service 2002). The young people responded by restructuring so that there was no single leader and instead everyone is viewed as leaders (Sanford 2006, 76).

The *Movimiento de los Niños por La Paz* (Children's Movement for Peace, MNP), led by youth and children, involved 2.7 million young people across Colombia in a symbolic vote called the 'Children's Mandate for Peace and Rights' in which the 'candidates' were children's rights drawn from the UNCRC (including the 'right to peace' and the 'right to love and family') (Carter and Shipler 2005). For the first time many Colombian adults realised the extent of the conflict's impact on the younger generation (Cameron 2001, 31). This demonstration of solidarity and political engagement, in combination with other work by the MNP, has led to various towns and regions involving children more frequently in decision making (Carter and Shipler 2005). By these actions, children and youth demonstrate the positive effects of political involvement and, it is argued, 'construct new modes of agency and citizen participation, which are necessary for peaceful resolution to the internal armed conflict as well as for post war reconstruction' (Sanford 2006, 78). Other, more localised efforts have involved young people in peacebuilding across Colombia, including Cali (Fundación Alvaralice 2016), Montes de Maria (McGill, O'Kane, and Giertsen 2015), and Choco Department (UNHCR 2017), among others. Often these efforts are small and local, and do not gain broader attention.

More recently, in the context of fierce public debate towards the end of 2016 following the surprise 'No' result in the peace deal plebiscite, student groups from universities and some high schools around the country, along with victim's rights organisations, organised marches and rallies (El Tiempo 2016; Sanchez 2016). In news reports and on social media, the message from young people was that their future was too important to waste this opportunity for peace. Alongside other social media campaigns the #PazALaCalle (#PeaceOnTheStreet) hashtag became a site of organising for student activists. In Bogotá, students set up camp in Plaza Bolivar, outside parliament. The 'Campamento por la Paz' (Peace Camp) promised to remain until the government and the FARC renegotiated a deal that was passed (El Espectador 2016). Such student organising has a long history in Colombia; this

Half a Century of Struggles for Peace 63

manifestation demonstrates the engagement and commitment of some young people around the country towards ideas of peace.

From symbolic votes, to collective protest, to leadership that provoked assassination, young people have long been actively involved in rejecting violence and working towards peace in Colombia. While children and youth have been disproportionately affected by the conflict they are not only victims. These few examples obviously do not capture the full ambit of engagements by young people and others in peace work in Colombia, and they cannot fully represent the everyday peace building that has occurred for decades, however they provide small glimpses into the radical action that can emerge from everyday lived experience of conflict. These radical actions are crucial, however, peace can also be fostered through mundane processes of everyday life. To explore the ways the mundane and radical intersect, this book focuses on the community of los Altos de Cazucá; to contextualise these discussions, the realities of everyday life in Cazucá are explored in the following section.

The Community of los Altos de Cazucá

Los Altos de Cazucá (often referred to simply as Cazucá) is part of Comuna 4 (the 4th 'region') of the municipality of Soacha in the Department of Cundinamarca. Soacha is located just south of Bogotá, although rapid urbanisation has made the division between the two difficult to distinguish. Cazucá exists right against the line dividing the two municipalities. The municipality of Soacha is divided into two largely rural territories and six urban *comunas*, which are divided into 347 *barrios*, of which eighteen are illegal settlements without appropriate land titles. Most of these illegal settlements are located in Comuna 4 and Comuna 6. Los Altos de Cazucá is one of these illegal *barrios* (Alcaldia Municipial de Soacha 2008, 8).[6] Only a few decades ago, the site where Cazucá is now situated was empty land, mostly steep, rocky hillsides alongside the highway south from Bogotá towards Soacha and on to the south of the country. Now there are over 50,000 inhabitants in Comuna 4. The comuna is one of the poorest in Colombia, and its poverty and segregation is immediately visible in its lack of paved roads, the shanty-houses, presence of garbage, tangles of electricity lines, and lack of curated or cared-for public space. The community of Cazucá is not unique in Colombia; there are similar places around the country's cities.

Occupants of Cazucá and nearby barrios refer to the space as *la loma*; literally 'the hillside', the use has a sense of community when invoked in conversation. People have been arriving to *la loma* since the 1970s, when the political violence throughout the country caused a massive surge in rural–urban migration. The subsequent industrialisation of Soacha through the 1980s and 1990s served to dramatically increase the urbanisation. The barrio communities started with Barrio Julio Rincon at the base of the hills, and since the 1970s have not stopped growing. This process involved violent confrontations with police, as much of the urbanisation occurred when people

64 *Half a Century of Struggles for Peace*

simply moved onto vacant land and established housing. For those who do not live in these communities, such practices are referred to as *invasiones* (invasions), invoking, with one word, many of the negative attributes ascribed by other Colombians of the act of arriving and the assumed attributes of occupants of these communities (see also Zea 2011).

Soacha in general, and los Altos de Cazucá in particular, is one of the highest recipient-communities in Colombia for people displaced by the conflict. Estimates suggest that over 50 per cent of the population is displaced; this statistic, however, is flawed because many people do not report themselves as displaced due to stigma and fear of further violence, and formal registers did not start until the late 1990s, meaning many more families may have been originally displaced but not recognised in statistics. However, many have now had children who have been born and raised in Cazucá, complicating an idea of 'return' to 'home' (see Berents 2015b). According to 2003 census data (the most recent comprehensive data available), Comuna 4 has just fewer than 50 per cent of all the displaced arrivals to Soacha, and its rate of growth is three times that of the general population (at 4.8 per cent, rather than 1.7 per cent) (DANE 2003). From government data for the Department of Cundinamarca approximately 45 per cent of arrivals are children under fourteen years old. In 2006, Cundinamarca received just over a quarter of the IDP population in Colombia (Pinzon Ochoa 2007, 284). Family life and structure is made more precarious as a consequence of displacement also. This is exemplified by fifteen-year-old Sofia – one of the research participants in Cazucá – in her explanation of her living situation:

> [W]ell I live with my grandparents. When I was nine my father was killed and my mother. ... I don't know. But before that we were displaced from [place name] and came here because my brothers could build a house here. So I have been here since I was about five.

The ongoing urbanisation of the area has led to other forms of land ownership/occupation, including the essentially 'pirate' sale of land, as Uribe and Vasquez term it (1995, 87) where land is sold on to new arrivals which provides right of possession but without appropriate legal titles. Generally, friends or relatives help those who arrive to acquire a small piece of land (often via the 'pirate' sale of land). Houses are built with whatever material is at hand, often initially cardboard and plastic sheeting, with more solid building materials such as tin, brick, and concrete added as time goes by; living conditions that are both figuratively and literally precarious.

In Soacha as a whole, 47.5 per cent of the population is classified as 'vulnerable' and in poverty conditions (this includes recognition of those displaced). Comuna 4 has the largest concentration of this demographic. While the Municipality recognises this as an issue, they noted in 2008 that their key program targeted at assisting these people, *Familias en Accion* (Families in Action), had only been able to assist just under 8 per cent of this population

(Alcaldia Municipial de Soacha 2008, 11). Because the establishment of settlements such as Cazucá occurred mostly illegally, the community has not been able to secure full and ongoing public services such as electricity, sewage systems, and, crucially, potable water.

While services have been gradually improving to the community, very few houses in Cazucá have running water, many do not have sewerage, and most illegally acquire their electricity via the tangle of wires which run up the hillside from the main power lines along the highway. The water the neighbourhood uses arrives irregularly, but generally twice a week, in tanks on the back of trucks. They fill vats for individual family use or that are used to feed into the hoses that share the water among houses and are visible lying across the ground all over the community.[7] Because sewers are lacking, the water often becomes contaminated while flowing through exposed pipe. Even the provision of water via these trucks is an improvement on five years earlier when there was no water apart from what was personally carried in. In conversations teachers mentioned that several years previously children were frequently very dirty and unable to clean themselves without travelling considerable distances to neighbouring communities or down the hill towards the road where water was available.

While Cazucá is one of the primary recipient communities of displaced people in Colombia, those who arrive are often disappear into the population that is already the most poor of the municipality and of the country more generally. In this environment the challenges are multiple, from navigating the complex system of government departments responsible for assistance in various ways, to securing employment and education for children, to dealing with the reality of the presence of the same armed actors present in the wider conflict, which are frequently the reason why individuals and families find themselves in Cazucá in the first place. Access to jobs, health care, and education is difficult. Many adult occupants are involved in the informal market, selling goods on the side of the road or are involved in other precarious forms of employment, begging, or taking part in illegal activities to help provide for their families. Many people in Cazucá cannot earn enough to provide sufficient food for their families, and although the government provides assistance for displaced people, including health care and education as well as living subsidies, the reality is many people do not access such benefits, either because they are not aware they are able to or because they are worried that being formally registered exposes them to the armed groups they are trying to escape (Médecins Sans Frontières [MSF] 2005, 2–3; Guerrero 2008). In 2005 COALICO (*Coalición Contra la Vinculación de Niños, Niñas y Jóvenes al Conflicto Armado en Colombia*, Coalition Against the Recruitment of Boys, Girls, and Youths to the Colombian Armed Conflict) estimated that over half the displaced families in los Altos de Cazucá could not access education or health care provided by the government (COALICO 2005). More recent indications are that this number has improved slightly since 2005.

The government does work to provide health and education services. However, the Colombian health system is very complicated. The subsidised

66 *Half a Century of Struggles for Peace*

Figure 2.1 Two views from the school *Minutos de Dios* over the community (photos taken by author). The barbed-wire fence of the school is visible in both. Also visible in both photos are the mixed building materials for housing in the community.

Figure 2.2

Half a Century of Struggles for Peace 67

health-care services (*régimen subsidiado*) that assists Colombians who cannot pay for their own health care, cannot meet demand (further complicating and frustrating the ability of the residence of Cazucá to access basic services). As a result of the overburdened primary system, another system has been developed for those who are 'linked' (*vinculado*) to the subsidised system, but not formally a part of it. People in this situation can receive emergency care and must pay a portion of the cost of certain services or medications (Human Rights Watch [HRW] 2005, 52).[8] In 2005, the International Committee of the Red Cross (ICRC) estimated almost 100,000 people were *vinculados*, attesting to the in-crisis situation facing the health-care system. These are people beyond the *regimen subsidiado*, which is already over capacity, and the overflow system is also over capacity (HRW 2005, 52; MSF 2005; Profamilia 2010). Long distances to reach medical care also present challenges to the occupants of the community, and people note that once they manage to arrive at a clinic or hospital they often have to stand in line for hours and perhaps not get in to see a doctor before it closes. If they do manage to see a doctor, they are sometimes turned away because they lack appropriate identification. Hospitals have no incentive to provide assistance to those not registered correctly because the government does not reimburse them for these services (HRW 2005, 56). Médecins Sans Frontières reports that respiratory and diarrhetic complaints are the most common ailments of the population of Cazucá, followed by foot infections, nutritional deficiencies, and psychological issues (2005, 9).

Primary and secondary education in Colombia was only made completely free from 2012. Previously some schools would charge students while many schools in poorer regions – including Cazucá – would offer *cupos* (places), which are subsidised by existing government programs but often still require some payment. This has meant that some young people were unable to access limited places or could not afford the fees themselves. President Santos announced the creation of a fund to provide free education, claiming it would provide 8.6 million Colombian students with entirely free education for primary and secondary school (El Espectador 2011; Colombia Reports 2012c). COALICO notes that conflict and displacement interrupt many young people's ability to attend school. Seventy per cent of children who have been displaced do not finish their schooling, predominantly because of economic reasons (they cannot afford clothes and supplies or they must help earn a living for their family) or because they are not registered with the government program, for the same reasons as described above (2005; see also HRW 2005, 41–46).

Death threats and fear of violence have been identified in a Human Rights Watch report as the two top reasons why displaced people have left their home communities in Colombia (2005). However, such problems are not left behind, but rather become a new lived reality in Cazucá itself. A piece of gang graffiti on a wall in Cazucá reads 'Parents, if you don't kidnap your children by dusk, we will do it for you'. Ana Milena Martinez, field coordinator for *Fundación Pies Descalzos* (the *fundación*) in Cazucá, says that such

68 Half a Century of Struggles for Peace

censuring by the armed gangs operating in the community was a common experience. In this environment, there is a high level of violence instigated by various armed groups, which, at its worst, results in many deaths and in families having to leave the community because they are put, for various reasons, on *'listas negras'* (black lists) that mark people for death (or threaten them into leaving). COALICO reports that between 2001 and 2004, almost 450 people were killed in Cazucá, over half of which were young men in their twenties, and males and females under eighteen (COALICO 2005).

The presence of illegal armed groups is ubiquitous in Cazucá, and is an oft-cited characterising feature of the community; with its peri-urban location, Cazucá is well placed as a route to traffic drugs and arms in and out of the city, and as a result is hotly contested by gangs. In research on education in Cazucá, Luisa Fernanda Duque (2009, 29) argues that the myriad of other problems that young people encounter in Cazucá – some few of which have been highlighted in this brief exploration – prompts young people to join various gangs. She argues that such actions become seen as valid because of the stigmatisation and the poverty that affects young people's lives (supported by Pinzon Ochoa 2007). Cazucá is affected by groups associated with the armed groups connected to the broader conflict. Since 2001, AUC paramilitaries gained significant presence in the area, taking over territory from the guerrillas (FEDES 2004), as well as *pandillas* (gangs), much more localised criminal organisations. Further, the community often experiences not only the practice of *'limpieza social'* ('social cleaning'), in which 'undesirable' elements of society are killed – which terrorises the population into submission (Lair 2003) – but also the violent imposition of the police and armed forces in raids and 'patrols'.

In the absence of the state, some of these other groups, through use of force, adopt the role of 'securing' and organising the community. For instance, armed groups often become implicated in the processes of selling and renting allotments (see Pinzon Ochoa 2007, 278). Medina and Téllez note that these groups use 'force on the pretext of serving the community or society's interests, to incapacitate them to control the escalation of conflict' (1996, 43). These violences are also connected to territorial control and control of the drug trade. The use of violence, the instilling of terror, and the control of space by armed groups in Cazucá profoundly affects the way in which people move through (or do not move through) the community and circumscribes the public spaces in which they might gather. Young people, apart from being at risk of recruitment to these groups, also must avoid being seen to be in the 'wrong place at the wrong time' on pain of death – as evidenced in the graffiti discussed above.

Conclusions

For the young people of Cazucá, overcoming the stigmatisation of the community is an immense challenge. Rosa Villamizar and Sara Zamora (2005,

Half a Century of Struggles for Peace 69

74) argue that such stigmatisation directly feeds into the negative practices of young people. Of course, the young people of Cazucá are a distinctly heterogeneous collective in age, background, sexuality, employment situation, educational achievement, ethnicity, family position, personal desires, and aspirations. However, many authors note that adults generally tend to perceive young people as 'transgressors' or as a 'problem' (Duque 2009; Villamizar and Zamora Vasquez 2005, 74; Pinzon Ochoa 2007, 288). The state, however, is often criticised for 'interpreting the realities of young people as problems', particularly in sectors like Cazucá. More than this, the government 'underline their [young people's] relationships with violence, insecurity and drug addiction, cataloguing the population as 'high risk'' (Pinzon Ochoa 2007, 288). As a result, while the state has not been entirely absent in formulating responses and assistance, it has been carried out in the 'best interests' of an imagined young person who they envision. The reality of everyday life is absent. As a result, this young person becomes 'representative, and thus [all] young people are represented' (Valderrama 2004, 166). Consequently, the actual realities and multiplicities of experience are erased.

It is this problematic, static, representation of young people in communities like Cazucá that is at the centre of this book. Existing literature points to the problems inherent in such a configuration, and this research echoes those claims. This chapter has explored the context of the conflict and briefly outlined the history and challenges of the community of Cazucá. It is against a background of endemic, protracted conflict – enmeshed in systems of social exclusion and cycles of violence within everyday life – that this book now turns to the task of finding more productive and inclusive ways of representing and engaging with young people's experiences and contributions.

Notes

1 There has been extensive research carried out on various aspects of the conflict and consequences in Colombia. Further to those referenced within this brief exploration, other research which is of particular value in exploring these themes includes but is not limited to the following: For further, detailed, exploration of the history of Colombia and its conflict see: Bushnell 1993; Palacios 2006; Sanchez and Chacón 2007; Richani 2002; Medina and Téllez 1996; Meertens and Sanchez 2001; Chernick 2001, 2009; Karl 2017; Dudley 2004; Pecaut 2000, 2006; Gamboa and Zackrison 2001; International Crisis Group 2009. For exploration of the consequences for the civilian population and efforts towards building peace see: Bouvier 2009; Arboleda, Petesch, and Blackburn 2004; Delgado, 2009; Haugaard 2008; Adell 2012; Mitchell and Hancock 2012; Solimano 2000; McGee 2017; Idler, Garrido, and Mouly 2015; McIllwaine and Moser 2007; Rettberg 2012; Rojas and Meltzer 2005; Tate 2007; Rettberg and Prieto 2010; Rodriguez 2016. For research focusing on children and youth in Colombia see: Riaño-Alcalá 2010; Berents 2015a, 2015b; Rodgers 2003; Sabogal Ruiz 2005; Sacipa et al. 2006; Watchlist 2004, 2008, 2012; Cameron 2000, 2001; CAP Colombia 2006; CIVIS 2010; Green 1998; Guerrero 2008; Mago 2011; Uribe Rueda et al. 2004; Ritterbusch 2011; UNICEF 2002.
2 Irina Mago conducted in depth interviews with former child combatants in Colombia in her Master's thesis which provide a rich understanding of the process

70 *Half a Century of Struggles for Peace*

of recruitment, participation, demobilisation, and return to civilian life (2011). For other, published, research on child soldiers in Colombia see Castillo-Tietze 2010; Andrade 2010; Ruiz Botero and Hernandez 2008; and Coalition to Stop the Use of Child Soldiers 2008.

3 A survey by the Comision de Seguimiento demonstrated that around 35 per cent of IDPs are not registered in the official government registry. Many IDPs do not declare their situation because of ignorance of the process, or fear of coming forward (2010). CODHES reported that for the year 2009 almost 290,000 people were displaced, compared to the government's claim of 120,000 (CODHES 2010). This is a significant difference, and demonstrates the precariousness of the position of IDPs in official discourse, before even examining the lived challenges that such people encounter.

4 The complete text of Article 44, which includes this quote reads as follows: 'The following are basic rights of children: life, physical integrity, health and social security, a balanced diet, their name and citizenship, to have a family and not be separated from it, care and love, instruction and culture, recreation, and the free expression of their opinions. They will be protected against all forms of abandonment, physical or moral violence, imprisonment, sale, sexual abuse, work or economic exploitation, and dangerous work. They will also enjoy other rights upheld in the Constitution, the laws, and international treaties ratified by Colombia. The family, society, and the state have the obligation to assist and protect children in order to guarantee their harmonious and complete development and the full exercise of their rights. Any person may request the Competent authority to enforce these rights and to sanction those who violate them. The rights of children have priority over the rights of others'. These rights are very similar to those granted by the UN Convention on the Rights of the Child (ratified in 1989). As evidenced previously in this chapter, many young people in Colombia do not in fact experience many of these rights.

5 This was emphasised by President Santos in 2012 as he announced new peace talks with the FARC. He noted that the constitution 'ordered' the pursuit of peace: "We have to do this together. As a society we have the obligation to do this, we are ordered to by the constitution. But we also do it because it comes from the heart,' said Santos' (Colombia Reports 2012a).

6 The occupants of the community referred to the general area in which I was working as 'Cazucá', however, while largely the official map and the discursive use of the name lined up, there are a number of barrios that were sometimes referred to within that designation. Most notably this includes barrio El Minuto, which sits higher up the hillside and was where the second school site was located. This is not to say there was confusion during my work in the community; occupants had a very clear understanding of the official designations for where they lived and the implications of their address for accessing support from the municipality.

7 Because Cazucá literally sits against the zoning boundary between Bogotá and Soacha, the neighbouring barrio receives its services from Bogotá's municipality who, in the case of provision of water, provide a 'better' service. Some of the hoses running through Cazucá, I was told, actually are poaching water from the better-supplied neighbouring community. Such acts make visible the tensions inherent in discourses around deprivation of services, and are discussed further in Chapter Four.

8 The *regimen subsidiado* is a tiered system in which people are ranked from Level Zero upwards (although the subsidised service deals with those from Level Zero to Level Two primarily). While more spaces have been made in the system, most are for Level One or Level Two. This excludes most displaced persons, who on this scale are Level Zero. As an International Committee of the Red Cross (ICRC) representative told Human Rights Watch (HRW) in 2005, 'At Level Zero, they have nothing. Level One means they have a roof over their heads' (HRW 2005, 54). The

cost of health care is subsidised on a sliding scale according to assigned level. Despite this system, many people still cannot afford the cost of medicine or, as previously noted, are not registered appropriately to receive the benefits.

References

1991. *Constitucion politica de Colombia*. Bogotá, Colombia: Estado de la Republica de Colombia.

2016. "Acuerdo final para la terminación del conflicto y la construcción de una paz Estable y duradera." Alto Comisionado Para La Paz. www.altocomisionadopara lapaz.gov.co/mesadeconversaciones/PDF/24-1480106030.11-1480106030.2016nuevo acuerdofinal-1480106030.pdf

ACNUR (Alto Comisionado de las Naciones Unidas Para los Refugiados). 2003. *La población desplazada en Bogotá: Una responsabilidad de todos*. Bogotá, Colombia: Alto Comisionado de las Naciones Unidas Para los Refugiados, ACNUR.

Adell, Borja Paladini. 2012. *From Peacebuilding and Human Development Coalitions to Peace Infrastructure in Colombia*. Berghof Handbook Dialogue Series No. 10. www.berghof-foundation.org/fileadmin/redaktion/Publications/Handbook/Dialogue _Chapters/dialogue10_paladini_adell_comm.pdf

Aguirre, Santiago S. 2014. *Queremos ser oídas: Obstáculos para la participación de las mujeres en los mecanismos de participación para la atención a víctimas del conflicto armado interno*. Bogotá, Colombia: International Center for Transitional Justice.

Albuja, Sebastián, and Marcela Ceballos. 2010. "Urban Displacement and Migration in Colombia." *Forced Migration Review* 34:10–11.

Alcaldia Municipial de Soacha. 2008. *Plan de Desarrollo 2008–2011: "Soacha para vivir mejor."* Soacha, Colombia: Alcaldia Municipial de Soacha.

Alzate, Monica M. 2007. "The Sexual and Reproductive Rights of Internally Displaced Women: The Embodiment of Colombia's Crisis." *Disasters* 32(1):131–148.

Amnesty International. 2004. *Colombia: Scarred Bodies, Hidden Crimes: Sexual Violence Against Women in the Armed Conflict*. London: Amnesty International, International Secretariat.

Amparo Sanchez, Olga, Jose Nicolas Lopez Vivas, Diana Rubriche Cardenas, and Maria del Pilar Rengifo Cano. 2011. *Campaign Rape and Other Violences: Leave my Body Out of War: Sexual Violence Against Women in the Context of the Colombian Armed Conflict 2001–2009*. Bogotá, Colombia: Casa de la Mujer.

Andrade, Gustavo Andrés. 2010. *Los caminos a la violencia: Viculación y trayectorias de los niños en los grupos armados ilegales en Colombia*. Bogotá, Colombia: Ediciones Uniandes.

Arboleda, Jairo A., Patti L. Petesch, and James Blackburn. 2004. *Voices of the Poor in Colombia: Strengthening Livelihoods, Families and Communities*. Washington, DC: The World Bank.

Aysa-Lastra, Maria. 2011. "Integration of Internally Displaced Persons in Urban Labour Markets: A Case Study of the IDP Population in Soacha, Colombia." *Journal of Refugee Studies* 24(2):277–303.

Ball, Patrick, Tamy Guberek, Daniel Guzmán, Amelia Hoover, and Meghan Lynch. 2008. *Assessing Claims of Declining Lethal Violence in Colombia*. Palo Alto, CA: Human Rights Program of the Benetech Initiative.

Berents, Helen. 2015a. "An embodied everyday peace in the midst of violence." *Peacebuilding* 3(2):115–125.

72 Half a Century of Struggles for Peace

Berents, Helen. 2015b. "Children, Violence, and Social Exclusion: Negotiation of Everyday Insecurity in a Colombian Barrio." *Critical Studies on Security* 3, no. 1: 90–104.

Benavides-Vanegas, Farid Samir. 2009. "Indigenous People's Mobilization and their Struggle for Rights in Colombia." *International Catalan Institute for Peace*, Working Paper No. 2009/8. https://papers.ssrn.com/sol3/papers.cfm?abstract_id=1884151

Bouvier, Viginia M. 2009. "Colombia Calls: Notes on a Nation's Struggle for Peace and Justice." https://vbouvier.wordpress.com.

Bouvier, Viginia M. 2014. "Victims Arrive in Havana for End of Round 30: Ver conferencias de prensa aquí." *Colombia Calls.* https://vbouvier.wordpress.com/2014/11/02/victims-arrive-in-havana-for-end-of-round-30-ver-conferencias-de-prensa-aqui/.

Bouvier, Viginia M. 2015. *Gender and the Role of Women in Colombia's Peace Process.* New York: UN Women.

Bushnell, David. 1993. *The Making of Modern Colombia: A Nation in Spite of Itself.* Berkeley, CA: University of California Press.

Cameron, Sara. 2000. "The Role of Children as Peace-makers in Colombia." *Development* 43(1):40–45.

Cameron, Sara. 2001. *Out of War: True Stories From the Front Lines of the Children's Movement for Peace in Colombia.* New York: Scholastic Press.

CAP Colombia (Children/Youth as Peacebuilders/Red Nacional de Jóvenes Constructores de Paz). 2006. *Niños & jóvenes como constructores de paz: III Encuentro Nacional.* Bogotá, Colombia: CAP.

Carter, L. Randolph, and Michael Shipler. 2005. "And a Child Shall Lead: Children's Movement for Peace and Return to Happiness in Colombia." In *People Building Peace II*, edited by Paul van Tongeren, Malin Brenk, Marte Hellema and Juliette Verhoeven. London: Lynne Rienner.

Castillo-Tietze, D. 2010. *¿De actoras en armas a sujetos sociales? Niñas excombatientes y procesos de desarme, desmovilización y reinserción.* Bogotá, Colombia: Terre des Homes (TDH), Fundacion Educacion y Desarrollo (FEDES).

Centro Nacional de Memoria Histórica. 2015. *Una nación desplazada: Informe nacional del desplazamiento forzado en Colombia.* Bogotá, Colombia: Centro Nacional de Memoria Histórica.

Chaowsangrat, Chaowarit. 2011. "Violence and Forced Internal Migrants with Special Reference to the Metropolitan Area of Bogotá Colombia (1990–2002)." Doctor of Philosophy, University College London.

Chernick, Marc. 2001. "The Dynamics of Colombia's Three-Dimensional War." *Conflict, Security and Development* 1(1):93–100.

Chernick, Marc. 2009. "The FARC at the Negotiating Table." In *Colombia: Building Peace in a Time of War*, edited by Viginia M. Bouvier. Washington, DC: United States Institute of Peace.

CIVIS. 2010. "Y vos joven, ¿a que le das voz?" http://civis.se/Y-voz-joven-a-que-le-das-voz.

CNN Español. 2017. "Los tentáculos de Odebrecht en Colombia: La red de los implicados en el escándalo." *CNN Español.* http://cnnespanol.cnn.com/2017/03/17/los-tentaculos-de-odebrecht-en-colombia-la-red-de-los-implicados-en-el-escandalo/#0.

COALICO (Coalición Contra la Vinculación de Niños Niñas y Jóvenes al Conflicto Armado en Colombia). 2005. *Alternative Report to the Report of the Government of Colombia to the United Nations on the Situation of the Rights of the Child in Colombia.* Bogotá, Colombia: COALICO.

Coalition to Stop the Use of Child Soldiers. 2008. *Child Soldier Global Report 2008: Colombia*. London: Coalition to Stop the Use of Child Soldiers.

CODHES (Consultoria para los Derechos Humanos y el Desplazamiento). 2010. *Número de personas desplazadas por Departamento de Llegada*. Bogotá, Colombia: CODHES.

CODHES (Consultoria para los Derechos Humanos y el Desplazamiento). 2011. *¿Consolidación de qué? Informe sobre desplazamiento, conflicto armado y derechos humanos en Colombia en 2010*. Bogotá, Colombia: CODHES.

Colombia Reports. 2012a. "Peace is More Than Ending Conflict: Santos." www.colombiareports.com/colombia-news/news/25829-peace-is-more-than-ending-conflict-santos.html

Colombia Reports. 2012b. "Colombia's Peace Framework Sends 'Dangerous Message': Amnesty." www.colombiareports.com/colombia-news/news/25984-colombias-peace-framework-sends-dangerous-message-amnesty.html.

Colombia Reports. 2012c. "Colombia Implements Free Primary and Secondary Education." http://colombiareports.com/colombia-news/news/21955-colombia-implements-free-primary-and-secondary-education.html.

Corte Constitucional. 2008. "Auto No. 251 de 2008." In *Corte constitucional: Sala segunda de revisión*. Bogotá, Colombia: Republica de Colombia.

DANE (Departamento Administrativo Nacional de Estadistica). 2003. *Censo experimental de soacha*. Bogotá, Colombia: DANE.

Delgado, Hernández Esperanza. 2009. "Resistencias para la paz en Colombia: Experiencias indígenas, afrodescendientes y campesinas." *Revista de Paz y Conflictos* 2: 117–135.

Derks, Maria, Hans Rouw, and Ivan Briscoe. 2011. *A Community Dilemma: DDR and the Changing Face of Violence in Colombia*. Peace, Security and Development Network. www.clingendael.org/sites/default/files/pdfs/20110700_briscoe_derks_colombia.pdf.

Domínguez Loeda, Gonzalo. 2017. "Colombia Peace Process: EU Prioritises Rehabilitation of Child Soldiers." *Euractiv.* www.euractiv.com/section/global-europe/news/colombia-peace-process-eu-prioritises-rehabilitation-of-child-soldiers/.

Dudley, S. 2004. *Walking Ghosts: Murder and Guerrilla Politics in Colombia*. New York: Taylor & Francis.

Duque, Luisa Fernanda. 2009. *Educacion y conflicto: Altos de Cazucá*. Bogotá, Colombia: Fundacion para la Educacion y el Desarrollo (FEDES).

El Espectador. 2011. "Educación pública gratis a partir de 2012." www.elespectador.com/impreso/vivir/articulo-314537-educacion-publica-gratis-partir-de-2012.

El Espectador. 2016. "Jóvenes acampan indefinidamente en Plaza de Bolívar para pedir que salven acuerdo con Farc." *El Espectador*, 6 October. www.elespectador.com/noticias/paz/jovenes-acampan-indefinidamente-plaza-de-bolivar-pedir-articulo-659031

El Tiempo. 2012. "Gobierno revisará cifras sobre reclutamineto forzado de niños." *El Tiempo*, 15 August.www.eltiempo.com/vida-de-hoy/educacion/gobierno-revisara-cifras-sobre-reclutamiento-forzado-de-ninos-_12131989-4.

El Tiempo. 2016. "Universitarios harán marcha del silencio para exigir acuerdo de paz." *El Tiempo*, 4 October. www.eltiempo.com/politica/proceso-de-paz/marcha-universitaria-en-silencio-por-la-paz-30502.

FEDES (La Funcación Educación y Desarollo). 2004. *Jóvenes de Altos de Cazucá, desplazamiento y muerte*. Bogotá, Colombia: FEDES.

74 Half a Century of Struggles for Peace

Fundación Alvaralice. 2016. *Jóvenes constructores de paz. Presentación de resultados de la experiencia de Mapas de Vulnerabilidad, Riesgos y Oportunidades en Potrero Grande, Cali.* Bogotá, Colombia: Organización Internacional para las Migraciones (OIM).

Gamboa, Miguel, and James W. Zackrison. 2001. "Democratic Discourse and the Conflict in Colombia." *Latin American Perspectives* 28: 93–109.

Garcia-Godos, Jemima, and Knut, Andreas O. Lid. 2010. "Transitional Justice and Victims' Rights before the End of a Conflict: The Unusual Case of Colombia." *Journal of Latin American Studies* 42: 487–516.

GMH (Grupo Memoria Histórica). 2010. *Bojayá: La guerra sin límites.* Bogotá, Colombia: Semana.

GMH (Grupo Memoria Histórica). 2011. *La tierra en disputa: Memorias del despojo y resistencias campesinas en la costa caribe.* Bogotá, Colombia: Semana.

GMH (Grupo Memoria Histórica). 2012. *Justicia y paz: Tierras y territorios en las versiones libres de los paramilitares.* Bogotá, Colombia: Semana.

GMH (Grupo Memoria Histórica). 2013. *¡Basta Ya! Colombia: Memorias de guerra y dignidad.* Bogotá, Colombia: Centro Naciónal de Memoria Histórica.

Gobierno de Colombia, and FARC. 2012. *Acuerdo General para la terminación del conflicto y la construcción de una paz estable y duradera.* http://pazfarc-ep.org/ima ges/Extras/AcuerdoGeneralTerminacionConflicto.pdf.

Green, Duncan. 1998. *Hidden Lives: Voices of Children in Latin America and the Caribbean.* London: Cassell.

Gruner, Sheila. 2017. "Territory, Autonomy, and the Good Life: Afro-Colombian and Indigenous Ethno-Territorial Movements in Colombia's Peace Process." *The Journal of Latin American and Caribbean Anthropology* 22(1):174–182.

Guerrero, Alba Lucy. 2008. "Internally Displaced Children Constructing Identities Within and Against Cultural Worlds: The Case of 'Shooting Cameras for Peace' in Colombia." Doctor of Philosophy, Education, University of California, Santa Barbara, CA.

Hanson, Marc. 2012. *Colombia: Transformational Change Must Include Urban IDPs.* Washington, DC: Refugees International.

Haugaard, Lisa. 2008. *The Other Half of the Truth: Searching for Truth, Justice and Reparations for Colombia's Victims of Paramilitary Violence.* Washington, DC: Latin American Working Group: Education Fund.

Human Rights Watch. 2005. *Colombia: Displaced and Discarded: The Plight of Internally Displaced Persons in Bogotá and Cartagena.* New York: Human Rights Watch.

Human Rights Watch. 2010. *Paramilitaries' Heirs: The New Face of Violence in Colombia.* New York: Human Rights Watch.

Human Rights Watch. 2011. "Chapter: Colombia." In *World Report 2011.* New York: Human Rights Watch.

Human Rights Watch. 2012. *"Colombia: Amend 'Legal Framework for Peace' Bill."* New York: Human Rights Watch.

Ibáñes, Ana Maria, and Pablo Querubín. 2004. *Acceso a tierras y desplazamiento forzoso en Colombia.* Bogotá, Colombia: Centro de Estudios sobre Desarrollo Económico, Universidad de los Andes.

Idler, Annette, Maria Belén Garrido, and Cécile Mouly. 2015. "Peace Territories in Colombia: Comparing Civil Resistance in Two War-Torn Communities." *Journal of Peacebuilding and Development* 10(3):1–15.

Half a Century of Struggles for Peace 75

IDMC (Internal Displacement Monitoring Centre). 2009. *Colombia: New Displacement Continues, Response Still Ineffective*. Geneva, Switzerland: Norwegian Refugee Council.

IDMC (Internal Displacement Monitoring Centre). 2016. *Global Report on Internal Displacement (GRID 2016)*. Geneva, Switzerland: IDMC.

International Crisis Group. 2008. "Correcting Course: Victims and the Justice and Peace Law in Colombia." In *Latin America Report No. 29*. Bogotá, Colombia: International Crisis Group.

International Crisis Group. 2009. "Conflict History: Colombia." www.crisisgroup.org/home/index.cfm?action=conflict_search.

International Crisis Group. 2012. *Dismantling Colombia's New Illegal Armed Groups: Lessons from a Surrender*. Bogotá, Colombia: International Crisis Group.

Jones, James C. 2009. "U.S. Policy and Peace in Colombia: Lost in a Tangle of Wars." In *Colombia: Building Peace in a Time of War*, edited by Viginia M. Bouvier. Washington, DC: United States Institute of Peace.

Karl, Robert A. 2017. *Forgotten Peace: Reform, Violence, and the Making of Contemporary Colombia*. Oakland, CA: University of California Press.

Lair, E. 2003. "Reflexiones acerca del terror en los escenarios de guerra interna." *Revista de Estudios Sociales* 15: 88–108.

Landmine Monitor. 2011. *Casualties and Victim Assistance*. Geneva, Switzerland: International Campaign to Ban Landmines.

Mago, Irina. 2011. "¿De niño combatiente a ciudadano?: Los retos de la reintegración política de niños desvinculados del conflicto armado colombiano." Masters in Political Science, Departamento de Ciencia Política, Universidad de los Andes, Bogotá, Colombia.

McGee, Rosie. 2017. "Invisible Power and Visible Everyday Resistance in the Violent Colombian Pacific." *Peacebuilding* 5(2):170–185.

McGill, M., C. O'Kane, and A. Giertsen. 2015. "Evaluating Children and Youth Participation in Peacebuilding in Colombia, DRC and Nepal: Lessons Learned and Emerging Findings." *Young* 11(1).

McIlwaine, Cathy, and Caroline O. N. Moser. 2007. "Living in Fear: How the Urban Poor Perceive Violence, Fear and Insecurity." In *Fractured Cities: Social Exclusion, Urban Violence and Contested Spaces in Latin America*, edited by Kees Koonings and Dirk Kruijt. London: Zed Books.

Medina, C., and M. Téllez. 1996. *Violencia parainstitucional, paramilitar y parapolicial de Colombia*. Bogotá, Colombia: Rodríguez Quito Editores.

Meertens, Donny. 2010. "Forced Displacement and Women's Security in Colombia." *Disasters* 34(S2):S147–S164.

Meertens, Donny, and G. Sánchez. 2001. *Bandits, Peasants, and Politics: The Case of 'La Violencia' in Colombia*. Translated by Alan Hynds. Austin, TX: University of Texas Press.

Meertens, Donny, and Margarita Zambrano. 2010. "Citizenship Deferred: The Politics of Victimhood, Land Restitution and Gender Justice in the Colombian (Post?) Conflict." *The International Journal of Transitional Justice* 4: 189–206.

Mejía, Daniel. 2010. "Evaluating Plan Colombia." In *Innocent Bystanders: Developing Countries and the War on Drugs*, edited by Philip Keefer and Norman Loayza. Washington, DC: Palgrave MacMillan and The World Bank.

Mejía, Daniel, and Pascual Restrepo. 2008. Unpublished manuscript, Universidad de los Andes.

76 *Half a Century of Struggles for Peace*

Ministerio de Defensa Nacional de la República de Colombia. 2011, May. "Política integral de seguridad y defensa para la prosperidad." www.mindefensa.gov.co/irj/go/km/docs/Mindefensa/Documentos/descargas/Documentos_Home/pispd.pdf.

Mitchell, Christopher, and Landon E. Hancock, eds. 2012. *Local Peacebuilding and National Peace: Interaction Between Grassroots and Elite Processes*. London: Bloomsbury Academic.

Mitchell, Christopher, and Sara Ramírez. 2009. "Local Peace Communities in Colombia: An Initial Comparison of Three Cases." In *Colombia: Building Peace in a Time of War*, edited by Viginia M. Bouvier, 245–270. Washington, DC: United States Institute of Peace.

Moser, Caroline O. N., and Cathy McIlwaine. 2004. *Encounters with Violence in Latin America: Urban Poor Perceptions from Colombia and Guatemala*. New York: Routledge.

MSF (Medicos Sin Fronteras). 2005. *Altos de Cazucá: Hasta cuando en el olvido*. Bogotá, Colombia: MSF.

O'Shaughnessy, H., and S. Branford. 2005. *Chemical Warfare in Colombia: The Costs of Coca Fumigation*. London: Latin American Bureau.

OECD (Organisation for Economic Cooperation). 2015. "Employment Outlook. How Does Colombia Compare?" www.oecd.org/countries/colombia/Employment-Outlook-Colombia-EN.pdf.

Oficina del Alto Comisionado Para la Paz. 2017. "Sistema integral de verdad, justicia, reparación y no repetición." www.altocomisionadoparalapaz.gov.co/procesos-y-conversaciones/proceso-de-paz-con-las-farc-ep/Paginas/PR-Sistema-integral-de-Verd ad-Justicia-Reparacion-y-no-Repeticion.aspx.

Palacios, Marco. 2006. *Between Legitimacy and Violence: A History of Colombia 1875–2002*. Translated by Richard Stoller. Durham, NC: Duke University Press.

Pearce, Jenny. 1990. *Colombia: Inside a Labyrinth*. London: Latin America Bureau.

Pecaut, Daniel. 2000. "Configurations of Space, Time, and Subjectivity in a Context of Terror: The Colombian Example." *International Journal of Politics, Culture, and Society* 14(1):129–150.

Pecaut, Daniel. 2006. *Crónica de cuatro décadas de política Colombiana*. Bogotá, Colombia: Grupo Editorial Norma.

Pinzon Ochoa, Nelson M. 2007. "Los jovenes de 'la loma': Altos de Cazucá y el paramilitarismo en la periferia de Bogotá." *Maguare* 21: 271–295.

Pizarro, Eduardo, and Pilar Gaitán. 2006. "Plan Colombia and the Andean Regional Initiative: Lights and Shadows." In *Addicted to Failure: US Security Policy in Latin America and the Andean Region*, edited by Brian Loveman. Lanham, MD: Rowman & Littlefield.

Presidencia Republica de Colombia. 2014. *Comunicado conjunto No. 42*. Bogotá, Colombia: Presidencia Republica de Colombia.

Presidencia Republica de Colombia, and FARC. 2015. *Comunicado conjunto No. 52: Avances del plan de descontaminación del territorio de explosivos*. 29 May. www.humanas.org.co/archivos/comunicadoconjunto52.pdf.

Prieto, Juan Diego. 2012. "Local Coexistence Among Victims, Ex-combatants, and Communities: Challenges for Social Reconstruction in Colombia." Paper presented at the ISA Annual Convention, San Diego, CA.

Profamilia. 2010. *Encuesta Nacional de Demografía y Salud – ENDS*. Bogotá, Colombia: Profamila.

Half a Century of Struggles for Peace 77

Profamilia. 2011. *Surveys in Marginalized Areas Sexual and Reproductive Health, Forced Displacement and Poverty 2000–2011*. Bogotá, Colombia: Profamilia.

Ramírez, Olga Lucía. 2013. *Agenda de las mujeres de la Ruta Pacífica para la negociación política del conflicto Colombiano*. Bogotá, Colombia: Ruta Pacífica de las Mujeres.

Red Nacional de Información. 2017. "Registro único de víctimas (RUV)." https://rni.unidadvictimas.gov.co/RUV.

Rettberg, Angelika, ed. 2012. *Construcción de paz en Colombia*. Bogotá, Colombia: Universidad de los Andes.

Rettberg, Angelika, and Juan Diego Prieto. 2010. "Víctimas, victimarios y vecinos: Proximidad social y actitudes de las víctimas frente a la reparación, la justicia y la paz." In *Reparación en Colombia: ¿Qué quieren las víctimas? Retos, desafíos y alternativas para garantizar la integridad*, edited by Ernesto Kiza and Angelika Rettberg, 107–132. Bogotá, Colombia: GTZ-ProFis.

Riaño-Alcalá, Pilar. 2010. *Dwellers of Memory: Youth and Violence in Medellín, Colombia*. New Brunswick, NJ: Transaction.

Ribeiro, R. 2003. *Gender Dimensions of Non-Formal Employment in Colombia*. Documentos CEDE No. 2003-04, Febrero. Bogotá, Colombia: Universidad de los Andes.

Richani, Nazih. 2002. *Systems of Violence: The Political Economy of War and Peace in Colombia*. Edited by James N. Rosenau, SUNY Series in Global Politics. Albany, NY: State University of New York Press.

Ritterbusch, Amy E. 2011. "A Youth Vision of the City: The Socio-spatial Lives and Exclusion of Street Girls in Bogotá, Colombia." Doctor of Philosophy, International Relations, Florida International University, Miami, FL.

Robles, Frances. 2017. "Colombian Anticorruption Official is Arrested in U.S. Bribery Case." *New York Times*, 27 June. www.nytimes.com/2017/06/27/world/americas/colombia-anticorruption-official-is-arrested-in-bribery-case.html?mcubz=1.

Rodgers, Dennis. 2003. "Youth Gangs in Colombia and Nicaragua – New Forms of Violence, New Theoretical Directions?" In *Breeding Inequality – Reaping Violence: Exploring Linkages and Causality in Colombia and Beyond*, edited by Anders Rudqvist. Uppsala, Sweden: Collegium for Development Studies.

Rodríguez, C. D. T. 2016. "Importancia de la construcción de paz en un contexto de guerra: Caso Colombiano en el periodo 2000–2016." *Revista Internacional de Cooperación y Desarrollo* 3(2):130–149.

Rojas, Cristina, and Judy Meltzer, eds. 2005. *Elusive Peace: International, National, and Local Dimensions of Conflict in Colombia*. New York: Palgrave Macmillan.

Romero, Mauricio, ed. 2007. *Parapolítica: La ruta de la expansión paramilitar y los acuerdos políticos*. Bogotá, Colombia: Intermedio.

Ruiz Botero, Luz Dary, and Martínez Hernández. 2008. *Nos pintaron pajaritos: El conflicto armado y sus implicaciones en la niñez Colombiana*. Bogotá, Colombia: Fundacion Cultura Democratica

Sabogal Ruiz, Viviana 2005. *Jovenes, conflictos urbanos y alternativas de inclusion*. Bogotá, Colombia: Plataforma Conflicto Urbano y Jovenes, CIVIS Suecia & ASDI.

Sacipa, Stella, Blanca Patricia Ballesteros, Juanita Cardozo, Monica M. Novoa, and Claudia Tovar. 2006. "Understanding Peace Through the Lens of Colombian Youth and Adults." *Peace and Conflict: Journal of Peace Psychology* 12(2):157–174.

Sánchez A, Nicholás. 2016. "¿Quiénes son los estudiantes que lideran las marchas por la paz?" *El Espectador, Colombia 2020*, 20 October. http://colombia2020.elespectador.com/pais/quienes-son-los-estudiantes-que-lideran-las-marchas-por-la-paz.

78 Half a Century of Struggles for Peace

Sánchez, Fabio, and Mario B Chacón. 2007. *Las cuentas de la violencia: Ensayos económicos sobre el conflicto y el crimen en Colombia*. Bogotá, Colombia: Grupo Editorial Norma.

Sanford, Victoria. 2006. "The Moral Imagination of Survival: Displacement and Child Soldiers in Guatemala and Colombia." In *Troublemakers or Peacemakers?: Youth and Post-Accord Peace Building*, edited by Siobhán McEvoy-Levy. Notre Dame, IN: University of Notre Dame Press.

SNAIPD (Sistema Nacional de Atención Integral a la Población Desplazada). 2010. *Informe del gobierno nacional a la corte constitucional sobre la superación del estado de cosas inconstitucional declarado mediante la sentencia T-025 de 2004*. Bogotá, Colombia: SNAIPD.

Solimano, Andres, ed. 2000. *Colombia: Essays on Conflict, Peace, and Development*. Edited by The World Bank, Conflict Prevention and Post-Conflict Reconstruction. Washington, DC: The World Bank.

Tate, Winifred. 2007. *Counting the Dead: The Culture and Politics of Human Rights Activism in Colombia*. Berkeley, CA: University of California Press.

Troyan, Brett. 2008. "Ethnic Citizenship in Colombia: The Experience of the Regional Indigenous Council of the Cauca in Southwestern Colombia from 1970 to 1990." *Latin American Research Review* 43(3):166–191.

US Department of State – Bureau for International Narcotics Control and Law Enforcement Affairs. 2006. "International Narcotics Control Strategy Report–2006." www.state.gov/p/inl/rls/mrcrpt/2006/vol11/html/62106.htm.

UN News Service. 2002. "Colombia: UN Envoy Embarks on Last-Ditch Effort to Salvage Peace Process." https://reliefweb.int/report/colombia/colombia-un-envoy-em barks-last-ditch-effort-salvage-peace-process.

UNHCR. 2012. "2012 UNHCR Country Operations Profile–Colombia." www.unhcr. org/pages/49e492ad6.html

UNHCR. 2015. "UNHCR Global Trends: Forced Displacement in 2015." www.unhcr .org/576408cd7.pdf.

UNHCR. 2017. "Forging New Leaders for a Colombian Region Torn by War." www. unhcr.org/en-au/news/stories/2017/4/58dd20a74/forging-new-leaders-colombian-regi on-torn-war.html.

UNICEF. 2002. *La niñez colombiana en Cifras*. Bogotá, Colombia: UNICEF, Oficina de Area para Colombia y Venezuela.

United Nations. 2012. "*Children and Armed Conflict: Report of the Secretary-General" (A/66/782–S/2012/261)*. New York: United Nations.

United Nations. 2016. "*Children and Armed Conflict: Report of the Secretary-General" (A/70/836–S/2016/360)*. New York: United Nations. www.un.org/ga/search/view_do c.asp?symbol=s/2016/360&referer=/english/&Lang=E.

Uribe, M., and T. Vásquez. 1995. *Enterrar y callar, las masacres en Colombia, 1980–1993*. Bogotá, Colombia: Comité Permanente por la Defensa de los Derechos Humanos.

Uribe Rueda, Nichola, Sara Victoria Alvarado, Sabine Markert, and Manuel Manrique Castro, eds. 2004. *Construccion de politicas de juventud: Analisis y perspectivas*. Bogotá, Colombia: Programa Presidencial Colombia Joven, Centro de Estudios Avanzados en Niñez y Juventud CINDE, Universidad de Manizales, GTZ & UNICEF.

Valderrama, A. 2004. "Una mirada a las singularidades juveniles." *Maguare* 18: 161–195.

Villamizar Rojas, Rosa, and Sara Zamora Vasquez. 2005. "Vivir juvenil en medios de conflictos urbanos: Una aproximacion en la zona colindante entre Bogotá y Soacha." In *Jovenes, Conflictos Urbanos y Alternativas de Inclusion*, edited by Viviana Sabogal Ruiz. Bogotá, Colombia: Plataforma Conflicto Urbano y Jovenes, CIVIS Suecia & ASDI.

Watchlist on Children and Armed Conflict. 2004. *Colombia's War on Children*. New York: Watchlist on Children and Armed Conflict.

Watchlist on Children and Armed Conflict. 2008. *Getting It Done and Doing It Right: Strengthening Monitoring and Reporting Activities on Violations of Children's Rights in Colombia*. New York: Watchlist on Children and Armed Conflict.

Watchlist on Children and Armed Conflict. 2012. *No One to Trust: Children and Armed Conflict in Colombia*. New York: Watchlist on Children and Armed Conflict.

White House, The. 2016. "Fact Sheet: Peace Colombia – A New Era of Partnership between the United States and Colombia." 4 February. https://reliefweb.int/report/colombia/fact-sheet-peace-colombia-new-era-partnership-between-united-states-and-colombia.

Zea, Juan Esteban. 2010. "Internal Displacement in Colombia: Violence, Resettlement, and Resistance." Master of Arts, Anthropology, Portland State University, Portland, OR.

3 Space, Power, and Terrains of Insecurity

FELIPE (16): … many people think that Cazucá … [exhales forcefully] … if you come here you'll be killed, if you arrive in Cazucá they'll rob you or attack you, or all of that. … And well if they actually came here they would see that isn't always true.

BRAYAN ALEXANDER (15): It's the stigma … of course there are problems here … but the social stigma is a massive issue … .

'Helen, there has been a *derrumba* in the community''. It was just early in the morning when I had phoned Ana Milena, *Fundación Pies Descalzos*'s field coordinator in los Altos de Cazucá to see if I could travel to the community that day. In Spanish *derrumba* literally means 'collapse'; in Cazucá it means landslide and, more than that, it means the wiping out of years of effort of families to stake out a small claim to a piece of land and build a life for themselves. Ana Milena told me that luckily, this time, no one had died. At the time of this phone call, I had been visiting Cazucá for about eight weeks, and Colombia was suffering through its wettest autumn in years. The steep sloping hills where these unsteady houses had been built couldn't hold the amount of water that had fallen. Landslides, such as this one, make visible the everyday precariousness of the lives of those who, for many reasons, find themselves living in Cazucá.

The landslide in Cazucá was one of innumerable landslides in similar communities around Bogotá and Colombia during my time there. In this case it affected approximately twenty houses, several of which had fallen entirely down the hillside to expose brightly painted or tiled rooms. Houses that were entirely uninhabitable were marked with spray paint: an 'X' inside a circle. Houses which had suffered severe damage or were at risk of also falling were marked with a '\' inside a circle (see Figure 3.1). People were being kept out of those houses, as the ground was too unstable to risk entering.

The inhabitants of the destroyed houses had nowhere else to go and so other families in the community took them in, and the local pastor assisted. The *fundación* did not normally provide emergency assistance, but in the absence of other help and in response to constant requests by mothers visiting

Figure 3.1 Aftermath of landslide. Danger sign visible on building (photo taken by author)

the *casita*, they organized meals and clothing for families whose children were in the school they worked with.

I spoke with Ana Milena about the consequences of the landslide when I arrived at the *casita* later on the day of our phone call. She said,

> [A]lthough most of the families have found somewhere else to stay, things will continue to be difficult. In losing their house they lost everything.

82   *Space, Power, and Terrains of Insecurity*

They built their houses from nothing, and now have nothing again. The government always talks big about helping such people but there will be very little help for these families. What are we here [at FPD] meant to do? People will help, but the insecurity of these people's lives makes it all so difficult. Where will they live? Where will their children study? How will they cook their meals? How will they keep their family safe if they do not have walls? They will be forgotten but continue to struggle.

Recounting this story here does not capture the impact of visiting the site with workers from the foundation. It was an intensely confronting and visible representation of the precariousness of the terrain of the community. Literally dangerous terrain, the neglect of the state in assisting with the disaster, as well as the fact such occurrences rarely merit a mention in any media (this one did not), all highlight the highly spatialised insecurity experienced by the inhabitants of Cazucá. Several weeks later, despite ongoing work by community members to clear the area and secure the ground, the houses remained where they had fallen, their occupants scattered and once again reabsorbed by the community in new ways.

The conflict in Colombia has always been profoundly spatialized. Historical antecedents can be seen in the division of areas of the country by identification with the Conservative or Liberal parties. The conflict through the second half of the twentieth century has seen people's ability to move around circumscribed. There are several different examples of this. One often repeated story amongst both Colombians and visitors has to do with travelling by vehicle along the main highway between Bogotá and Medellín. Particularly during the 1990s and into the early 2000s it was generally understood that if you had not seen a vehicle pass you in the other direction for ten minutes to turn around and return where you came from because it was a fairly reliable sign of a roadblock or other activity by armed actors preventing travel along that road. The highway was known for kidnappings in particular. For those who could afford it, air travel became the best way of moving between the two cities, but for many Colombians it was an unavoidable risk. Similar stories exist for roads and locations around Colombia. For foreigners, Colombia's conflict is mapped by degree of danger by foreign governments' foreign affairs departments so travellers know where they can or cannot travel (or with how much security they can expect to do so).

The Pastrana government's failed attempts to allow FARC a zone to operate in as part of the peace process in the early 2000s – where part of the agreement for peace talks was a geographical region of FARC control, which the FARC largely used to regroup while peace talks deteriorated (Arnson et al. 2006, 8–9) – is another example of the way the conflict is experienced and described spatially. Additionally, the creation of 'peace communities' and zones of peace by locals living amongst the worst of the conflict (Sanford 2003; Mitchell and Ramírez 2009; Rojas 2007; Hancock and Mitchell 2007) demonstrates civilians organizing the spaces of the conflict within their lives. These communities, existing in particularly affected areas of the country, collectively

Space, Power, and Terrains of Insecurity   83

decided they would be sites in which no armed actors or weapons would be permitted. Such action creates a consciously spatial reading of the violence; many of the armed groups, as well as state forces, challenge the creation of these communities, and in many cases individuals have been killed for their involvement.

The story of the landslide illustrates a different kind of spatialized danger for the inhabitants. However, not only do those who live in Cazucá have to negotiate a physical terrain of insecurity, but a figurative terrain in which the narrative and stigmatization of the community reinscribes violence. The dominant construction of *barrio* communities such as Cazucá as places of violence perpetuates justifications for exclusion, which in turn increases the violence and insecurity in those communities. The absence of constructive state intervention in these spaces, or the fact it only enters in particularly violent, repressive ways circumscribes the ability of those who live within the spaces to participate meaningfully in broader civic life. By exploring how young people see the spaces they occupy, this chapter contributes to this book's conceptualization of a politics of the everyday that is located within young people's daily navigation of their everyday environments. It asks: what might a politics of space might mean when read through the lives of young people marginalized by conflict and disenfranchised by the state? How can their reading of the everyday terrain of insecurity which they negotiate can contribute to making young people present in notions of everyday peace?

This chapter begins with the conversations and formal planning documents, in which those beyond the community frequently identify the area in which Cazucá is located as a place of danger. It is the construction of this stereotype and young people's responses to it that occupy the first section. Spatial insecurity and the rendering of groups of people as powerless is a visible manifestation of structural violence in which institutions exclude people from the political process, deny them access to services and benefits, and exploit them for economic or political gain (see Farmer 2004). It can be seen as a 'nonplace' (Nordstrom 2004; Auge 1995), a place that is beyond the bounds of supposed civilised 'made' space of the city. Such narratives reinforce a culture of social exclusion, which has profoundly damaging effects on notions of community and cohesion. Such a construction of Cazuca as a 'non-place' permits a profound othering of its occupants which enables the state to exercises its power in particular ways. Springer envisions 'virulent imaginative geographies' (2011) that inform the deployment of power by the state in places characterized as beyond the bounds of controllable 'civilised society'. Such spaces are constrained and patrolled in (often violent) ways that enable the ongoing authority of those in power. The negative stereotyping of geographically defined areas is embedded in a neo-liberal discourse about civilized and non-civilised spaces, endorsed by deliberate acts of 'not-knowing' (Nordstrom 1999, 2004, 37–38) about the reality of life within *barrios* such as Cazucá. The rendering of spaces as inherently violent and 'uncivil' justifies their ongoing exclusion and particular forms of violent and militarised

84   *Space, Power, and Terrains of Insecurity*

intervention as well as the emplacement of invisible 'boundaries' that contain the violence but do not endeavour to address its causes. Young occupants characterise these interventions by the state as corrupt, neglectful, and violent, and it is these sentiments that are unpacked in the next section of this chapter. Young people articulately critique the state's (non)engagement with the occupants of the community, express sentiments of profound injustice, and emphasize their distrust of the police who are the state's most visible representation in Cazucá. Such engagements increase the insecurity of the spaces people must live in and also circumscribe an individual's abilities to participate in the collective life of the country.

Having looked 'from the outside in' and analysed how those outside it understand a community such as Cazucá, and the nature of its occupants, this chapter then turns to how the physical space of Cazucá is navigated by young people themselves. Space is fluid, contingent, and negotiated. Spaces can transition from private to public, from sanctioned to transgressive, from 'hot' to 'dead', and from safe to dangerous, in complex and rapid succession. In this discussion, centering young people's accounts of spatial insecurity makes them present as agents in the spaces of the everyday, and contributes to recognizing their understandings as important for building notions of everyday peace in such insecure terrains. Exploring how the inhabitants of Cazucá understand the spaces they occupy opens a space for a politics of the everyday that starts at the bodies of young people. It contributes a way of conceiving the politics of space in the context of the embodied everyday lives of young people affected by social exclusion and insecurity.

A 'Non-Place'

Places are a product of interrelations that are 'constituted through interactions' (Massey 2005, 9). They also achieve a notion of status through a defining of what they are *not*. Central in the creation of place is a firming of a notion of places that are 'other'. Edward Said argues that the creation of identity in this sense occurs through the practice of 'designating in one's mind a familiar space which is 'ours' and an unfamiliar space beyond 'ours' which is 'theirs'' (1995, 54). In such configuration 'our' space is understood as a sanctioned space – while it may hold negative connotations (a house can be 'prison-like' just as much as it can be 'home-like'), it is a space that is understood, ordered, and controlled. Place in this sense is a 'spatial metaphor [that] is a vehicle for the fabrication of identity' (Gregory 1995, 455). It is this understanding of space as controlled and sanctioned that highlights the link between spatial understandings of identity and structures of knowledge and power.

Said discusses 'imaginative geographies' as triangular interactions and interrelations of power, knowledge and, crucially, geography. While this includes the physical, topographical rendering of space, it also includes the fluid and contested nature of space as *imagined*, strengthening the interface between 'ours' and 'theirs', 'here' and 'there', and 'controlled' and 'uncontrollable'.

Space, Power, and Terrains of Insecurity 85

The starkest recognition of sanctioned places is to describe them in opposition to 'non-places'. Carolyn Nordstrom argues that the making of places as visible sites of belonging, power, or meaning depends on a 'non-recognition of non-places' (2004, 37). This term, originally used by Marc Auge, here follows Nordstrom's discussion of the phrase. Auge is interested in the huge places of movement and transit that supermodernity has created, such as airports, highways, refugee camps and holiday resorts. These non-places exist in collective consciousness as unable to be defined as 'relational, historical, or concerned with identity' (Auge, 1995, 76). For Nordstrom, the intriguing aspect of non-places is their applicability to illicit spheres in conflict zones. If places are given meaning and substance, they are made in opposition to all that is *elsewhere*, to that which is 'constructed in popular thought as the province of misery and danger ... the homeless, the criminal, the illicit, the marginal' (Nordstrom, 2004, 37).

While Nordstrom is more interested in the paths and implications of vast extra-legal networks that operate in conflict and post-conflict zones, her interpretation of Auge's non-place is useful when considering the presence of large populations that exist in a state of marginality and precariousness on the literal edges of the civil, *made* place of cities such as Bogotá. Cazucá, along with the other *barrios* around it, are 'invasions' (*invasiones*), illegal settlements encroaching upon the assumed civility and security of Bogotá itself. Rengifo Castillo notes that

> these zones do not exist in the collective imagination of the big cities as spaces of struggles for social inclusion, or the right to belong to the city, rather, they are recognised for their marginality, for the high rates of violence and for the danger, real or imagined, that they represent for the rest of the inhabitants of the city.
>
> (2005, 61)

Such 'non-places', understood by those *beyond* of the geographical location of the hillside, can only be conceived of as an absence of place, beyond civil society, outside of meaning; and those who inhabit such space are 'shadowy figures' (Nordstrom 2004, 37) who are unable to fully participate in the plurality of place making in civil spaces (see Massey 2005, 9). Those who occupy such a place are unable to participate in the creation of understandings of their own experiences and thus are described rather than describing their own sites of being. Springer notes that the manner in which we recognize a place is 'dependent on the stories-so-far to which we have participated in forming that place, but equally, and indeed wholly for places that we have never visited, the imaginings that have been circulated, rendered, and internalized or rejected in forming our cartographic understandings' (2011, 94). To this end, the effect of media and public 'information' on the peri-urban barrios that occupy the supposed 'non-place' along the highway between Bogotá and Soacha greatly influences understandings of these places.

86 Space, Power, and Terrains of Insecurity

The construction of such non-places as the 'province of misery and danger' can be clearly seen in the description of popular opinion in the Regional Advocacy Resolution #003 released by the Public Defender, responsible for attention to human rights under Article 282 of the Colombian Constitution. In this document it is noted that for the citizens of Soacha 'the populations of los Altos de Cazucá and Ciudadela Sucre [a nearby *barrio*] are considered foreigners and invaders. In the worst of cases they are seen as delinquents, paramilitaries or guerrillas ... a danger for the Municipality' (Resolucion Defensoria 2002, 3). Such an understanding can be seen to not only problematize a spatialized conception of the issue, but problematize those who occupy that space also. Fear and threat of violence, tied to a specific place is fundamental to our understandings of the constitution of spaces. Negative understandings of a place can prompt a 'visceral and emotional charge to our ontological and epistemological interpretations' (Springer 2011, 94). Those who live within Cazucá are aware of this attitude. Sixteen-year-old Christian recognises that the external opinion of Cazucá is negative; however, he challenged that observation by noting that if people came here they would see there is more to the community than the negativity:

> Here we also learn how to be very fair people. Everything isn't violent. Here we learn how to be a good person and that. Well, in Bogotá, the opinion of Cazucá is shit. But that is because they do not try and speak with us. But we do try to find other ways of being good people.

Of course, here is the crux of the issue around the creation of 'non-place': because it has been classified as beyond civil society it can be ignored or deliberately 'non-recognized' to borrow Nordstrom's phrasing, making it unnecessary for those outside of Cazucá to attempt to question or challenge their conception of the space and those who live within it.

This deliberate non-recognition of non-place, which has the effect of profoundly othering the occupants of such places is evident further in the Regional Advocacy Resolution No. 003, which goes on to note that the inhabitants of Cazucá are generally seen to 'not consider los *soachunos* [citizens of Soacha] their countrymen, nor Soacha their municipality' (2002, 3). Not only does such a pronouncement problematize the very existence of the *inhabitants* as well as the physical territory of Cazucá, but it also links perceived nonconformity to a lack of a sense of citizenship and has the effect of isolating those who live in Cazucá as *other* to the *soachuno* or *bogotáno* (or even 'proper' *colombiano*), who performs and conforms as citizen. The explicit and implicit understanding of places such as Cazucá as non-places have the effect of disconnecting the problems experienced by those who occupy these places from the broader political forces in the country that have brought these people there; it figuratively destabilises the terrain in which they live. The problem becomes constructed as located in a bounded geographical terrain, which erases or hides the *placing* that occurs in that process.[1]

The Consequences of a 'Virulent' Imaginative Geography

There is an inescapable tension in the process of rendering somewhere as 'other'. The practice of place making – and its concomitant process of reading other spaces as 'non-place' – is not a neutral act, but rather is an act of power. The exercise of power operates partly through a 'social segregation of the excluded', which divides the urban space into 'civilised zones' and 'savage zones'. In the former the state acts in a democratic manner, but in the latter it can act as 'a predatory state without even the slightest regard' for the law or the well-being of the occupants of that zone (Santos 2002, 453). The 'placer' – the person who *others* spaces like Cazucá as non-place – is outside of that space, and is also in a position whereby their designation both contributes to, and grows from a broader tacit agreement on which spaces are sanctioned and which are not. It is a vast array of the Colombian population who falls into these liminal categories and precarious terrains. These include Colombia's IDP population, struggling rural communities, urban unemployed, and young people unable to access education or work. Coleman argues these groups are 'completely excluded' (2007, 208) by the construction of non-places, and exist in a state of perpetual anxiety about the future because of this exclusion. Santos describes these people as the 'uncivil civil society' because while they are formally citizens, 'in practice they have no rights' (Santos 2002, 451, 457). Such a reading of the state's power pushes Said's configuration of 'imaginative geographies', asking instead how they can be read as 'virulent' imaginative geographies (Springer 2011). Springer's understanding and use of the word virulent is particularly relevant here. He explains its use in the following manner:

> First, I seek to emphasize those imaginative geographies that invoke a profound sense of hostility and malice, which may thereby produce tremendously harmful effects for those individuals cast within them. Second, through the simplicity of the essentialisms they render, some imaginative geographies may be readily and uncritically accepted, thus making them highly infectious and easily communicable among individuals... and in this way they operate as symbolic violence.
>
> (2011, 93)

Finally, he argues that in a linguistic sense virulence is derived from the Latin word man (*vir*) and virulence is 'informed by masculinist modes of response and engagement'; thus, 'the cultural coding of places as sites of violence is thus imbricated in gendered ideas about master ... colonial control' (2011, 93–94). Springer argues that this is a 'discursive emasculation' which is itself a form of symbolic violence, and results in those within the virulent imaginative geographies unable to manage the violence themselves. This conceptualization of imaginative geographies as 'virulent', connected to Santos' 'uncivil civil society', partially explains the state's behavior in Cazucá and similar sites.

88 *Space, Power, and Terrains of Insecurity*

Furthermore, the gendered connotations of a virulent imaginative geography – of a state as master and in control of a submissive, feminised, population – have important consequences for the occupants of these communities.

The state's intervention into the spaces Santos' frames as 'civilised society' are different from much of the state's involvement in the peri-urban communities such as Cazucá, where the physical presence of the state is through the bodies of military and police. The division of the way space is inscribed and understood by the state enables 'the exercise of power and violence over those represented as the savage, underdeveloped 'other'' (Coleman 2007, 207). The members of the uncivil civil society exist in 'savage' zones where they remain constantly exposed to police, military, and gang violence. The profound disjuncture between the demands *on* the state by those displaced and their host communities and the willingness and ability *of* the state to provide adequate and required services is not only a deep structural violence, but obfuscates the efforts of people in these environments to not just resolve ongoing everyday violences but to live amongst them.

In Cazucá the most obvious daily presence of the government is a secured van staffed by law-enforcement officers, which sits low on the hill of the community ostensibly (although not often practically) as a form of engagement with the community. As seventeen-year-old Laura notes 'the police are useless here on the hill (*la loma*). Their only use is as decoration. That's the truth'. Members of the community noted that the law enforcement presence makes the physical space and their presence within that space *more* dangerous as they are aware the van is constantly watched by the various illegal armed groups that regulate the space of the community also. Interaction, even inadvertent with law enforcement personnel, can have severe personal consequences if the illegal armed groups see that interaction as a threat. In many ways the presence of the van is a physical marker of an enforced boundary for the occupants of the community, as well as a point of entry for the state. Conversely, the police also claim a freedom of movement not available to the occupants when they entered the community to raid or otherwise impose forceful authority (these interventions are discussed below). These interactions and risks highlight the 'hostility and malice' (Springer 2011, 93), as well as masculinst forms of violent control, inherent in understandings of such spaces as 'virulent' imaginative geographies. They reinforce external notions of inherent violence that is tremendously harmful to the occupants of such spaces.

Hunt highlights that the nation-state is not the base of a 'civilised' international order, rather – following Agamben, as well as and Hansen and Stepputat – she argues that the 'very power [of the nation-state] is garnered from excessive and exceptional violence and the ability to create and exclude 'bare life'' (2009, 35). But more than this, such violence also regulates and creates structure and meaning. While state failure is defined in general terms as the inability of rulers to govern even their core areas, Colombia demonstrates the complexity of such claims. While the state continues to hold power and maintain legitimacy, unlike in other situations of countries with internal armed conflict, this power is fraught, violent, and constitutive of the relationship between the institutions of government and the citizenry in general. Davis and Pereira (2003) note that irregular armed forces (from paramilitary forces through to privately hired security) are now a widely accepted part of modern states and modern processes of governance. The institutionalized (if now illegal) links between government forces and paramilitary groups are well documented and Coleman argues that this 'military-paramilitary violence both reproduces and is reproduced by a neo-liberal regime of inclusion for a minority of the population and exclusion for the majority' (2007, 208). Hunt (2009) also shows that the violence in Colombia is worst in the areas where the government is 'most present', in particular where the government is evident through police or military presence but also in other areas through the government's use of paramilitary or private forces. The enactment of inclusion/exclusion is profoundly spatialized. Rural citizens are problematized as primitive and in need of coercion by the state in order to develop, while other spaces are categorized as violent, rebellious and in need of force to bring the space back under control (a phrase that in many cases is a fantasy as Colombia's history of violent partisanism means that many physical geographical spaces have never sat comfortably under state control). Thus, these populations – those that remain in these spaces, those who fight, as well as those who flee – are 'already non-includable' within the neo-liberal project of development and state control. As Coleman observes, 'The imaginative geographies have been created which make possible the violent imposition of neo-liberal capitalism' (Coleman 2007, 209). In these narratives the government 'owns' and 'controls' the space, wrestling it physically from those who are 'uncivil' or 'uncontrollable' through supposedly civil means.

With the undertaking of the peace process, and the vacating of certain territories by the FARC in early 2017, a new dimension of this tension has become evident: the state has been slow to enter these territories, and control has been claimed by paramilitary groups imposing a new form of violence. Rhetoric from the state has reinforced a sense of inevitability of further violence in these areas as the state moves forces in to 'regain control'. These virulent imaginative geographies commence in the countryside, where the conflict created impossible challenges for farmers and peasants who live with the consequences of ongoing violence and the attempts of the state to exert control. However they make their way into urban environments as those displaced by the conflict establish communities like Cazucá, and as people find employment scarce, resources unavailable, and services nonexistent.

Those characterized as 'uncivil' or 'savage' in the imaginaries of those in power are not unaware of the problematic nature of the construction of these terrains of insecurity. Those marginalized by the state and most affected by conflict make claims to belonging; protests by IDPs occur within the civic spaces of Bogotá (Zeiderman 2013, 2016), and in the everyday spaces of Cazucá, individuals recognize that being in the peri-urban *barrio* allows them a visibility they lack in the countryside (see Berents 2018). Ana Milena, the

90   *Space, Power, and Terrains of Insecurity*

fundación's coordinator in Cazucá, contextualized this sentiment that I had encountered in several conversations with adult occupants of the community:

ANA MILENA: Yes, yes of course. And a part of this is that its also … that its also been promoted that violence starts in the countryside. But still, the state doesn't reach even here [Cazucá] … and if the state abandons us, well obviously there are going to be other groups, recruiting … say, changing people's minds. Yes? Then, of course, obviously the government sees the space as a problem. But look, for example at Bogotá, all of Bogotá and where is the urban zone and the rural zone? Part of it [Bogotá] is on the border with farmers and so on. Yet they are so rarely recognized, they are paid very little, they are able to learn very little. Yes?
HB: … lack of opportunities…
ANA MILENA: Yes! Of course, that is it. It is the total lack of care of the government for the rural zones … where one is not appreciated as much as the other. Mmmm. So, well, if you imagine here is difficult, over there [in the countryside] it is lots harder, I mean in those zones people can only achieve basic levels of education, no more …

This discussion with Ana Milena highlights the difficulty in categorizing spaces in different ways, as the territory of Cazucá itself can be read as both urban – through the presence of people living there – and as rural – through zoning decisions and the nonengagement of the state. Ana Milena's discussion of the rural and urban spaces in and around Bogotá demonstrate the way in which the government sees these issues as a problem of space – more particularly a problem of proximity, locality or geography, all of which render people invisible rather than recognizing the embodied experiences of those *within* the spaces. The rendering of spaces as of less concern to those in authority, and consequently to those who have fled, as seemingly irredeemable or lost manifests in sentiments of profound disenfranchisement and articulations of the failing by the state of its obligations.[2] As bodies-out-of-place, the imposition of violent categories forces such people 'into the savage spaces within an urban topography divided by logics of hyper-exclusion and hyper-inclusion' (Coleman 2007, 209). This disjuncture renders the space as violent and justifying of exclusion, while eliding the activities and actions of those in this space would challenge such narratives.

Violent State Intervention and Stigmatisation of the Community

Cazucá is the site of contestation between gangs (in many cases linked to the armed groups of the broader conflict) and the security apparatus of the state, namely the police and army. For many inhabitants this situation is reminiscent of the kind of environment they fled from, and more than that, it makes everyday life insecure. Many young people are sceptical of the ability or desire of the police to intervene in situations and in almost all interviews someone

Space, Power, and Terrains of Insecurity   91

made mention of the inaction or unwillingness of the police, or accused them of being corrupt rather than caring for the community; evident in this exchange between seventeen-year-old Laura, and fifteen-year-old Rosa:

LAURA: ... if you go to [the police] with a problem they just say 'so what do you want me to do about it?' and do nothing.

ROSA: It is because the police now, are busy being thieves. They are just thieves dressed like police. Because they also rob you or say you need to pay for help from somewhere else.

Several other young people echoed Rosa's comments, saying that the police would do nothing if contacted. These stories include one in which the police were called because of a situation of domestic violence and they said they could not do anything, and this subsequently made the situation worse according to the young people I spoke with. Rosa, Laura, and their friend fourteen-year-old Camila Andrea also spoke about the police in the context of drug problems:

LAURA: Yes, the drugs pass through and the police don't do anything ...

CAMILA ANDREA: And so people think we are drug addicts or involved in some way ... which means we get punished as a community...

ROSA: [interrupts Camila Andrea] Under-age kids come past with a little bag [of marijuana]. But the police don't do anything!

Such stories are common amongst both the young people and the adults around them. Similar accounts were given by members of the *fundación* and the unwillingness, or inability, of police to effectively govern the *barrio* was a clear concern. When the force of law is applied to the community, it often takes the form of late night raids on suspected gang members' households, which sometimes lead to shootings, knifings, or other violence on the streets. These sweeps are often publicized by the police via television and newspaper after the fact, and often solely in quantifiable terms (amount of drugs seized, weapons confiscated, people arrested) and without reflection on the consequences of the raids on the fragile (in)security of the community. During a conversation in 2010 with several students in a lunch break at school, referring to a police action in the neighbourhood, they told me that one of their older brothers was refused a job the next day because he came from the neighbourhood that had just been on the news and thus was seen as potentially connected to the drug violence.

The relationship between the police and the occupants of Cazucá is not unique, but rather repeats a frequently cited experience of those who live in poor and marginalised communities. Elizabeth Leeds, in work in *favelas* in Rio de Janeiro, Brazil argues that the occupants of the *favela* are caught between local drug gangs and the police who do not remain neutral in their dealings – often being paid off, or participating in extortion of the gangs

92 *Space, Power, and Terrains of Insecurity*

(2007). Police rarely attempt to build relationships with the community and Leeds argues that 'the role of the police in perpetuating drugs trading is a crucial variable in the ongoing dynamic of exclusion-violence-exclusion' (2007, 28). Other research in Colombia identifies the police as the main source of mistrust because not only would they not provide 'formal' security (that they were meant to do as part of their job) but they would extort people for bribes, cut deals with local gangs, and also become complicit with violent occurrences (McIllwaine and Moser 2007, 131). Picon, Arciniegas, and Becerra note that in *barrios* like Cazucá the management of the community manifests as a 'chain of legalities and illegalities that local politicians, public functionaries, and agents of the state participate in; and which is partially accepted by the inhabitants of the *barrio*' (2006, 14). They go on to argue that an individual's position in the execution of power depends on their 'ability to comprehend and manage the logics of bureaucratic processes and evade the official norm'. The complexities of such a process complicate daily life and make negotiations of the spaces in which individuals live more insecure and potentially transitory.

While a majority of the occupants of Cazucá are not involved in the drug trade and would prefer it did not occur, the violent interventions by the state security forces in which all occupants are seen as potentially implicated and thus potentially violent only increases the distrust and disdain for the police. Such distrust increases the space in which the gangs can operate and decreases the security for all members of the community. In furthering Springer's articulation of 'virulent imaginative geographies', the ability to represent and imagine particular terrains and the inhabitants in one way and not another is the powerful operationalization of rules of norms. Such configurations allow the space for violence and, as Springer notes, '[sanctioning] certain acts of violence as 'rational' while condemning others as 'irrational' can be discerned as a primary instrument of power insofar as perceived rationality becomes misconstrued with legitimacy' (2011, 93). Hunt argues that the manifestation of the power of the state can be conceptualized as ruling both 'violently and non-violently, legally and illegally, equally and unequally' (Hunt, 2009, 68). These apparent contradictions and the differentiation of citizens as more or less deserving of protection (despite the contradictory negative outcomes such protection may bring) highlight the presence of those on the margins of society. The violent intervention of the state in the community is rationalized as necessary and appropriate by the state. These dilemmas underscore the difficulties facing young people living in Cazucá in a position of constantly reinforced marginality and structural powerlessness.

Here I turn to discuss young people's feelings towards the Colombian government broadly conceived, as well as its interactions in Cazucá in light of this othering and violent intervention. Young people were acutely conscious of the disparity in the way in which the state engages with its citizens in 'civil' spaces and 'non-places'. Most frequently such frustrations were articulated as a sense of profound injustice. The sense of insecurity in the *barrio* is seen as a

Space, Power, and Terrains of Insecurity   93

systemic problem in which the challenges faced within the community are either largely ignored, or largely seen as unimportant. Lack of support structures for local initiatives, or even for everyday living, are seen as fundamentally interconnected within the terrain of violence. This perceived ability of those in positions of authority to negate the suffering within the *barrio* can be read as a deployment of deeply embedded power relations. Young people articulated a deep sense of frustration that not only does the state appear to not help, but that they *could* help and do not. The operation of these relations are intimately tied to broader issues of corruption, class struggle, clientelism, and insufficient consultation with local communities, resulting in misuse of resources meant to flow into the community. Some complaints were loud and blatant, such as fourteen-year-old Camila Andrea: 'Ooshh! You know what makes me so angry?! The amount of corruption there is here'. Further to Camila Andrea's frustration, other young people articulated connections between inequality, corruption, and power. Sixteen-year-old Felipe lay the blame with the government, finding fault with corruption that allows those with money to dominate positions of power:

> In my opinion Colombia has world potential, but what has happened here is that no one knows how to govern ... there is lots of delinquency, lots of corruption. And so, because of this, the people high up in society are from over there, and they have the money and not the poor people. And so we can't say anything because it is corrupt and we have no money.

For sixteen-year-old Juan Carlos the link between money and power that Felipe noted is significant, but it results, in his opinion, in an unfair playing field where merit, intelligence, and values are not seen as having worth. Corruption is linked to injustice:

> What you have to understand is here what counts is who has more money or who has more power, those who have more of that, and well ... Look, what you do in society is based on who has more power is apparently going to be more just or good or make things better. Because you have more money and that. Intelligence doesn't matter, or the values of the person, only the power and money is what matters. This isn't true and it isn't just or fair to be like this.

The issue of structural inequality arose in relation to later discussions around peace, too. Juan Carlos returned to his previous comments about power and justice to note that for him, peace is justice: 'Now many governments are robbing money from people. You pay taxes and this money never arrives in any form. And so for me, justice like this, that would be peace'.

Explicit accusations of corruption were mentioned frequently in connection with taxes and the provision of services by the government, with many young

94 *Space, Power, and Terrains of Insecurity*

people using the word 'corrupt' in conversations. Seventeen-year-old Laura argued, 'The state robs everyone, robs us'. Fifteen-year-old Rosa agreed and added that for her 'it also seems unfair because they pretend to fix the *barrio*, but it is us who fix it ourselves'. Rosa followed this comment with a discussion of how various families in the community organized to purchase new bulbs for streetlights when the local government had repeatedly failed to deliver. While there were not many streetlights, their functioning was vital to increase security a small amount after dark. In our discussion, teacher Ana Martinez highlighted the absence of basic services as another way the government fails the occupants of Cazucá. She explained that

> to live in Cazucá is to live in a very basic state, without public services, without minimal opportunities for many things. ... One thing you [speaking to me, the researcher] have seen as well: water. Water is such a vital element, yet in the schools we do not have water in the bathrooms for example. There isn't a way for the children to wash their hands.

The absence of such a basic necessity constituted for Ana Martinez a fundamental failure of the state to its citizens. During a workshop called *Promotores de Paz* (Peace Promoters) run by CESTRA-USIP with community-nominated leaders from Comuna 4,[3] potable water was one of the key topics focused on by the participants. Again, the 'indifference of the state' was mentioned, and the lack of delivering on promises was described as a 'lack of respect' for the occupants of the Comuna. For the participants the solution was two-fold: to organize in a way to put forward people to manage the politics and lobby for improvement, and concurrently, to find ways of caring for the existing resources of the community and building capacity to collective resolve the issue of lack of, or inadequate, water provision. One smaller group during the workshop had a conversation in which they recognized the liminality of the spaces the Comuna occupied and were geared towards finding practical ways of resolving the issues; this conversation was emotional and heated at times as these people care deeply about their communities. Basic services such as water, sanitation, and electricity, seen as fundamental rights for citizens, are largely absent in the community. While – as Laura and Rosa above noted and this example from the CESTRA-USIP workshop demonstrates – the occupants of the community attempt to fix such things themselves, it is telling of the way in which the state abdicates its responsibility to this particular group of its citizens.

When I asked in one interview with a group of young people whether they felt the government could do more to help with problems in the community, fifteen-year-old Maria Patricia started to answer before I had even finished the question:

> Yes. Because ... Um ... I have heard or seen many things. I've seen that the government doesn't help people. They say they do but its all lies. The

Space, Power, and Terrains of Insecurity 95

government gives the police millions to help but what happens with that money? In my opinion they keep it. They share it between themselves when they should be helping people ... but instead they do nothing.

Maria Patricia makes direct accusations of corruption, but the sense that the state does not care about the young people in Cazucá was mentioned multiple times. Laura and Rosa also discussed the ways in which people suffer, in particular the lack of sufficient food, and the many ways the government could assist. Ultimately they argue that the government seems to care about itself and not about those living in Cazucá.

LAURA: ... and there are people who go hungry. If they have food for breakfast they don't have anything for lunch or dinner. Or if they have food for dinner, they don't eat all day.
ROSA: ... and they [the government] pretend to help. But rarely they do, and there are so many things they could help with. Like food for children.
LAURA: ... water ...
ROSA: ...the materials we bring to school. And well, it is apparently our fault, because the government only takes for itself and not for us.

There is frustration and anger in these conversations; they are reoccurring sentiments when speaking with many different young people. Young people care deeply about their community and are acutely aware of the inequality and abandonment by the state of many people. Susana and Brayan Alexander, both fifteen years old, commented on the problems and causes of such problems. These comments are reflective of broader attitudes and discussions I was part of:

SUSANA: Well, my opinion of Colombia, well, I think it is a wonderful country overall. It is a very pretty country, but it still lacks, it lacks a lot, like opportunities for the people, I mean, the poor people, and we still do not have many opportunities to find work, or if we want to study ... for people who need to work, for children who often can't eat, we don't have the chances. We are lacking opportunities in this country, so while it is all pretty, we lack opportunities. This is what we are missing.
BRAYAN ALEXANDER: ... And I think more than opportunities is justice. As in, justice not only if you commit a crime, but equally that it is not fair if I, say, was born in a poor barrio that I have to continue living my whole life like this, you know, with violence and with. ... I don't know what else. This isn't fair. Justice is: fine I am poor, but I have the same opportunities as other people from other classes. And then, if equality comes, justice ... that is what would be fair. But for now we do not have that equality.

Here it is evident that unequal access to opportunities for people based on their economic and geographic location is experienced and articulated as a

96 *Space, Power, and Terrains of Insecurity*

profound sense of injustice. For Brayan Alexander, it is not even the basic provision of services that is at the heart of his complaint, but simply the lack of equal opportunity to advance and absence of a 'fair' or 'just' system of education and employment in the country. The effect of violence on these opportunities is exacerbated by a perception of the government's indifference to the challenges facing the lives of these young people. This is not the abstract planning of a state, but the reality of marginalised people who experience that neglect tangibly in their everyday life.

When speaking with some of these young people again in 2016 the focus was on the anticipated announcement of a successful agreement in the peace talks taking place in Havana between the FARC and the government. The proposed amnesty provisions within the talks were particularly highly discussed by mainstream outlets and on social media. 'God help us Helen, they are still only thinking of themselves and not of us', Alejandro, now in his early twenties, exclaimed to me when the peace talks were mentioned in conversation. This sense of corruption or abandonment was mentioned unprompted – I had simply asked what he thought of the peace talks – and was followed by further conversation about broad and specific injustices Alejandro saw inherent in the peace process. This was echoed by several others who saw the provisions as evidence that the state and its elites were still prioritizing themselves above the citizens they were professing to help. Some young people from Cazucá circulated memes and political cartoons on their Facebook pages highlighting the perceived farce of talks of 'justice'. This disconnect between the elite process and the experiences of daily life of these now-young-adults reinforces a sense of injustice.

Speaking from the 'Non-Place'

The marginalization of liminal communities is exacerbated for young people who are portrayed mostly via discussions of their deficiencies and the potential danger they pose. A constriction of the ability to publicly express themselves, and the stigmatization and criminalization of young people from areas such as Cazucá are broad ways in which young people become read as victims in the social, political, and symbolic violence that permeates their lives. However, against an external discourse that fails to account for the complexity of life in Cazucá and that explicitly excludes consideration of such lived experiences, Cazucá's young people recognize the liminality of the space they occupy in Cazucá. Located on the municipal boundary line between Soacha and Bogotá, rejected in many ways by both cities, they say, 'We aren't from either, we are from the hill (*la loma*)'. At the same time many young people reaffirmed their love of Colombia, and spoke of positive characteristics of being Colombian. Belonging for many of these young people is articulated in specifically spatialized terms – terms that reject the power dynamics of those in power, either in Soacha or Bogotá, or the meta-narrative of the state (see Berents 2014, 2015).

Spaces of violence in the Colombian conflict are characterized by movement, variation, and unpredictability. From the requirement to abandon homes; to the uncertain spaces of peri-urban communities such as Cazucá; to the shifting space of home life as family members separate to find work, are disappeared, or killed, the space in which violence is enacted and experienced varies. However, intertwined with these shifting terrains there is an enforced rigidity to spaces conventionally understood as fluid. Violence fixes boundaries that 'may or may not be visible but which nevertheless people recognize as life risking frontiers should they transgress them' (Pearce 2007, 27). Fear of violence has 'gradually come to curtail, fragment and annul' (Restrepo 2004, 179) many of the crucial social spaces of the city, resulting in a weakening of social capital and the interactions between citizens that in turn strengthen ties and sense of community.

Sixteen-year-old Daniela, when asked about the most difficult things about being young in Cazucá replied without hesitation: 'insecurity ... more than anything. Seriously. To be young'. Experiences of living in Cazucá are regularly described by the young people as specific experiences of insecurities.[4] When asked about the negative aspects of life in the community eleven-year-old Andrea and twelve-year-old Sebastian noted that the potential of robbery and assault is one of the most difficult things to live with:

ANDREA: ...or when it gets dark the shops have to close ...
SEBASTIAN: ...their doors...
ANDREA: Yes everything. ... They close up the shops, because they come and rob them.
SEBASTIAN: Yes. They rob them!

The two went on to discuss personal assaults also:

ANDREA: ...and there are many problems with thieves ...
HB: And have you experienced this?
ANDREA: My mother, yes. Me, no. Thank god.
SEBASTIAN: My parents also.

Later after I had finished the interview with the two of them, Andrea came to talk to me in the playground. She told me that the experience of her mother's robbery, in which they took her bag and 'all the money for our food', now means that her mother is very protective of Andrea and her siblings. For Andrea this insecurity manifests as two main concerns: the first being concern for her family's wellbeing, and the second as an impediment to being able to socialize with her friends because her mother often did not want her to go to friends' houses that were 'too far away'. Andrea was not alone in discussing the problems of insecurity in spatialized terms, where the potential for violence resulted in a restriction of movement. In response to being asked what they dislike about living in Cazucá, or what is difficult about living here, these three young people had immediate examples:

98 *Space, Power, and Terrains of Insecurity*

PAOLA (15): Well, what I don't like is the insecurity (*la inseguridad*). You have to be very aware. Of everything and …

ALEJANDRO (17): For me, well, no, it is that there are many thieves, and yes, the insecurity. That you can't even go to the corner sometimes.

JULIANA (17): Yes, for me the insecurity also. More than anything. And the houses where no one lives.

A sense of insecurity, for these three, is not an abstract concept, but bound up in practices and places which they inhabit. Empty houses are seen by the community as potential sites of danger because they are not 'claimed' or sanctioned and so can be occupied by 'less friendly neighbours' as one teacher euphemistically noted, referring to the criminal gangs and smaller scale drug vendors in the neighbourhood. Also, much of the violence perpetrated by armed actors in Cazucá is prompted by the actors' stakes in both the drug and illegal arms trades. The presence of drugs in the community formed a background to many comments made by young people, and drug addicts and the sale of drugs were invoked as negative things about the community. Several young people and teachers made mention of the fact that drugs were sold outside the school in the afternoon, and also near sites of transport – street corners near stops for the *colectivo* taxi-buses were often described as *muy caliente* (very hot), referencing their implicit danger to those passing by.

The restriction of movement is clearly illustrated through the articulation of the issue of street corners in Cazucá, where violence fixes boundaries that may be invisible but have potentially deadly consequences for transgression. Alejandro, above, is not the only one to draw attention to street corners as potentially dangerous. Several other young people mentioned it anecdotally and the *fundación's* field coordinator, Ana Milena (who is not originally from Cazucá), articulated just why they present such a danger to the inhabitants:

Look, when I was young it was really easy to stay out until 11 or 12 at night, playing basketball, being with my friends or my siblings, and I knew it wasn't dangerous … I knew that I could stay in a park at that time, chatting, without anything happening. Here [Cazucá], no. … Not only because the kids are more vulnerable to attacks or being assaulted, but because at times they are stigmatized, and many young people assume that if you are on a corner you are an informant. … In los Altos de Cazucá, in some parts more than others, the presence of illegal groups is very evident. And so these groups have the idea that life has to be how they imagine it. And a kid who is on the corner is there because they are getting high, or doing something else that they shouldn't be doing.

Consequently young people not associated with the illegal gangs avoid being located in that space. The control by the gangs over the nominally public space is explicit. Ana Milena notes that 'they say 'you have to be inside at this time' or 'you have to be at your house' ... then they simply kill many young people because they make a mistake'. Spaces come to be defined by these risky, life-threatening frontiers, defining and circumscribing not only where and how but also *when* young people can move through the community, and young people must become skilled in knowing how and when they can navigate through their community (see Berents and ten Have 2017). To navigate their everyday life is to navigate these terrains of insecurity.

Compounding these insecurities is the literally insecure terrain of the community, which is prone to disastrous landslides. When there are deaths it is often many members of the same family are killed in these situations, causing added distress to survivors who not only lose their residence, but often most of their relatives. While the government does offer assistance to victims of landslides in these communities, including living support or rehousing people, it can often be difficult to access, or take an unreasonably long time to do so. On my first visit to the school after the landslide in 2010 I was asked by almost all the students I spoke with whether I had heard about the event. Upon asking if they knew people affected, almost all of them responded in the affirmative. One girl told me they were looking after a mother and several children who had lost their house. It meant there was 'almost no space to move' in their house at that time.

The violent insecurity of daily life was compounded by this literal form of insecurity. My conversation with Sebastian and Andrea occurred just after the landslide. For Sebastian, even at twelve years old, it was a clear indication of the connections between spatial insecurity, abandonment of the state, and the difficulties of living in Cazucá: 'Because look ... this landslide, the landslide that happened, they [the government] aren't relocating anyone, and they are left in the street'. Our conversation continued, as Sebastian noted that the houses had fallen a long way down the hillside, before Andrea mentioned another landslide in a nearby community, and that no one had been helped there either: 'The government is not helping with anything'. Both of them were conscious of the risks of living in such housing, but also aware of the lack of alternatives. For Andrea it was clear that the government should help, and that it made things worse and more insecure when they did not assist:

> ... More than anyone it is the government that has to help. Because they have the money and the skills to help. But people are in the street and at risk, and the government is nowhere.

The problems caused by landslides highlight the multiple, interwoven insecurities of Cazucá including being rendered beyond civil society and thus outside the concern of the state, the violent and corrupt engagement of the state in the community, and the physical danger of moving through and living in the barrio. These multiple insecurities are significant and present in everyday life for young people.

Conclusions

In this chapter's explorations of the politics of space and place the complexities of the everyday terrains occupied by Cazucá's young people are visible. Multiple forms of violence circumscribe and alter the way in which young people can interact both with each other and with their environment. The lack of attention to the security of the occupants of the *barrio* by government officials exacerbates the insecurity of those who live there. Both corruption and impunity have consequences which fold back on the occupants who are not involved in illicit activity, as they become bound up in conceptions of the entire space being one of 'misery and danger' (Resolucion Defensorial Regional 2002) and all those who live there as being delinquents, drug dealers, and violent criminals who choose not to participate. Virulent imaginative geographies proliferate externally to Cazucá and limit how the occupants can participate in broader civic life. Young people are particularly affected. Not only are their daily lives affected by experiences of spatialized insecurity, but by being frequently homogeneously described as key actors in the violence and insecurity, they are further written out of dialogue and denied opportunities to appear in the political, public realm in productive ways.

There are layers of complexity at play in this discussion. On one level is a conceptual denial, deliberate acts of 'not-knowing', which permit Cazucá to be defined in the collective imagination of those who occupy the 'civil(ised) society' as a 'non-place', the 'province of misery and danger'. The profoundly negative *placing* conducted through popular discourse, and the way in which the state's involvement swaps from abandonment to violent intervention are often elided or not discussed. However, the young people, and their families and teachers, are very conscious of this, and articulately note the consequences of such interactions. There are other practical consequences of the characterization of Cazucá as a 'non-place'. The inadequate provision of basic services is seen by the young people and by adults from the community as profoundly unjust, and as a violation of basic rights. It is the territory of Cazucá, as an *invasión*, as liminal, and as of marginal concern to the broader polity that allows this ongoing disregard for those living within the community. While the community often works together to fix problems such as broken lights or the inconsistent supply of potable water, their absence from inclusion in broader discussions and discourses is a form of violence and is an injury to young people's articulations of belonging.

It is in the everyday lives of these young people that the spatial dimension of insecurity and restriction of movement is most manifest. Fear of violence circumscribes young people's movements and experiences of their community. The presence of the police van invokes boundaries and a sense of threat, as does the more ephemeral presence of, but very real threat posed by, gangs throughout the community making particular areas hot (*caliente*). Further to the notion of fear is the unpredictability of much of the spatialized violence. Corruption renders unreliable those who are meant to police the

Space, Power, and Terrains of Insecurity 101

boundary and adds further tension. Threats against homes by armed gangs violate notions of secure boundaries and 'safe' places. Combined, the tensions, threats, and fear present in the everyday render spaces insecure and fraught.

Young people, as they describe in their own words, are profoundly aware of the challenges of insecurity and of the damaging external labelling of the community. However, structural power systems render them largely powerless, writing them out of consideration, and abandoning them to negotiate such challenges to the best of their individual abilities. The practices of deliberate 'not-knowing', the violent intervention of the state, and ongoing risk and violence within everyday terrains reinforces narratives of passivity. However, the occupants of Cazucá are aware of these spatialized insecurities and work within their everyday lives to negotiate them. Notions of violence and the multiple, compounding ways it affects young people, must be brought in to conversation with understandings of everyday peace. This is the terrain of social exclusion, insecurity and fear that in part is why everyday peace must be conceived of as *amidst-violence*. In exploring the acts of power that delineate such spaces as 'non-places' this chapter has illustrated the forms and contours of the terrain of insecurity occupied by young people in Cazucá. The subsequent chapter takes this understanding and uses it to underpin a discussion of the way the violences that move through this terrain are experienced within and through the bodies of young people.

Notes

1 The term 'placing' here comes from work carried out by Diana Bocarejo on multicultural politics in Colombia. She describes placing as the ways in which different institutions or people mobilized 'their 'lived and imagined' places to reshape ... their political scope' (2008, 3). But more than this placing implies that space emerges within political relationships and does not exist a priori and thus 'not only must we examine spaces as political activities but we must also describe authority in terms of the spaces it assembles' (Smith 2003, 77 in Bocarejo 2008, 3).
2 For discussion on the consequences of characterising communities like Cazuca in these ways, and displaced people's response to such characterisations see Berents 2018. See also Zeiderman 2016 and Zea 2010.
3 The workshops were run by local NGO CESTRA and supported by the US Institute of Peace and consisted of approximately thirty people (mostly adults, although there was one seventeen-year-old) from the various barrios that comprised Comuna 4 of Soacha who had been nominated or selected by their community to participate – usually because of their work in a particular area (for example there was a woman who had been involved in local agriculture efforts, and an indigenous man who was very active in indigenous advocacy, as well as the head of the parents' committee at a local school). The program was designed as a capacity and skills raising endeavour, as well as a forum to link community leaders and hopefully strengthen grassroots community projects. It ran once a week for several months. I attended four sessions during my time in Colombia. Those who registered received reimbursement for their travel as well as coffee and snacks during the workshops – this was seen as reasonable and helped those who otherwise would perhaps not be able to make it.

102 *Space, Power, and Terrains of Insecurity*

4 Negative experiences were not totalising for the young people I spoke with, and all offered positive experiences of living in Cazucá, associated with friends, school, playing, sport and even pride in the people who make up their community. These reflections are discussed in more detail in Chapter Five, but its important to note here, that in conversations I often first asked about positive experiences, before asking about more negative aspects, and often conversations were framed by young people through the tensions inherent in these two engagements with their lived experience.

References

2002. Resolucion Defensorial Regional No. 003. Soacha, Colombia: Defensoria del Pueblo.

Arnson, Cyntia J., Jaime Bermúdez, Father Darío Echeverri, David Henifin, Alfredo Rangel Suárez, and León Valencia. 2006. "Colombia's Peace Processes: Multiple Negotiations, Multiple Actors." In *Latin American Program Special Report.* Washington, DC: Woodrow Wilson International Center for Scholars – Latin American Program.

Auge, Marc. 1995. *Non-Places: Introduction to an Anthropology of Supermodernity.* Translated by John Howe. London: Verso.

Berents, Helen. 2014. "'It's About Finding a Way': Children, Sites of Opportunity, and Building Everyday Peace in Colombia." *International Journal of Children's Rights* 22(2):362–384.

Berents, Helen. 2015. "Children, Violence, and Social Exclusion: Negotiation of Everyday Insecurity in a Colombian Barrio." *Critical Studies on Security* 3 (1):90–104.

Berents, Helen. 2018. "Right(s) From the Ground Up: Internal Displacement, the Urban Periphery and Belonging to the City." In *The Politics of Identity: Place, Space, and Discourse*, edited by Chris and Dean Keep Agius. Manchester: Manchester University Press.

Berents, Helen, and Charlotte ten Have. 2017. "Navigating Violence: Fear and Everyday Life in Colombia and Mexico." *International Journal for Crime, Justice and Social Democracy* 6(1):103–117.

Bocarejo, Diana. 2008. "Reconfiguring the Political Landscape after the Multicultural Turn: Law, Politics and the Spatialization of Difference in Colombia." Doctor of Philosophy, Department of Anthropology, The University of Chicago, Chicago, IL.

Coleman, Lara. 2007. "The Gendered Violence of Development: Imaginative Geographies of Exclusion in the Imposition of Neo-liberal Capitalism." *British Journal of Politics and International Relations* 9: 204–219.

Davis, Diane E., and Anthony W. Pereira. 2003. *Irregular Armed Forces and Their Role in Politics and State Formation.* Cambridge: Cambridge University Press.

Farmer, Paul. 2004. "An Anthropology of Structural Violence." *Current Anthropology* 45(3):305–324.

Gregory, Derek. 1995. "Imaginative Geographies." *Progress in Human Geography* 19 (4):447–485.

Hancock, Landon E., and Christopher Mitchell, eds. 2007. *Zones of Peace.* Boulder, CO: Lynne Rienner.

Hunt, Stacey Leigh. 2009. "State Fragmentation and Citizen Education: Creating a Culture of Citizenship in Bogotá, Colombia." Doctor of Philosophy, Political Science, Rutgers, The State University of New Jersey.

Space, Power, and Terrains of Insecurity 103

Leeds, Elizabeth. 2007. "Rio de Janeiro." In *Fractured Cities: Social Exclusion, Urban Violence and Contested Spaces in Latin America*, edited by Kees Koonings and Dirk Kruijt. London: Zed Books.

Massey, Doreen. 2005. *For Space*. London: SAGE.

McIlwaine, Cathy, and Caroline O. N. Moser. 2007. "Living in Fear: How the Urban Poor Perceive Violence, Fear and Insecurity." In *Fractured Cities: Social Exclusion, Urban Violence and Contested Spaces in Latin America*, edited by Kees Koonings and Dirk Kruijt. London: Zed Books.

Mitchell, Christopher, and Sara Ramírez. 2009. "Local Peace Communities in Colombia: An Initial Comparison of Three Cases." In *Colombia: Building Peace in a Time of War*, edited by Viginia M. Bouvier, 245–270. Washington, DC: United States Institute of Peace.

Nordstrom, Carolyn. 1999. "Wars and Invisible Girls, Shadow Industries, and the Politics of Not-Knowing." *International Feminist Journal of Politics* 1(1):14–33.

Nordstrom, Carolyn. 2004. *Shadows of War: Violence, Power and International Profiteering in the Twenty-First Century*. Oakland, CA: University of California Press.

Pearce, Jenny. 2007. "Violence, Power and Participation: Building Citizenship in Contexts of Chronic Violence." In *IDS Working Paper No. 274*. Brighton: Institute of Development Studies.

Picon, Yuri Romero, Liliana Arciniegas, and Javier Jimenez Becerra. 2006. "Desplazamiento y Reconstruccion de Tejido Social en el Barrio Altos de la Florida." *Revista Tendencia & Retos* 11: 11–23.

Rengifo Castillo, Carmen. 2005. "Balance Comparativo: Conflictos por territorio, Conflictos por Participacion Politica y Jovenes en las Comunas 7 de Barrancabermeja, 13 de Medellin, 15 de Cali y Cazuca (Soacha) y la Estancia (Ciudad Bolivar-Bogota)." In *Jovenes, Conflictos Urbanos y Alternativas de Inclusion*, edited by Viviana Sabogal Ruiz. Bogotá, Colombia: Plataforma Conflicto Urbano y Jovenes, CIVIS Suecia & ASDI.

Restrepo, Luis Alberto. 2004. "Violence and Fear in Colombia: Fragmentation of Space, Contraction of Time and Forms of Evasion." In *Armed Actors: Organised Violence and State Failure in Latin America*, edited by Kees Koonings and Dirk Kruijt. London: Zed Books.

Rojas, Catalina. 2007. "Islands in the Stream: A Comparative Analysis of Zones of Peace Within Colombia's Civil War." In *Zones of Peace*, edited by Landon E. Hancock and Christopher Maitchell. Boulder, CO: Lynne Rienner.

Said, Edward. (1978) 1995. *Orientalism*. London: Penguin Books.

Sanford, Victoria. 2003. "Peacebuilding in a War Zone: The Case of Colombian Peace Communities." *International Peacekeeping* 10(2):107–118.

Santos, Boadventura de Sousa. 2002. *Towards a New Legal Common Sense: Law, Globalization and Emancipation*. London: Butterworth.

Springer, Simon. 2011. "Violence Sits in Places? Cultural Practice, Neoliberal Rationalism and Virulent Imaginative Geographies." *Political Geography* 30: 90–98.

Zea, Juan Esteban. 2010. "Internal Displacement in Colombia: Violence, Resettlement, and Resistance." Master of Arts, Anthropology, Portland State University.

Zeiderman, Austin. 2013. "Living Dangerously: Biopolitics and Urban Citizenship in Bogotá, Colombia." *American Ethnologist* 40(1):71–87.

Zeiderman, Austin. 2016. *Endangered City: The Politcs of Security and Risk in Bogotá*. Durham, NC: Duke University Press.

4   Embodied Everyday Violences

[I]t is such a stupid violence. Why? Because everyone fights for things without thinking of the cost ...

> - Laura, seventeen-year-old occupant of los Altos de Cazucá

A child of Cazucá, from when they arrive in this zone have to learn to defend themselves against others ... because living in Cauzcá is not easy. To live in Cazucá is to live amongst people who may be violent towards you at any moment.

> - Ana Martinez, teacher in los Altos de Cazucá

The small group of young women had spent the time before class started sitting on the concrete steps in the playground crying and dabbing their faces to try and stop their make-up from running. One of the young women seemed particularly upset and the others, while also unhappy, were consoling her. Sarah – one of the other volunteers with *Fundación Pies Descalzos* (the *fundación*) – and I had been sitting in on various classes helping out where necessary, but today the teacher for this class of fourteen- to sixteen-year-olds had given me permission to speak more about my research and get the students to answer some basic introductory questions for my work.

The young women remained upset throughout the class while I ran the activity, and the teacher spent much of the lesson with a girl up the front, at the teacher's desk. The two seemed unrelated, however, neither Sarah nor I had much time to consider what was happening as we were wrangling a class of almost forty students into paying attention and doing the task. Our discussion with the class revolved around the young people's thoughts about the positive and negative aspects of Cazucá, the things that need to change in the future, and their understanding of what the idea of 'peace' means. One group of young men argued that there needs to be 'many more opportunities for Colombian people, including changing poverty which breeds vandalism, narco-trafficking and disorder'. In the opinion of one fifteen-year-old girl, things not only needed to be spoken about but also action needed to occur to change things in the country. Often slipping into boisterousness, and with tangential conversations about how things were in my home country

(Australia), and Sarah's (the US), the young people were collectively excited to speak about these things. They raised many examples from their own lives. It was early in my time with the community and it enthused me to have started these conversations. I was looking forward to speaking more with various members of this class in the following weeks.

The group of young women participated in the class despite their distress, and when we asked the teacher whether we should be concerned, she told us to just continue. After the class ended and the students had left we asked the teacher what had been happening with the young women. She told us the girls were crying because the night before a twenty-year-old boy had been killed in the neighbourhood. The teacher kept using the phrase '*el era malo*' (he was bad), and spoke of taking drugs. It was not an accident or suicide; he had been killed. The girls were friends with him and that was why they were upset; he was the ex-boyfriend of one of the girls, amplifying the sadness and pain they were feeling.

The teacher explained that the other upset girl who had been at the front of the room with her during the class thought she might be pregnant to her boyfriend. He was in his final year of school, but on drugs and often did not come to class. The teacher had been explaining to the girl who was fifteen about the timing of menstrual cycles using a small calendar from her purse. Apparently, despite having had sexual education classes, the young girl had not really understood how menstrual cycles worked. Sarah and I asked what she would do if she was pregnant. The teacher said most likely she'd keep the baby and leave school. We asked what the boyfriend would do and the teacher threw up her hands and said 'who knows with him'.

The content of our conversations with the class suddenly took on a different light with this very real, very emotional glimpse into how these young people navigate daily routines of relationships, school, and friendships alongside the powerful and deadly consequences of violence in the community. It was a confronting introduction to the realities faced by these students, and the way that various forms of both direct and indirect violences have embodied consequences that reverberate through friendship groups and classrooms. It also highlighted the ways that violence affects collective understanding and meaning-making, and how it isolates individuals in the midst of ongoing lived experiences.

In the previous chapter I explored the spatial nature of social exclusion and the way in which spaces such as Cazucá are constructed as 'non-places' beyond the bounds of 'civil' society. Such places and their occupants are characterised and stigmatised as the origins of broader violence and crime in the city. It is undeniable that such places are violent and insecure, but such constructions of violence are profoundly spatialised in nature as the previous chapter demonstrated. This chapter builds on that critique, but moves from structural, spatial terrains of violence that shape the landscape of the everyday lives of young people in Cazucá to explore how violence is embodied and physically manifests against and within the bodies of these young people. Violence affects the intersubjective negotiation of lived experience and shuts

106   *Embodied Everyday Violences*

down potential for challenge and response. While violence and violent acts are frequently portrayed as anomalies or deviations from 'appropriate' or 'normal' life, such a portrayal de-links the act of violence from its social and political context. It cannot be imagined as the mechanism of a relationship that is implicitly oppressive, marginalising and silencing. Exploring the intimate, daily, embodied experiences of individuals locates violence within the everyday. It allows a questioning of how the everyday can be read as a site to comprehend how individuals respond to mundane and radical violence in both mundane and radical ways.

This chapter first discusses the ways in which the terrain of insecurity impacts on the lives and bodies of young people in Cazucá. This focus draws attention to the consequences of the invisible yet pervasive networks of power, violence, exclusion, and belonging that operate in this context, and which disproportionately affect young people. Violence and the experience of fear and pain isolate individuals, yet, in many ways, the violences experienced by the occupants of Cazucá are not extra-ordinary but are simply part of the everyday. The second section of this chapter explores the various ways violence manifests as an embodied experience, against and within the bodies of young people in Cazucá. Blackmail, robbery, and death threats are common forms of interaction with the armed gangs in the area that have lasting impacts. Young people in the community also experience the violations of sexual assaults more often than the national average. These experiences can be profoundly isolating, as the violence is intimate and can be deeply traumatising. In another vein, while some intimate relationships are positive and fulfilling, others encounter multiple challenges from violence, to pregnancy and the risk of sexually transmitted infections. Sexual relationships are linked to discussions of being *present* and having purpose or meaning, but the risks and challenges raise questions of these other kinds of everyday violences, which are closely connected to broader violence and conflict as consequences of poverty, lack of health services, and social exclusion. Ruptures in family relationships, from domestic violence to absent parents, pose other challenges in negotiating fraught and violent situations. Lastly, this chapter explores how these different forms of embodied violence pose challenges to social cohesion in an environment already fractured and insecure. As noted, violence inhibits social relationships and an ability to express and contribute to notions of 'togetherness'.

Power, exclusion, and belonging are caught up in expressions of violence that manifest in the everyday lives of young people in multiple ways. Violences stem from broader social and political issues and exclusions, as well as impacting on the lifeworlds of individuals and their ability to maintain connections and contribute to collective life. This understanding allows the intimate, embodied experience of individuals to be read as profoundly political, and the everyday to be understood as a more accountable site for questioning how individuals can respond to mundane and radical violences in mundane and radical ways. A crucial component of thinking through how an everyday peace is constituted within insecure terrains is therefore an understanding of how young people understand and negotiate forms of violence and risk present in their daily lives.

Violent Implications of a Terrain of Insecurity

Nancy Scheper-Hughes and Philippe Bourgois (2004, 2) argue that while violence performed on 'grand' scales, such as war, massacre, or state-sanctioned oppression, is 'graphic and transparent', it is the 'everyday violence of infant mortality, slow starvation, disease, despair, and humiliation that destroys socially marginalised humans with even greater frequency [and is] usually invisible or misrecognized'. This idea of violence incorporates those violences experienced by people in extreme poverty and violence of being out-of-place through migration. It also includes other forms of powerlessness 'imposed' by the systematic denial of such people's presence and agency. This reading of violence and of violent acts does not require the act to be conscious and proactive (see Farmer 2004, 307). Rather, such structural violence arises from systems of oppression that are operationalised simply through the condoning and perpetuating of certain social orders.

While much literature on structural violence focuses on the structures themselves, I follow Arthur Kleinman, Veena Das, and Margaret Lock in their application of the term 'social suffering' (1996). This draws attention to the effects of violence that such social orders 'bring to bear on people', including violence 'to the body and to moral experience' (Kleinman 2000, 226). It is this form of violence, an attack on an individual's existential groundedness or presence in the world, which is an assault on the 'personhood, dignity, sense of worth or value of the victim' (Scheper-Hughes and Bourgois 2004, 1). In Michael Jackson's words, this violence occurs when a person's 'status as a subject is reduced against his or her will to mere objectivity' (2002, 45). Such symbolic violence can flow as a consequence of a physical manifestation of violence – such as a robbery, sexual assault, or an attack on the home – and these are discussed further below, but can also result from structural violence that stigmatises particular people for the location they live in. Such stigmatisation has consequences that incorporate everything from exacerbating poverty to damaging self-esteem and increasing pressure on family members, including children, to contribute to survival.

The profoundly spatialised terrain of insecurity that operates in this context is not isolated, but rather deeply interlinked with the structural forces that instigate and normalise the multiple violences which are experienced in and through the bodies of those experiencing 'social suffering' in highly contingent, individual ways. Considering violence in this way responds to Nancy Scheper-Hughes and Philippe Bourgois' (2004) call to recognise the 'slipperiness' of the concept of violence (this draws on Taussig 1987). Such a consideration challenges a straightforward reading of violence and complicates understandings of what kinds of experiences are mediated by violence. This approach is similar to Kleinman's discussion of social violence's 'multiple

108   *Embodied Everyday Violences*

forms' in which he argues current taxonomies, such as 'public versus domestic, ordinary as against extreme political violence', are inadequate (2000, 46). Jackson recognises that 'violence ... occurs in the contested space of inter-subjectivity, [and thus] its most devastating effects are not on individuals *per se* but on the fields of interrelationships that constitute their lifeworlds' (2002, 39 italics in original). Sketching violence in this way disrupts readings of violence as extra-ordinary and rather moves to locate it in the everyday. This does not seek to excuse the violences discussed, nor to minimise the suffering caused, but rather the opposite: to account for everyday-violences in an embodied sense, in order to better accentuate what an everyday-peace-amidst-violence looks like.

Young people are disproportionately affected by these attacks on their sense of self, where violence shapes the way young people understand their lives, selves, and the world around them. Natalia Martinez from *Fundación Restrepo Barco* notes:

> So there are some who have their rights violated because of the conflict, there are others that have their rights violated on account of poverty. And so, and so I think these are, they are very related. ... I think the youth population has been a victim of the conflict. Violence affects children in a radical way because it interrupts the process of their construction as a person, of knowing as a person, and the construction of their life. It interrupts its process ...

Later in the interview she pointed out that

> it is not only at the level of the government, and the situation of conflict which strengthens the use of weapons, it is that violence is there, daily, every day – the father that hits the mother, the father who hits their son, teachers who use really strong language with students – and I think we need to strengthen this day to day also. The day to day of the city. Because otherwise children are introduced to ... to ..., they are growing in an environment that is violent, and then soon they will start doing it also.

There is an everyday challenge in Natalia's observations to recognise the way that violence becomes part of the day-to-day existence of young people, and circumscribes understandings of their environment and experiences. Violence removes the recognition of self in the context of relationships with others. Such a challenge is particularly acute for young people, who are seen as passive recipients of culture and experience. The vulnerability and marginality of young people in Cazucá is exacerbated by a deeply entwined interrelationship between the structural violence of marginalisation and negation, and the threat and experience of physical violence in the community. Such violences are compounded by the effects of a 'symbolic' violence, which denies the active presence of young people, their experiences, and sense of self.

Embodied Everyday Violences 109

Violence is not just denial of experiences and presence or the negative stereotyping of a community. It is linked to visible actions that are committed against the bodies of others. The *pandillas* (gangs) that operate in the community are the most direct manifestation of physical violence, as extrajudicial killings are frequent and generally carried out with impunity. In addition to the actuality of deaths in the community, such groups also reinforce their threats against the broader community through highly visible graffiti, such as 'parents, if you don't kidnap your children by dusk, we will do it for you'. In addition to the organised threat of gangs, violence against people's property is common through robberies at gunpoint or (more commonly) knifepoint, both on the street and in the home, as well as acts of vandalism. Young people also navigate the challenges of drugs and associated physical costs of both addiction and the risks their trade presents to daily life. For young women, sexual violence profoundly affects their sense of self, their confidence, and their articulation of belonging to the community. Specific manifestations of violence in an everyday context are a consequence of the 'pervasive indifference, endemic oppression and sense of abjection that can make a person feel as though he or she is a mere object ... of no account' (Jackson 2002, 44).

For sixteen-year-old Felipe the daily experience of violence impacts his ability to see himself as able to effect change: 'The violence, well, I think it affects whoever it wants no? ... I can't do anything because the violence never leaves us'. Fifteen-year-old Brayan Alexander echoes a similar sentiment to Natalie from *Fundación Restrepo Barco*, above, when he highlights how violence becomes normalised and thus difficult to change, despite its damaging consequences:

> [A]nd it's that, there are so many problems and people can't realise what is normal, like they kill someone and it is normal. It is because of this we need to solve these problems, the actual situation, because it can change but we need to realise what is wrong to change it.

Similarly, seventeen-year-old Laura calls Colombia's violence 'dumb' and 'stupid', and blames fear and powerlessness as obstacles in responding in nonviolent ways:

LAURA: Oooii! [In Colombia] we have a dumb violence (*una violencia boba*), it is such a stupid violence. Why? Because everyone fights for things without thinking of the cost. And if you don't want to fight, well, they'll kill you because. And if you say anything against it they'll kill you. This is what I don't like. The stupid and unjust violence.

Physical violence, imbricated in a broader relationship of symbolic violence against the community and the self, poses profound challenges for maintaining a sense of self. I turn now to accounts of immediate expressions of violence, committed against the bodies of others.

110   *Embodied Everyday Violences*

Armed Actors: Robbery, Vandalism, and Death Threats

The presence of gangs and actors associated with the broader armed conflict in the community dramatically increases the sense of insecurity young people experience. As discussed previously the public spaces of the community are circumscribed by both the threat and presence of armed actors (both illegal and state sanctioned), but more than this, the domination of these actors occurs through acts of violence against those who move through these spaces; such acts include assassinations, robbery, sexual assault, extortion, and bribery.

Paramilitaries associated with the broader conflict control large parts of the community through targeted threats and assassinations in response to acts or comments that displease or threaten the gangs, or, as some occupants explained, seemingly for no reason at all. So-called *listas negras* (black lists) will be slipped under the door of a house or posted publicly. Such practices serve as notice of death and generally result in the named party (and often their entire family) leaving the community. The practice of black listing and gang violence is not limited to Cazucá, but occurs throughout Colombia in both poor *barrio* communities, and in regions under control of non-state-armed groups. Seventeen-year-old Laura and fourteen-year-old Camila Andrea spoke of friends or neighbours that had left because of such threats:

LAURA: … and if someone doesn't keep quiet from fear they, they take you. They say 'You have twenty four hours to leave the barrio'. And you have to go, because if you don't go, well, goodbye my friend.

CAMILA ANDREA: Yes, you have to go with your family, if you don't they kill them. This happened to one of our classmates.

LAURA: Yes.

CAMILA ANDREA: It's that you have to go, you don't even know why. There is only one option: leave or get killed.

While the threats of violence that cause families or individuals to leave the community are significant, the issues such departures invoke further complicate young people's lives and make their existence more insecure. Ana Milena, from the *fundación*, pointed out one way the issue is complicated:

[F]or many boys and girls in this sector the situation of violence is intolerable, I know of families where three people have been killed. And they say, well we have to leave here. So the government has to guarantee if those children leave that they will be linked to a new school.

Ana Milena's comment highlights the fact that often finding a school with space to take on new students can be difficult, and so in addition to the fear and trauma that is involved in forced relocation, young people often find their opportunities limited or closed. For the occupants of the community there is a sense that such violence is also carried out without consideration of the

Embodied Everyday Violences 111

consequences. Fifteen-year-old Rosa invoked family and property as things that suffered as a result of gang violence:

> There is a saying that they 'kill without knowing'. For example, they kill someone and they don't know the pain that their mother feels, or they break windows in a poor family's house. It is all with impunity.

Such individual consequences are often not seen or considered in exploring these violences that are seen at a more generalised disembodied level.

Black-listing is linked to the practice of '*la limpieza social*' ('social cleansing'), a superficially mundane term for the often horrifically violent murders of targeted community members. Social cleansing is a fundamentally urban phenomenon, a 'systematic practice of assassination ... directed against a group of people who have in common a membership in a socially marginal sector' (Rojas 1996, 23). It is a practice rooted in the disillusionment of marginal sectors in the government's ability to successfully assure security. Frequently, police and other state-security members are seen as sanctioning the behaviour. However, with its use now throughout Colombia, it has become implicated in the practices of *sicaros* (assassins) in poorer communities. While it is frequently described as the removal of so-called 'undesirables', such as beggars, sex workers, and drug addicts (all implicitly political statements in their own right), its practice gains further political connotations with the targeting of community leaders, union leaders, and other outspoken citizens (see Rojas 1996, 23; Pinzon Ochoa 2007). Young people, who can be seen as dangerous or displaying some form of 'immoral behaviour', are particularly vulnerable. The paramilitary forces in Cazucá use the threat of such 'social cleansing' to maintain control of the neighbourhood. Duque (2009, 30) notes that the reluctance of the police to venture up the hillside in Cazucá creates impunity for the illegal actors, and constant uncertainty, insecurity, and fear for the other occupants of the community. While these ideas were explored in the previous chapter in relation to the spatial terrains of insecurity, that insecurity obviously manifests as physical and emotional violence and risk for the inhabitants of those spaces. It is exacerbated and continued by the practices of individuals and groups, which have formal and informal modes of power and control.

Seemingly contradictorily, at times the armed actors in the community can create a pretence of security for the population; at times even solving issues in the community, by performing tasks usually associated with police services, such as mediating disputes, and addressing other community concerns. However, while these actors may resolve small problems as they arise, such solutions are predominantly violent and do not lessen the generalised terror and insecurity of the community. Additionally, Pinzon Ochoa notes that in different *barrios* the threat varies; sometimes they are more affected by the *pandillas*, sometimes by the '*limpieza social*', sometimes by paramilitaries. However, the security of the population depends on their ability to exist in a state of

112 *Embodied Everyday Violences*

'generalised prevention' with people they do not know because they might be informants (2007, 284). In such an environment the contradictions, tensions, and insecurity contribute negatively to social cohesion and can result in increased levels of violence, both actualised and anticipated.

Belonging to a gang can provide security and access to services and materials that are often scarce. Such gangs may be affiliated with armed actors, or act alongside them dealing in drugs and extortion of the local population. Several authors, writing specifically on Cazucá or neighbouring barrios, note that affiliation with gangs can provide young people with a sense of security and protection (Duque 2009, 29–31; Sabogal Ruiz 2005, 70; Pinzon Ochoa 2007, 283). Affiliation with a gang, as Sabogal Ruiz points out, can provide social cohesion and belonging (2005, 70), and provide a way of living amidst the violence day to day. However, stability and cohesion is actually prevented in the broader communities they operate in precisely because of their presence.

In interviews, young people often did not distinguish exactly who, or which group, was responsible for attacks and violence. In speaking with a group of young people during lunch break at school they told me that there often 'wasn't a point to separating who did what', and generally there was a feeling that coping with the results of an attack or robbery was more pressing. This is not to say, however, that those who frequently rob or vandalise the neighbourhood are unknown to the young people, their families, and those who work at the school. Such behaviour, whether connected to the actions of the paramilitaries, or the *pandillas*, was usually generalised. Most young people had an experience, or had family who had been the victim of some form of violence, such as eleven-year-old Yamila: 'Where I live, next to where I live there almost always are thieves'. Eleven-year-old Javier also echoed similar sentiments: 'Well, here it is bad because there are many robbers and there are many people who kill lots of people'.

Yamila and Javier's accounts of violence are general, but draw links back to spatial conceptions of violence, and also of the insecurity presented by other people. For fifteen-year-old Luz Milena and sixteen-year-old Daniela, violence has been an immediate experience against their own bodies:

LUZ MILENA: Since I've lived here in Cazucá, well, yes, I have been the victim of attacks and of violence.
DANIELA: Yes, like my friend said … the same.

These brief accounts all bear witness to the normalisation of physical violence in these young people's lives. The other form of connected violence is against property, as evidenced in Camila Andrea's account:

In my case I live in a square and on the other side is the kitchen, and we had a problem because [the attackers] broke the windows on that side because we wouldn't sell the house, almost all of the windows. But we couldn't do anything and who do you complain to?

The sense of helplessness articulated in Camila Andrea's acknowledgement of 'who do you complain to?' underlines the insecurity and everyday nature of the violence in the community. The threats of violence posed by armed actors in the community are manifold, from death to robbery, attacks, and vandalism. Such experiences are common and shared.

Intimate Violences

Violence is not always public, carried out by armed actors. Young people spoke also of much more intimate forms of violence, from intimate partner violence and sexual assault, to navigating teenage relationships, pregnancies, and risk of disease. These more private violences are no less impactful than the more public violence described above, and in some cases they form a large part of young people's experiences of daily life. This section firstly deals with sexual violence and risk of assault and other threats, before turning to the complexities of romantic relationships.

During the interview process young people were not asked specifically about sexual violence in the community. However the frequency with which the topic was mentioned showed that it is an issue that is very present in young people's lives. This is important to note. It is impossible to fully account for the silences and omissions in the interviews, although there were several times when the young person would change the topic rapidly or simply decide they had no more to say. For example, one young woman, in conversation about experiencing violence, swapped tone and said, 'I've been a victim of that, and now, well, it is very hard to live here with my family and well, no, I don't want to say anymore on that'.[1] Silence is characteristic of much to do with sexual violence both in Cazucá and more broadly among IDP populations and throughout Colombia; similar stories have been noted by others.[2] Yet sexual violence against women and girls in Colombia is a recognised tactic of violence in the country's armed conflict (United Nations 2001, 12; Cespedes-Baez 2010; Amnesty International 2004; Meertens 20062010). Sexual abuse and exploitation of women and girls is used in Colombia to create fear and terror in communities and prompt displacement, to control populations, to assist in the acquisition of land, and as a form of revenge. The extreme violence of the conflict has long played out on women's bodies, and initiatives to combat it have been largely ineffective.

The issue of sexual violence has been underresearched in the context of the conflict in Colombia, although there is a regular report conducted by Profamilia (*Asociación Probienestar de la Familia Colombiana*, Colombian Association for Family Welfare) that includes statistics on gender-based violence and sexual assault. The most recent one was conducted in 2010. However, in 2011, a report conducted through the framework of the campaign 'Rape and Other Violations: Leave my Body out of the War' was released (Amparo et al. 2011). It was the result of a study of women and girls aged fifteen to forty-four across Colombia between 2002 and 2009, and concluded that in

114 *Embodied Everyday Violences*

municipalities with an active presence of armed actors the rate of sexual violence was 17.58 per cent. In real numbers that means that almost half a million women were victims of sexual violence in those nine years. It also found that 82 per cent of those women did not report their abuse, and three quarters cited the presence of armed actors as a major obstacle to reporting (Amparo et al. 2011). Additionally, over half noted that they didn't think there was adequate support for them if they did report it, and they were scared of repeat attacks, or other kinds of violence against themselves or their families (Amparo et al. 2011). Such a study highlights the broader context of sexual violence, as it explicitly seeks links between acts of sexual violence and broader violence associated with the conflict. It includes in its discussion of sexual violence, not only physical rape but other experiences including forced pregnancy, forced abortion, forced prostitution, sterilisation, and sexual harassment, bringing attention to the broader spectrum of sexual and gender-based violence experienced by women and girls.

Violence against women and girls who have been internally displaced is also a large but underreported and underresearched issue. Accounts indicate the degree to which attacks against displaced women go unreported (see Alzate 2007, 140). Sexual violence occurs outside the household, perpetrated by groups of unknown men, members of armed groups, and that young adolescent women are particularly vulnerable (see Alzate 2007; Amnesty International 2004; Cespedes-Baez 2011). Other reports highlight the increased rates of domestic violence and abuse of young people within households (Profamilia 2010; Arboleda, Petesch, and Blackburn 2004, 39–40). These two forms of violence upon the bodies of women and girls – sexual violence and other forms of domestic violence – are related. Similarly to other conflict zones globally (see Hynes et al. 2004), they point to a broader gendered dimension to violence and exclusion across all of Colombia, one that is particularly felt by young women[3] in communities such as Cazucá.

The manner in which sexual violence is practiced and silenced has a disproportionate impact on the lives of women and girls, as it makes the interrelation of violences acutely apparent (see Cespedes-Baez 2010, 282). In conversations with young people, sexual assault was frequently cited as one of the things that makes Cazucá a dangerous place, and one of the things that is 'not so good' about Colombia. Interestingly, it was also the younger participants who more frequently mentioned it specifically as a threat.[4] These following four snippets of different conversations indicate how it was often discussed by young people:

HB: … And what about things that aren't so good about Colombia?
SEBASTIAN (12): The violence.
ANDREA (11): That there are lots of robbers.
SEBASTIAN: And many rapists and killers of children …
ANDREA (11): We are affected by the violence more than anything. For example, sometimes you go for a walk and they kidnap you, sometimes they take girls and violate them also.

HB: How do you think the violence in Colombia has affected young people?

INGRID (12): Um, well, because sometimes with the conflict children sometimes, well, they end up with the guerrillas.

DAVID (11): Children get killed, or kidnapped ...

LUIS FERNANDO (11): Or they are violated ...

DAVID: Yes. Exactly.

SUSANA (15): My opinion of Cazucá well ... there is a fear of being robbed or being attacked, because here there is lots of violations of children...

HB: Are there bad things about Cazucá also?

MARIA (11): Yes.

HB: Like what?

MARIA: Robbery, murder, violations ... and other things ...

In all these accounts, mention of sexual assault occurs alongside other forms of violence in response to general questions about negative or 'bad' things about the community or the country. In all but the final quote above, sexual assault was also linked explicitly to experiences of children and young people. When it was mentioned in general discussions of violence, it was often left undiscussed, or mentioned only in relation to external, 'large' violences that were seen to affect everyone.

However, while twelve-year-old Alicia mentioned it as something that would be absent in a Colombia that is at peace, she also tied it to domestic abuse as an intimate violence within the house:

[F]or me peace would be an end of violence, that there is not abuse; that parents don't violate their children, that robbers don't attack or kill. ... If there was no more violence for me, that would be peace.

Similar recognition was given by fifteen-year-old Maria Patricia who saw domestic violence and child abuse as something she could work towards helping. As she says: 'Where I live there is violent abuse, I have seen how other people are abused and to me I think: 'hopefully this ends'. ... So I want to study'. Fifteen-year-old Rosa also mentioned domestic violence or child abuse and complained that there 'are people who hit women, or hit their children when they fight, and other people say nothing when they know it is happening'.

My conversation with eleven-year-old Andrea and twelve-year-old Sebastian highlights the connections between threats of sexual violence, broader physical violence, and the terrain of insecurity. Andrea and Sebastian were going to be moving from *Colegio Minutos de Dios*, that is located higher up the hillside, to *Gabriel Garcia Marquez* the following year when they went up a year at school. Previously, Andrea had mentioned a general worry about this move, and it came up again in this conversation about a particular individual:

116 *Embodied Everyday Violences*

ANDREA: Well, around here there is a man who asks [pauses and turns to Sebastian] ... What is his name?
SEBASTIAN: Who?
ANDREA: The man who violates children . . .
SEBASTIAN: Ahhh. ... 'Chupamiel'?
ANDREA: Yes. It's that he takes the kids ... he takes them and violates them. It's because of him that I don't want to go to the school below [*Marquez*].

In this conversation, the potential for violence was located in the knowledge or belief of this threatening man who was located physically down the hill at *Marquez;* he was central in the spatial ordering of her world, where he embodied her understanding of terrains of insecurity. Teachers had also mentioned the problem of 'unwanted' people hanging around outside the gates as children arrived and left; however, no one else could confirm the existence of this particular character, although I mentioned it to several adults who worked in the two schools. Whether or not 'Chupamiel' exists as a particular individual, the threat he posed – of sexual violence against young people's bodies – circumscribes the physical space of interaction and reinscribes regimes of fear in the collective and individual consciousness of the young population at *Minutos*. It alters their lifeworlds, their ability to be and move through these spaces.

While many challenges continue to exist for displaced and poor young women in accessing information about their rights, the *fundación*'s field coordinator, Ana Milena, highlights both sexual abuse, and abusive relationships as particular issues facing young people in Cazucá:

> For example things such as sexual abuse. Yes? Sometimes it becomes normalised as well [in the context of broader violence being normalised]. And there is a lot of ignorance ... it can be normal for men to think that women are their property. Yes? That you can't go out with whoever, you can't have friends. And it is obvious how damaging this can be to families.

Yet she also draws attention to the fact that situations of displacement can cause people to become more aware of their rights and provide them platforms to claim those rights:[5]

> If we could say there is any advantage, an advantage of people in situations of displacement is that they recognise and say 'thanks to displacement, I know my rights. I didn't know I could do that, that the state had to give me that, or that I could also work, or now it is good that I can plan [in reproductive terms], because my mother didn't know these things'. So, sometimes they say 'ooof, it's taken the blindfold from my eyes, and I've discovered that I have rights, that I am a subject with rights'. But the problem is the ignorance.

Embodied Everyday Violences 117

The issue of sexual violence in the lives of young people in Cazucá is imbricated in broader networks of violences. High rates of sexual violence in such a community is not a mark of the people themselves as more deviant or violent, but rather a reflection on the structural situations which contribute to and sustain an environment where violences are present and systems are not in place to adequately educate for prevention.

While some sexual encounters are unwanted assaults, young people in Cazucá also choose to form and pursue relationships just like their peers in other places globally. However, there can be additional challenges, issues, and difficulties around both intimate relationships and knowledge about positive sexual health practices for young people who experience social exclusion and marginalisation. Young people I spoke with were quick to note that some young men and women entered into sexual relationships to try and assert a 'sense of themselves'; such observations are not uncommon in broader research around young people's sexual practices. However, in Colombia, the challenges and risks for displaced and marginalised young people are exacerbated through a lack of access to information and knowledge about positive relationships and positive sexual practices. A Human Rights Watch (2005) report notes that two out of three displaced adolescent girls in Colombia become pregnant by age nineteen. A Profamilia survey found that rates of pregnancy with first child continue to be higher in regions facing conflict or economic marginalisation (Profamilia 2010, 77–82, 85–88, 2011; see also Rios 2008, 352). While most people under twenty-five had participated in sexual education activities their ability to access such activities, or provision of such activities was limited in both conflict zones and zones of increased poverty (Profamilia 2010, 476; Women's Commission 2002, 30). Other research found that 81 per cent of sexually active young IDPs do not use any contraceptive method (Pacheco Sanchez and Enriquez 2004, 31). Further than this, maternal health services are often lacking in communities such as Cazucá or, despite their subsidisation by the government, are too expensive for many young women to access (Women's Commission 2002; Amnesty International 2004; Bosmans et al. 2012). These challenges endure even though sexual and reproductive health, particularly of IDP communities, is recognised as a human right in the 2003 *Política Nacional de Salud Sexual y Reproductiva* (National Sexual and Reproductive Health Policy) (Ministerio de la Proteccion Social 2003).

In daily life at school pregnancy was a recurring topic. Young women shared stories of friends or family members becoming pregnant while at school and who often had to drop out to care for the baby. While teachers and *fundación* employees were quick to note that sexual health education was an integral part of schooling, they also cited multiple examples of young women becoming mothers, or facing 'impossible decisions' about what to do upon discovering they were pregnant. Colombia's abortion laws remain significantly limiting, even though the total ban on abortion was lifted in 2006 (see Reutersward et al. 2011); additionally, social stigma, the influence of Catholic faith amongst many Colombians, and the aforementioned cost of

118 *Embodied Everyday Violences*

any medical procedure prevents many young girls from seeking abortions (Alzate 2007, 139). The other aspect of this problem is that girls and women seek illegal, unsafe, and potentially fatal abortive procedures (Women's Commission 2002). A teacher told me in conversation that young girls in Cazucá 'knew where to go', but that frequently 'the results were not what anyone would want'.

Lack of knowledge about safe sex practices is a key factor in the high pregnancy rates amongst young women in Cazucá. More than this, the responsibility for ensuring safe sex is practiced is seen as the responsibility of the woman, and as evidenced anecdotally in the stories above, pregnancies are frequently unplanned or not understood. The young women I spoke to were hesitant to speak about some of these issues and the conversations would frequently be framed with reference to other girls in the community – friends, cousins, and anonymous stories they had heard. Among the teenage girls interviewed there was acute awareness of the problem facing their companions and themselves – for example, this story from fourteen-year-old Camila Andrea:

> Well there are people, young people like me, like my friends, who end up pregnant because they don't know how to look after themselves; and because at a party they go off with whoever. Look, it's like they don't have a sense of themselves. I have a friend, well not a friend, basically a cousin, and she doesn't know how to respect herself. At a party she goes with one, and then another. Its like pretending to have a sexual life … until it becomes real because she is pregnant and the guy doesn't want to know. … It is also the guy's fault as well. No. It's like: you have to look after yourself, because you … because you are the woman, it's you who is going to get pregnant.

In Camila Andrea's discussion, many of the risks and challenges discussed above are evident. She also recognises the social pressures on women in particular, who are held responsible for behaviours and for outcomes such as pregnancy. While she notes that young men are also culpable, in the experiences of many young women the responsibility and culpability falls on their shoulders. One of Camila Andrea's friends, fifteen-year-old Rosa, recounted that after her sister and her sister's boyfriend had fought and broken up she went to a party and ended up with a new boyfriend who 'disrespected her' and was 'bad':

ROSA: …everyone said [the breakup] was her fault.
CAMILA ANDREA: Because she didn't know how to look after herself properly.
ROSA: … and so we knew where it could go. And we told her 'take care, take care'. … But no. No, she went to a party and got drunk and when her friends tried to get her to leave she would not go. And so, she didn't know how to look after herself, protect herself. And well, the guys don't care.

Embodied Everyday Violences   119

The lack of responsibility of young men towards young women as sexual and romantic partners was a reoccurring theme in discussions with young women. Sexual relationships and resultant pregnancies are a significant issue when they arise for both young women and young men, and frequently negatively impact both their lives.

However, pregnancy and motherhood, as well as active sexual practice should not be seen as inherently negative phenomena. Relationships can provide young girls with a sense of stability. In the context of a lack of opportunities, motherhood is seen as a way of securing a place in the community. Previous to her work with the *fundación*, Ana Milena had been working with a sexual health program in Cazucá and was acutely aware of the challenges for young people in the community, and the obligation for more information and support to be provided. This lengthy quote is important and illustrative of the complexities here:

> [A]nd speaking of relationships, and the role of women. There are still young men who continue to claim that women have to stay in the house, look after the kids. Yes? It is really normal for girls, after leaving school to think 'Now I want to have children'. Because ... well, I spoke with a girl and she said to me 'I want to have a baby' ... and I said 'Well, when are you going to have one, when do you want to have kids?' She said 'When I leave school'. And we did an exercise, I got them to think about when they want to be mothers and fathers. And a majority said once they leave school, or when they are eighteen or maybe twenty. And to myself, I am like, 'What? I couldn't imagine my life, like that, at 18 with a kid!'. ... But they do see things like that. And it is because motherhood represents for young people a possibility of being. As in, 'With this, I will have respect. I will have something to fight for, a home, I will have a name that will continue . . .' It's like 'We've been together as boyfriend and girlfriend for a while, we want to demonstrate our love in a sexual way'. Yes. I think ... well, good, I wouldn't censor them for thinking that. Sexuality is something delicious you should enjoy and use how you wish. But. But! It is that they have to think if they are protecting themselves or not. If they are sure or not. Yes? But many young people are parents and they say 'I wanted to have a kid and yeah ... now my life has changed, I want to go out, but I can't, and I can't make things the way they were before'. We really have to start being conscious of what we say, and how we talk about pregnancy.

Ana Milena drew attention to how the stability of motherhood and an active sexual life can be empowering for young women. Internally displaced adolescents around Colombia interviewed by Women's Commission (2002) noted that a child not only gave them someone to love, it brought emotional and financial support from family and friends – although not always from their sexual partner. In research conducted in a *barrio* with similar socioeconomic

120 *Embodied Everyday Violences*

conditions to Cazucá located in Cali, researchers noted that motherhood is taken on as a 'role that becomes characteristic of them' (Sabogal Ruiz 2005, 122) as a way of establishing a certain autonomy as adults in an environment in which opportunities to advance other talents are absent.

It is primarily lack of support, knowledge, and ability to access services that means that pregnancy provokes so many challenges in Cazucá. Pregnancy and motherhood at an early age not only causes physical health concerns but also impedes the ability of young women to complete their education and progress to more stable, better-paid employment later in life. While the situation persists, structural inequity perpetuates vulnerability and the potential for various embodied violences – such as complicated pregnancies, lack of medical aid, and illegal abortion procedures – against young women, and their partners and families.

Fractures in Family Relationships

As well as individual experiences of violence and risk, young people often find the assumed site of security – the family – actually presents risks, tragedy, and violence. Fifteen-year-old Rosa's account of violence and tragedy not only tells of broader issues but also was a profoundly difficult story for her to recount:

ROSA: …It is not good for anyone. There are people who arrive [in Cazucá] dying, almost dead. Pregnant. At that point …
CAMILA ANDREA: [interrupts] They die sometimes.
ROSA: [continues] … little grandmothers [*abuelitas*, an affectionate diminutive] … Aiii no, it's that people, many people, die because of the doctors, hospitals. For example, in my case, my mama lost her girl who was two because the doctor didn't think about the drug she would have to buy. It cost [an enormous, impossible sum relative to income] each time … and so the doctor was the one who killed her. How was my mother meant to save her? There are many people who do damage to people and they don't care because…
LAURA: [interrupts] They don't have a heart.
HB: …mmmm …
LAURA: [quietly] And it happens more than once to the same family.
ROSA: [simultaneously] … the poor. And so, my mama almost went crazy because of this doctor, and ooshh my mama hated all the time she had to go to hospital for that, it was a terrible time. She would say: my life, my money, these aren't costs, but my daughter and my pain, it is too high … [Rosa speaks very fast and quietly here, the end of her comment is inaudible before becoming loud and insistent in the following] And what? For what? Still my sister is gone.
  [Silence]

The imposition of the violent and tragic consequences of social exclusion, poverty and marginalisation are starkly visible in Rosa's story. At its heart it speaks of a family tragedy, the loss of a sibling, and the depression of her mother, which is experienced as a profound pain. However, it is embedded within systems that prevented Rosa's mother from seeking adequate and affordable health care. Those who occupy positions within that system are seen as uncaring and indifferent to the violence and pain experienced by families such as Rosa's. The story commenced with an apparent generalised observation about the embodied suffering of those arriving to the community, but quickly it became apparent that this was not a generalised comment but a personal experience. Stories that circulate as commonly held understandings of collective life lose their specificity; however, these webs of understanding in the community are rooted in shared, specific experiences of tragedy and loss. Rosa's experience can also be linked to other conversations and stories during my time in the community. Together these stories draw out observations about how the shape and experience of family life can be deeply affected by structural violences, and social exclusion, which play out in various ways on the bodies of women and their children.

Family can, however, also be an explicit site of violence. As noted in the previous chapter, in one case of reported domestic abuse the abdication of responsibility by the police led to a continuation of the violence. Young people also commented that parents were frequently absent for long periods because of the nature of work they undertook to provide for their families, and that often their presence was authoritarian or was so brief as to be almost worthless. Twelve-year-old Alicia said that while her parents sometimes offered to help with homework or listen to her, sometimes they would not because 'they would arrive so tired from work'. Ana Milena (from the *fundación*) highlighted intrafamilial violence as a significant obstacle for young people. The understanding of women as men's 'property', she argued, is prevalent in the community, and parents who behave in this manner teach these behaviours as appropriate to their sons. Fifteen-year-old Sofia argues that adults often 'do not know how to listen':

> And often the parents don't listen to what they do, or they just hit them and tell them off. How is that going to teach them? All that will do is that they will grow knowing to tell lies and continue with their bad activities.

Obviously, such accounts are not meant as a generalised commentary on all experiences of young people with their families. Many young people told of parents who tried very hard to provide for their families in difficult conditions and provide support and assistance whenever it was needed. Parents were also described as role models and as important figures in young people's lives, and these intergenerational relationships and transfers of knowledge are a key site of resilience. However, the difficulties of the environment and the occasions of domestic violence are experienced as profoundly negative experiences by

122　*Embodied Everyday Violences*

young people in Cazucá, who often feel abandoned in responding to and ameliorating such situations. Families, then, are the sites of tensions between the desire for supportive and secure environments, and the location of tragedy and violence, which are experienced both on the bodies and through the everyday lives of these young people.

'Violence Generates Violence': Challenges to Social Cohesion

As evidenced by the accounts of many young people, physical violence is not experienced solely physically but has consequences for the social fabric of the community and the way occupants perceive their environment. This inter-relation between physical violence and rupture of social cohesion within the community is clearly articulated by fifteen-year-old Susana:

> Well, I think violence affects everyone. Because, look, there are people who kill others who have nothing to do with it, who aren't to blame ... now the police kill many people for being in conflict with, like, FARC, the guerrillas, with gangs, with everyone. Children are killed. People are killed who have nothing to do with the problem, who are simply passing or are in their house and are shot and they die from it. Because, look, often people don't know how to solve problems between themselves, or they have to do it violently. You can't fix thing by speaking, like through having a meeting or something. But everyone is ... well, they think it has to be violent and things aren't like that. Because they kill others as an opportunity for a fight at least, and that badness, it touches us all. We have lost many people in this *barrio* ...

In this quote, Susana demonstrates the way in which individual (and at times random) acts of violence reinforce each other and create a culture where violence becomes a legitimate form of expression and a way to solve pro-blems, while simultaneously limiting the possibility of other forms of engage-ment such as speaking. It also touches on how such violence affects whole communities and their intersubjective being, as well as the individual bodily encounters with violent action. Other young people expressed similar sentiments:

BRAYAN ALEXANDER (15): ... well, they attack someone and people say: 'Ai! Why did you kill that person?' And they say, well, because they killed someone I know. ... And, well, this isn't the solution. They say they will keep killing people but no, that isn't the solution ...

FELIPE (16): Violence generates violence ...

BRAYAN ALEXANDER: Exactly! If they are going to act violently here we will get more violence ... perhaps we can arrive at solutions but continuing more and more violently, that won't work.

Embodied Everyday Violences 123

The feeling that the prevalence and continuance of violences leads to further violence also echoes Jackson's (2002) argument about the most devastating effects of violence being on the 'lifeworlds' of individuals – their relationships with others and sense of connectedness. A notion of what is possible in the everyday experience of people's lives depends on the interrelationships between people, that their embodied experiences affect one another, and the webs of relationships they build and maintain. Varying forms of violence curtail this relational experience and break communal bonds. The risk against body and life is seen as too great to challenge.

Elaine Scarry speaks of violence as a silencing act, noting that the inability of the victim to relate their experience forms part of the pain of the event. For Scarry, 'pain does not simply resist language but actively destroys it' (1985, 4). The threat, or previous experience of violence silences people and further engrains the violence experienced as a deeply embodied trauma. Seventeen-year-old Laura directly describes this:

> [P]eople stay quiet. They are told 'No, you shut up or we'll kill you'. And they continue to shut up because they are scared of what the cost will be. And so no one can help.

Such violence does not manifest in isolation or without cause. Frequently, both adults and young people would speak of the lack of opportunities in Cazucá, in particular for young people. There are links in these observations to the structural inequality and social exclusion, and resultant insecurity, discussed in the previous chapter. However, more than this, such powerful imbalances and exclusions on structural levels have lived consequences in the everyday. Young people faced with limited options, make tactical choices they see as best improving their lives. Ana Milena notes this:

> If, for example, a young guy starts selling drugs, or falls into delinquency, it is because he didn't have opportunities, because he didn't have work, or the ability to study. ... I think it is also a little bit to do with the vision that is constructed about what is possible or not. In that this then starts to become realised. And they start to naturalise, normalise these types of conduct. ... It is a bit circular.

Ana Milena also linked this normalisation of violence to the tendency not to trust those who are unknown, or strange, whether that be those arriving displaced, or even, she noted, LGBT (lesbian, gay, bisexual, transgender) persons.[6] Such intolerance and delinquency are linked to the censoring by gangs in the community as well as intrafamilial violence: 'So then, where children grow up in an environment of violence you see them at school, they are the most aggravated, the one who hits the most. It is all connected'. The insecurity of place, the presence of potential violent actors, the threat of embodied violences, all contribute to ongoing processes and actions of violence and insecurity.

124 *Embodied Everyday Violences*

Conclusions

As evidenced by the accounts of many young people, violence is not experienced solely against the body but *is* embodied. It is both enacted against physical bodies and also contributes to the ongoing process of embodied lived experiences, which constitute identity, habit, and everyday life. Such embodied violences are embedded in challenges to the cohesion of the community and the way occupants perceive their environment. This interrelation between the physical environment and the rupture of social cohesion within the community highlights the ways in which such violences affects the webs of relationships between individuals as well as individual sense of self.

It is difficult to isolate the particular and multiple manifestations of violence in Cazucá, as their causes and consequences are all enmeshed. However, this chapter has identified several different 'forms' of violence, all experienced against and through the bodies of young people, and all of which affect their sense of being. The violences enacted by armed groups and gangs have the most resonance with spatialised insecurity discussed in the previous chapter. However, their actions do not just foster terrains of insecurity that restrict movement, but often are enacted upon the bodies of young people. The consequences of such behaviour are a fundamental breakdown in trust within the community and extremely elevated levels of fear. Direct violence as a result of gangs, the drug trade, or state intervention is experienced as entwined with more intimate violences, including sexual assault, as well as the risks and violences present in some intimate partner relationships and family settings. While not all situations are violent or risky, the combination of systems that are unsupportive of marginalised individuals along with the challenges of poverty and social exclusion, increase the likelihood of various violences. Although disparate, these stories resonate in discussions of the difficulty of claiming an embodied and meaningful 'sense of being' in an environment that contains so many everyday violent risks to the body and lives of young people.

Present throughout this chapter are discussions and ideas about the space in which violence affects individuals' abilities to be present and participate in the collective of relationships. Jackson notes that violence inhibits these relationships and Scarry notes that pain and violence actively destroys language. These tensions, insecurities, and risks negatively impact social cohesion. The result of this is cyclical: violence, both actual and anticipated, is increased. Violence impacts lifeworlds, and thus embodied experience must be understood as the realm of the political – not invisible or taken for granted, but rather interrogated, engaged with, and imbricated within the fabric of the everyday. The violences described through this chapter shape particular experiences of lived, situated daily life; these are not extreme violences that occur elsewhere, but rather form the background of daily life. It is embodied. Taken together, this chapter and the previous chapter have detailed how the multiple forms of violence and insecurity experienced within the everyday lives of the occupants of Cazucá can be understand as an embodied-everyday-amidst-violence.

Embodied Everyday Violences 125

This attention to the way the dangers and violences are experienced and understood by young people should not be read as a totalising narrative. All occupants of Cazucá, including young people, find ways of negotiating and living with such violences as well as identifying the limits of current approaches and requirements for more productive engagements. It is important to recognise that although the violences of everyday life contribute to the problems experienced by young people, this definitely does not mean that all young people are somehow made violent or dangerous simply because their existence is bound up in the same spatial territory. Without exception, all adults I spoke to in Cazucá affirmed the resilience of young people who 'in the middle of family difficulties, poverty, continue to move ahead' (Ana Milena). Recognising this fact moves beyond the concept of dangerous or passive youth toward examining the ways young people find spaces and manners of coping with, and ameliorating the effects of, violence and envisioning peace. It is this recognition that is explored in the following chapters.

Notes

1 This quote comes from an interview participant. After discussion with her following the interview, I have used her quote here but not her pseudonym. She noted that she really wanted me to be able to discuss it but did not want it to 'affect what else she had to say about other things'.
2 A 2012 report by the Watchlist on Children in Armed Conflict reported that fear of stigma or retaliation prevented many survivors of sexual assault from speaking up or seeking help. They cite a survey by Oxfam and *Casa de la Mujer* (Women's House Foundation) discussed in text (Amparo Sanchez, Lopez Vivas, Rubriche Cardenas, and Rengifo Cano 2011). Additionally, Watchlist notes that lack of legal action against perpetrators compounded the inability of survivors to report their assault (Watchlist 2012, 22–23). On this, see also Bosmans et al. 2012; Amnesty International 2004; and Women's Commission 2002, 18–19.
3 This section focuses particularly on the experiences of young girls and young women. I acknowledge the nature of the discussion, and the absence of consideration of sexual violence against boys and young men. However, as these explorations stem from interviews and conversations in the field, young men and boys' sexual vulnerability was not specifically discussed. Obviously, I cannot speculate on the actual reason for this, but in light of other conversations about gender in the field, I would note that its absence in discussion does not imply its absence from actual lived experience. The only time young boys were invoked was in the context of a few conversations about family/domestic abuse, and these conversations were not specifically about sexual abuse but broader themes of neglect and physical violence.
4 While it is speculation to query why this is the case, I suggest perhaps it has to do with the age at which many young women become sexually active, which often occurs between the ages of the younger (eleven- to twelve-year-olds) and older young people (fifteen- to sixteen-year-olds) I spoke with. Once a young woman has had sexual experiences (consensual or forced) there is perhaps a different form of 'silencing' around the manner in which sexual encounters are discussed. This also links to broader discussions in this chapter about young people developing a 'sense of self', shaped by both positive and negative experiences. Sexual experience form part of that exploration and development of 'self'. Sexual assault has been recognised in some cases to challenge fundamental assumptions about self and place.

126 *Embodied Everyday Violences*

Perhaps these observations help explain, at least in part, this notable difference in the young people's engagement with the topic.

5 The sentiment – of becoming aware of rights – was also expressed by community leaders in CESTRA-USIP's *Promotores de Paz* (Peace Promoters) workshops.

6 Ana Milena commented: '… and obviously the issue of gender. It's very easy to see … not only with physical violence but how I might position myself as a women, or maybe as LGBT in a society which discriminates against me. It's like what is different is strange, it's bad, it's against the norm. And then, also, it makes intolerance in relation to anyone unknown or strange, from new people to different sexualities …'.

References

Alzate, Monica M. 2007. 'The Sexual and Reproductive Rights of Internally Displaced Women: The Embodiment of Colombia's Crisis.' *Disasters* 32(1):131–148.

Amnesty International. 2004. *Colombia: Scarred Bodies, Hidden Crimes: Sexual Violence Against Women in the Armed Conflict*. London: Amnesty International, International Secretariat.

Amparo Sanchez, Olga, Jose Nicolas Lopez Vivas, Diana Rubriche Cardenas, and Maria del Pilar Rengifo Cano. 2011. *Campaign Rape and Other Violences: Leave My Body Out of War: Sexual Violence Against Women in the Context of the Colombian Armed Conflict 2001–2009*. Bogotá, Colombia: Casa de la Mujer.

Arboleda, Jairo A., Patti L. Petesch, and James Blackburn. 2004. *Voices of the Poor in Colombia: Strengthening Livelihoods, Families and Communities*. Washington, DC: The World Bank.

Bosmans, Marleen, Fernando Gonzalez, Eva Brem, and Marleen Temmerman. 2012. "Dignity and the Right of Internally Displaced Adolescents in Colombia to Sexual and Reproductive Health." *Disasters*. www.biomedsearch.com/nih/Dignity-right-internally-displaced-adolescents/22329483.html.

Cespedes-Baez, Lina Maria. 2010. "Les vamos a dar por donde más les duele: La violencia sexual en contra de las mujeres como estrategia de despojo de tierras en el conflicto armado Colombiano." *Revista Estudios Socio-Juridicos* 12, no. 2: 273–304.

Duque, Luisa Fernanda. 2009. *Educacion y conflicto: Altos de Cazucá*. Bogotá, Colombia: Fundación para la Educacion y el Desarrollo (FEDES).

Farmer, Paul. 2004. "An Anthropology of Structural Violence." *Current Anthropology* 45, no. 3: 305–324.

HRW (Human Rights Watch). 2005. *Colombia: Displaced and Discarded: The Plight of Internally Displaced Persons in Bogotá and Cartagena*. New York: Human Rights Watch.

Hynes, Michelle, Jeanne Ward, Kathryn Robertson, and Chadd Crouse. 2004. "A Determination of the Prevalence of Gender-Based Violence Among Conflict-Affected Populations in East Timor." *Disasters* 28(3):294–321.

Jackson, Michael. 2002. *The Politics of Storytelling: Violence, Transgression and Intersubjectivity*. Copenhagen, Denmark: Museum Tusculanum Press, University of Copenhagen.

Kleinman, Arthur. 2000. "The Violences of Everyday Life: The Multiple Forms and Dynamics of Social Violence." In *Violence and Subjectivity*, edited by Veena Das, Arthur Kleinman, Mamphela Ramphele and Pamela Reynolds. Oakland, CA: University of California Press.

Kleinman, Arthur, Veena Das, and Margaret Lock. 1996. "Introduction." *Daedalus* 125(1) (special issue titled *Social Suffering*): xi–xx.

Meertens, Donny. 2006. *Colombia: Brechas, diversidad e iniciativas. Mujeres e igualdad de género en un país en conflicto.* Bogotá, Colombia: ASDI, Embajada de Suecia.

Meertens, Donny. 2010. "Forced Displacement and Women's Security in Colombia." *Disasters* 34(S2):S147–S164.

Ministerio de la Protección Social. 2003. *Política nacional de salud sexual y reproductiva.* Bogotá, Colombia: Ministerio de la Protección Social.

Pacheco Sanchez, Carlos Ivan, and Carolina Enriquez. 2004. "Sexual and Reproductive Health Rights of Colombian IDPs." *Forced Migration Review* 19: 31–32.

Pinzon Ochoa, Nelson M. 2007. "Los jovenes de 'la loma': Altos de Cazucá y el paramilitarismo en la periferia de Bogotá." *Maguare* 21: 271–295.

Profamilia. 2010. *Encuesta nacional de demografía y salud – ENDS.* Bogotá, Colombia: Profamila.

Profamilia. 2011. *Surveys in Marginalized Areas: Sexual and Reproductive Health, Forced Displacement and Poverty 2000–2011.* Bogotá, Colombia: Profamilia.

Reutersward, Camilla, Par Zetterberg, Suruchi Thapar-Bjorkert, and Maxine Molyneux. 2011. "Abortion Law Reforms in Colombia and Nicaragua: Issue Networks and Opportunity Contexts." *Development and Change* 42(3):805–831.

Ríos García, Ana Liliana. 2008. "Alcance de las políticas públicas en el área de salud sexual y reproductiva dirigidas a los adolescentes en Colombia." *Salud Uninorte* 24 (2):351–358.

Rojas, Carlos Eduardo. 1996. *La violencia llamada "limpieza social."* Bogotá, Colombia: CINEP.

Sabogal Ruiz, Viviana 2005. *Jovenes, conflictos urbanos y alternativas de inclusion.* Bogotá, Colombia: Plataforma Conflicto Urbano y Jovenes, CIVIS Suecia & ASDI.

Scarry, Elaine. 1985. *The Body in Pain: The Making and Unmaking of the World.* Oxford: Oxford University Press.

Scheper-Hughes, Nancy, and Philippe Bourgois, eds. 2004. *Violence in War and Peace: An Anthology.* Oxford: Blackwell.

Taussig, Michael. 1987. *Shamanism, Colonialism, and the Wild Man: A Study in Terror and Healing.* Chicago, IL: University of Chicago Press.

United Nations. 2001. *Consulta con mujeres desplazadas sobre principios rectores del desplazamiento.* Bogotá, Colombia.

Watchlist on Children and Armed Conflict. 2012. *No One to Trust: Children and Armed Conflict in Colombia.* New York: Watchlist on Children and Armed Conflict.

Women's Commission for Refugee Women and Children. 2002. *Unseen Millions: The Catastrophe of Internal Displacement in Colombia: Children and Adolescents at Risk.* New York: Women's Commission for Refugee Women and Children.

5   Resilience and Resistance

HB: What do you think of the future here? What will it look like?

MARIA PATRICIA (15): That Colombians learn soon to change their way of being. That there are many people who say, 'Ooo, I will help', but they are lying, and we should be a part of a change. So that everyone has a life, has their health.

SOFIA (15): I agree with Maria Patricia. But we need to change the way we think, because sometimes we don't think. People think only of the violence, or only of themselves. We can do better than this. That is what I think.

'To speak about the rights we have, to share our belief in everyone's ability to guarantee those rights, this is how we become stronger as a community'. This was how, during a break between sessions, one young female student explained the importance of the event we were attending. As a volunteer with the *fundación*, I, along with the two other volunteers, had been asked to participate in the school's first human rights forum (*Primera Foro de Derechos Humano: Una Mirada Desde el Colegio*) in 2010. The atmosphere was almost festive, with the courtyard of the school covered in posters made by the students explaining each of the human rights in the UN Declaration on Human Rights.

Young people talked articulately about different aspects of human rights to classrooms full of their peers, teachers, guardians, and representatives from the local government and various NGOs working in the community. In contrast to the difficulties and everyday violences that surrounded the school, the space within the school this day was vibrant, encouraging, and engaging. It had young people's voices at the heart of events.

More than the focus on concepts of human rights, what was significant about the event was the presence of adults – parents, teachers, and NGO workers – who were sitting listening to young people. In a community so often fractured by violence, the sense of being together, and the commitment to dialogue and collaboration stood out. Later in the day one of the student speakers described with passion why, in his view, days like the forum were so important:

Human rights have to be a reality, not idealistic. Our rights are important and we have an obligation to ensure they are achieved. Things like this forum are important to help that because it allows us all, students, parents, teachers, to come together to discuss why they are important and how we can make them a reality. Abuse of human rights is not new, but it happens in new ways, where the internet can complicate fights between gangs or between individuals. And in our environment, where there is such violence, little children in our *comuna* grow up seeing violence and thinking 'This is acceptable, this is how you solve problems'.

He went on to make the point that there was a real need for older students to model respect for younger students, arguing that it is important to educate young people as well as possible so they can be good citizens, so that doors open for them and they can contribute to a better society. Although framed around human rights, this student was invoking a sense of community, and of communal responsibility for responding to and resisting narratives of violence and exclusion.

All day I kept thinking about the negativity that so often characterises the community externally and the individual experiences of the young people I had spoken with. Here, for a day, such negativity and the very real and serious issues that exist were not ignored, but they were not dominating either. It was the potential to affect those negative things, to respond to violence, to build stronger communities and recognise young people as actors in those

Figure 5.1 The human rights forum at *Instituto Educativo Gabriel Garcia Marquez*. Visible in the background are typical dwellings of the community (photo taken by author).

130 *Resilience and Resistance*

activities that were centred, and which created so much enthusiasm and excitement. After an energetic and inspired demonstration from a local youth hip-hop group who rapped and danced to an original track about young people's ability to make change, a student in his final year at the school ended the day by summing up the experiences in a single, simple idea: 'We are what we do, and above all, we are what we do to change what we are'.

The radical potential of a notion of everyday peace is its ability to recognise individuals' attempts to negotiate violence, address material needs, and to find sites of resistance and solidarity. Much of the previous two chapters have focused on the way in which exclusion and violence function to exacerbate insecurity and impact lived experience. Here I am interested in the converse, in how young people find space that responds to the circumscribing of public space, and their liminal space in collective consciousness.

The exploration of structural marginality, pervasive social exclusion, and violence experienced through everyday embodied experiences in the previous two chapters is not meant to totalise the experience of the occupants of Cazucá. Rather, paying attention to how such marginality, exclusion, and violence manifest and are understood by the young people opens space to question how existing narratives uncritically locate the problem within the bodies of Cazucá's occupants and the networks they inhabit. Having outlined and explored the challenges facing the young occupants of Cazucá in the previous two chapters, this chapter asks how young people resist and respond to these challenges, building individual and communal resilience. In doing this, it locates the site of the everyday within the narratives and lives of the young people who live in the community, and allows an opening to see what discourses preoccupied with liberal peacebuilding narratives might miss. It finds places and sites where notions of the everyday are visible in young people's efforts to resist violence and seek places where violence is ameliorated and the collective potential for building webs of relationships is enhanced. It is in such spaces that the importance of routine and everyday activity can be seen; young people's lives are not only characterised by violence, but contain routine and 'normal' events that foster resilience. Young people speak of the community generally as well as the school and the *fundación* as such places. Such sites can be seen as spaces of opportunity where, although imperfect, violence is reduced and young people's actions and experiences can be recognised. Together these explorations identify ways in which young people resist the multiple violences of their lives and conceive of spaces where notions of peace have weight and can be fostered. It recognises the importance of fraught sites of resilience and draws attention to the value of including young people's own accounts of experience in exploring and proposing an everyday-peace-amidst-violence.

Notions of Resilience and Resistance

Individuals give meaning to their daily practice, constituting an everyday life. Within this practice, resilience and resistance are crucial. Resilience has come

Resilience and Resistance 131

to mean an individual's capacity to mediate risk, adapt, and remain strong. Masten, Best, and Garmezy (1990) identify resilience as good outcomes despite high-risk environments, sustained competence despite ongoing threats, or successful recovery from a traumatic event. Resilient young people are seen to be proactive in solving problems, to be positive and optimistic about the future, and contain a sense of purpose concerning their life (Apfel and Simon 1996; Boyden and Mann 2000). Additionally, the support and positive encouragement of peers, family, and teachers, as well as environments that are considered secure, reinforce young people's ability to cope (Wessells 2006; Boyden and Mann 2000). Such configurations have merit in the broadest sense but must not be considered fixed or universal. Resilience then, as conceived of within this chapter, is not primarily located in the mental-health and health-sciences discourses as something individualised in response to trauma with measurable, quantifiable outcomes. Viet Nguyen-Gillham et al., in research about Palestinian youth (although I argue their point is more broadly applicable), note that while this work is important, it must be accompanied by broader, qualitative explorations of resilience, as 'a lexicon of pathology not only stigmatises, it precludes this population from potential life-affirming outcomes' (2008, 292).[1]

Increasingly research recognises a notion of resilience beyond an individual quality of a particular young person and values the resources within communities, and young people's social context (see Ungar 2004, 2008; Summerfield 2002; Luthar 1993, 2005). Jo Boyden and Gillian Mann argue the terminology around the idea of resilience itself is limited and imprecise, that the notions of risk and resilience are 'culturally and normatively loaded' (2000, 10), and that much of the research on resilience has been conducted with children in the industrialised global north, and finally that young people's own accounts have been conspicuously absent in much of the discussions and analyses (2000, 8–11). It is critiques such as this that underpin a reluctance to over-specify a definition of resilience here. Rather, it is used as a guiding concept to inform the exploration of the choices and justifications young people give in responding to their environments and articulating future aspirations. Furthermore, such a choice responds in part to Boyden and Mann's criticism of overly adultist understandings of children's resilience by considering their own explanations. Resilience should be recognised as a 'useful metaphor' (Boyden and Mann 2000, 20), that is variable and contingent and not reductive. Instead of being seen as a specific interventionist tool, resilience is a useful concept to recognise young people's own capacities and understandings.

In strengthening and complementing this understanding of resilience as recognising young people's capacities, this chapter also adapts the idea proposed by Nguyen-Gillham et al., which reconstitutes resilience as 'a wider collective and social representation of what it means to endure', positioned within a context of 'social suffering' rather than pathologised individualism (2008, 292). In conceiving of resilience in this fashion, this chapter is able to account for the human agency present in meaning-making amongst insecure

132 *Resilience and Resistance*

terrains and amidst ongoing violence. This understanding of resilience responds to the consequences of fear and violence such as those outlined in previous chapters, and overcomes the foreshortening of the future imposed by violent acts (see Restrepo 2004) and disruption to relationships. Resilience can be seen partially to be an act of endurance.

Ryan Burgess, in work within Comuna 4 where Cazucá is located, argues that resilience can be understood in the way young people are aware of the manifestation of violences, are able to judge the seriousness of threats, and their creation and exploitation of opportunities to resist or respond to such violences and threats (2008, 189; see also Berents and ten Have 2017). These broad categories, similar in parts to my discussion below, demonstrate the broad applicability of a notion of resilience, without a reductive or individualising understanding of young people's engagement with their environment and their relationships with others. Resilience is a part of an individual's everyday, their negotiation of daily violences, reliance on those around them for support, and tactical responses to structural exclusion and threat.[2] It helps in understanding the reality of an idea of an everyday peace, particularly *amidst* violence.

To speak of resisting, of resistance, is also not to fully adopt Richmond's understanding of resistance as the way of responding to, and in some cases rejecting, orthodox peace (2010). While Richmond argues that resistance at a local level can be a mechanism to reconceptualise people in 'contextual and everyday terms' (2010, 686–689), he reinscribes the 'local' with a fundamental alterity. Such a flattened reading of the spaces of the everyday limits their potential. I seek more nuance and recognise that it is possible – from a position of marginalisation – to desire those things offered by a liberal contract, but to articulate frustration, anger, and disenchantment with the denial of this obligation by those structures that hold power over your life. This complicates the idea of resistance offered by Richmond, as discussed in Chapter One. As will become evident in this chapter, many young people are not rejecting the *ideals* of liberal peace but rather are rejecting or speaking with anger about the *inequalities* and the *inherent contradictions* of their everyday lives within these framings.

Young people, located in 'everyday' practice, unaffiliated with civil society organisations or other formal modes of 'liberal-local' engagement want or expect the things that liberal peacebuilding and the liberal state tells them they are entitled too – things such as education, health care, respect for human rights, and security – and yet they are able to critique the actuality of experience in which powers and structures operate to deny such things to young people in the 'non-places' (to invoke Nordstrom and discussions in Chapter Three), in the spaces excluded from broader social and political life. Resistance is instead conceptualised here as a response to the conditions of marginalisation, violence, and threat, in part caused or exacerbated by the state, but in which tactics can be developed to ameliorate or minimise risks and violences. This then is a different way of conceiving of resistance that acknowledges the expected role or the state while criticising its failings and that builds and supports resilience within the everyday.

This chapter outlines *ideas of resilience* – against both immediate, everyday threats and the distant state – which is fostered in spaces where violence is ameliorated, and the notion of *resisting* structures and powers which deny the obligations and relationships present in an idea of post-liberal peace. Together, these strengthen the argument for understanding everyday forms of peace as constituted through the meaning young people give their daily practice in spite of marginalisation, violence, and suffering.

Spaces of Resilience and Resistance

Amongst persistent everyday violences there are spaces where violence is lessened, ameliorated, or held at bay. Central in young people's articulations of such spaces are notions of community and belonging. If violence disrupts or denies our ways of belonging and becomes woven into everyday being, then finding spaces and ways which run counter to that violence can provide more stable grounding for claims of belonging, and the authority that is held to make those claims. The young people of Cazucá find such grounding in various ways through school, organised spaces provided by the fundacion and other NGOs, and at times through the coming together of the community for particular purposes.

Such spaces are also locations where young people's contributions are recognised as valid, in a way that is not recognised in other everyday contexts. They can function, imperfectly, as reprieves or responses to the effects of violence that denies the presence and actions of young people. These spaces can be formal such as the regulated structure of the school and the interactions within, or informal, such as the casual conversations that occur around and between scheduled meetings or events through the *fundación*. Villamizar and Zamora (2005, 70–71) point out that 'new forms of expression' arise in places of encounter that are quite often public. Spaces such as the 'houses of leaders, school and NGOs' are sites in which 'public action is developed, youth initiatives are promoted and spaces of participation are provided'. These spaces also allow the establishment of 'more horizontal relationships with the adult populations' (Villamizar and Zamora 2005, 71).

In addition to the securing aspect of such spaces, part of the importance of their existence are as sites where normal routines can be embedded and practiced. Writing about young people living amongst ongoing violence in Jerusalem, Pat-Horenczyk, Schiff, and Doppelt (2006) argue that maintaining routines increases a sense of autonomy and reinscribes the normalcy of everyday life. Similarly, the strength of a notion of everyday peace existing *amidst* violence, rather than as a dichotomising understanding of peace *or* (or *only after*) violence, draws upon demonstrable evidence that young people in Cazucá establish and maintain normality and routine in their everyday lives. In order to recognise everyday peace, it is important to recognise that narratives of violence and insecurity are not totalising. When asked what they liked to do in their free time outside of school young people told me they did many

134   *Resilience and Resistance*

things. This included playing games (such as eleven-year-old Johan David who particularly enjoyed playing hide-and-seek with friends at school); doing homework; helping make food; listening to music or practicing an instrument; or visiting family (like sixteen-year-old Juan Carlos, who regularly visits his grandmother). Sixteen-year-old Felipe likes to party (in conversation he used the slang, *rumba*) while seventeen-year-old Alejandro often helps his father in their small shop. Such activities are notable for their commonness, and the way in which they are located in the spaces and interactions of the everyday.

Beyond the routines and practices of everyday life there are spaces where youth participation is supported or encouraged. Such spaces exist in tension with spaces in which actions are violent or transgressive.[3] Locations where violence is ameliorated are also often locations where possibility emerges, and resultantly where the challenges young people face in their everyday lives can be negotiated, redefined, and managed. What is key here is recognising that young people's efforts to engage are strengthened if they are acknowledged or given space. It is more than a simple need for recognition but rather a need for some kind of balance between personal experience and the broader network of relationships 'such that one's voice carries and one's actions have repercussions in the state, nation or community with which one identifies' (Jackson 2002, 40). For young people in Cazucá, their voices might rarely have repercussions at the state level, but they can and do make changes in the local community. I now explore the sites and spaces (physical and conceptual) that enable and foster young people's resilience and resistance.

The Community

The collective space of the community can be dangerous. However, this is a simplistic account, because it is also the most important location for interaction and for creating cohesion against the violences that impose themselves. Yuri Picon, Liliana Arciniegas, and Javier Becerra, speaking of a *barrio* community near to Cazucá argue that 'the barrio is a space of collective life, a space of decision, opposition and confrontation between people who share common ground and carry out activities that permanently intersect' (2006, 16). The difficulties of collective space are well recognised by young people. Fifteen-year-old Susana is aware of the difficulties of navigating opinion and experience of Cazucá, but argues for the capabilities and potential of young people within that difficult space:

> My opinion, in regards to Cazucá, is that it can be a nice space. Because people say it is a *barrio* of street people, of poor people, but it does have beauty. Education, the creation of each individual, the development of thinking. But of course, there is fear of being robbed or attacked, because here there is a lot of violations of under age children. But, well, you need to take care and pay attention that nothing happens; and don't socialise with lots of people you don't know. Because that's when I think bad

things happen. But there is much goodness and kindness here also, and amazing young people.

The tension between the dangers and the potential of the space of the community is evident in Susana's discussion, and the physical space she evokes is described with human emotions: 'goodness and kindness'. Michael Jackson draws on Simone Weil to note that rootedness, this connectivity, is unable to be unlinked from an individual's participation in a community (2002, 12). Susana's recognition of individual development which she links to the positive attributes of the community highlight these relationships and the rootedness, or connectedness, to others.

Due to the time of year I was in the community, Christmas was on the minds of many young people I spoke with. The celebrations associated with Christmas were often mentioned as an example of a positive aspect of the community, and more than that, as a time when the community acts collectively in a positive manner. When eleven-year-old Andrea was asked what she liked about Cazucá she replied:

> Well we have nice neighbours. ... When it is Christmas we all decorate many of the houses and it is great (*chevere*). Almost everyone gives a bit of money to fix the neighbourhood for Christmas. All the houses.

Not only is Christmas seen as a fun activity but also Andrea notes that in the community there is a collective contribution and commitment to the event. For fourteen-year-old Camila Andrea, the positives of events like Christmas help balance the negative aspects of the community:

> I think Cazucá has a little of everything. Sometimes here in Cazucá it is violent ... [but] it has, sometimes, happiness. Like soon it will be Christmas, and everything will be happy, everyone will be dancing ...

More broadly than particular celebrations, several young people made positive associations with their neighbours, or other young people near where they live. As always, tempered by the recognition that there are also negative aspects, but strong relationships with neighbours was mentioned several times, as in this comment by twelve-year-old Sebastian: 'Cazucá has both good and bad things. For example there are some great neighbours. It is fun to spend time together'.

A collective notion of community is not only present in isolated events, but forms a collective of resistance against obstacles. During a conversation with several young people about the way in which the government abnegates their responsibility for provision of services and improvements to the community fifteen-year-old Rosa observed that

> We have to do everything. All of the community gave money to fix things. If the streetlights break, well we fix them because it is safer that way. But it is always us.

136　*Resilience and Resistance*

What followed this observation was a discussion of how it is 'unjust' that the responsibility falls on the community, but that there was a sense of pride that people in the community worked to solve their own problems, and put aside their own issues to collectively make improvements for all.

The notion of 'community' is an intangible one, and not one that is simple to define. For these young people, the importance of collectively engaging with their neighbours, friends, and broader community strengthens their positive associations with their environment and their ability to participate in change-making activities. Such articulations also make evident the claim by Nguyen-Gillham et al. (2008) that resistance has a wider collective interpretation of constructive endurance. There is, in these young people's discussions, the idea that there can be a notion of resilience that is embedded in and strengthened through the networks of relationships that hold disparate people together in difficult circumstances.

School and Education

For the young people involved in this project, school underpinned everyday routines and provided a space where violence was ameliorated. The physicality of protection offered by the two school sites: through the walls of *Garcia Marquez* or high chain fence at *Minutos* – topped with broken glass and barbed wire respectively – as well as the presence of a guard at *Garcia Marquez*, and a padlocked gate at *Minutos*, establishes the visibility of protection. In addition the emotive and creative space built and promoted by the teaching staff assists in encouraging young people to build routines of everyday life.

It is perhaps to be expected that the physical site of the school was frequently mentioned in discussions of the positive aspects of the community. It is after all, where the young people involved in this project spend a majority of their time when they are not at home. It is important to recognise however that attendance and matriculation rates for the young people of Cazucá are often low and these experiences and sentiments about school and education would not be common to all young people in the community. Due to experiences of high poverty, displacement, and limited space in schools, as well as the insecurity of the distance sometimes needed to travel to arrive at school, many young people do not attend.[4]

While the young people involved in this project spoke highly of the school, it is true that educational institutions are not always seen as positive, facilitatory sites, but can be the location of fractious relationships, combative encounters with authority, and diffuse encounters with the powers of the state. Yet for many of the young people I spoke with, school was a site that offered potential, a space where young people could pursue individual goals and work collaboratively with others. While educational sites may be seen as part of a formal delivery and maintenance of institutions emphasised (crucially and validly) by traditional peacebuilding practices, it is interesting that the school also occupies an 'everyday' role as a space of collective resilience for young people. Notions of everyday-peace are located fundamentally in the sustaining of the routines and practices of the everyday; for young people, school is foundational to everyday life. It can, at least for some students, function as a 'site of opportunity' where young people can develop relationships with peers and associated adults, and which provides a space of lessened violence (see Berents 2014). Psychological research on conflict-affected young people highlights similar conclusions. Betancourt and Khan (2008, 323) note that schools provide a sense of predictability, but also can foster 'enriched social networks ... between children, staff and other adults in the community'. Colombia Villamizar and Zamora (2005) and Burgess (2008, 273–284) make similar observations about the role of the school as a focal point of support and resilience.

Teachers are aware of this role of the school, and their part in it. For Ana Martinez, a teacher at the school, there is a clear link between the provision of education and the promotion of resilience in young people. Education, for Ana Martinez, was important not only for academic knowledge but also for the ability of young people to improve their quality of life in the present and into the future:

> At least during their time at school it helps create reflections for their life, for the construction of their world, and provides better opportunities in how to be human. To say, 'I can study more, I am a clever person, I can give more, each day I can learn something new, if I wanted I could leave this space and create a new space, I can improve my quality of life, not have ten kids like my mother, but only one that I can educate'. It is these things that are at the centre of what we do in the school. But in a way that is real, that stays inside you. Not only to be written on a piece of paper, but that is lived and that they take within their chest and say, 'Hey, I am going to take the middle road, because that road is sensible, and I won't be a parent at fifteen, and I won't have to go looking for food day to day for my child, but I am going to wait and give myself space to educate myself a little more, to have better stability, before starting a family'. And so this is what we [as teachers] work on, that they internalise all those things and improve their quality of life.

Here it is evident that while Ana Martinez sees herself in a pastoral role to a large degree, she recognises the internal competencies of young people to make informed and positive choices. Resilience is an embodied practice, emerging through their bodies, not bestowed by institutions. This ability is strengthened by the physical presence of the school also, which is a protected site, as Ana Martinez notes:

> The school is a space of refuge. Where there is less violence. This is because of the control of the teachers, because of discipline and because

138 *Resilience and Resistance*

the children feel it is a space that is better supported and safer. I am sure you have seen outside these walls there is lots of insecurity. ... But a child within this space feels protected to a certain degree. Because they know that no one is going to hurt them, or hit their face, and if they get into conflict with a peer there is always mediation.

The sense of the school as somewhere protected, where violence is lessened is evident in this exchange between fifteen-year-old Rosa and fourteen-year-old Camila Andrea:

ROSA: I do like school. At times I didn't like it because before I was at another school where there were lots more fights than here ... there isn't violence here like in the other place. ... I also like it because my classmates are very nice, and teachers are helpful, and people don't pull out knives at school.
CAMILA ANDREA: I like school because you can learn lots of things, and also I've gotten to know friends. There isn't so much violence as with people outside school.

Rosa's understanding of her environment is in comparison to a previous community she lived in where, as she mentioned several times during the discussion, there was more violence in general. The space of the school here is linked to the behaviour of the teachers, of other students, as well as the relationships that are built in the space made less violent and as a space whether they can be more supported.

The school is also a site where young people can individually achieve their potential. As well as generally positive comments from most young people when asked what they thought of school, Alejandro explicitly noted the spatial nature of the school as important to assist in achieving aims:

Well, yes, education is good because if you want to learn you learn and those who don't, well ... [trails off]. But for me, education is good, and I want to keep studying, and the school provides a space to follow that goal.

Alejandro recognises that it is an individual choice to want to pursue education, and recent events before this discussion bring extra attention to that observation. A friend of Alejandro's had recently got his girlfriend pregnant and had – according to schoolyard rumours – turned to 'bad events' to help support her as well as very infrequently attending school. This change in his friend's situation reinforced Alejandro's commitment to seeing through his high school degree (*bachilerato*) and graduating.

Fifteen-year-old Paola echoed the individual commitment required to make use of the positive potential of the school environment when she commented that 'education at this school is good, [but] it depends on us if we do our part and want to learn or not ...'. Susana also noted the role of the teachers in supporting young people. There is a requirement for actions to be acknowledged to have an affect, the actions of young people in this space are recognised and validated, and this creates a positive environment:

HB: And why do you like school?
SUSANA: Because you are treated well. There are many good teachers, well not all, but most, and for example I have an attachment to almost all the teachers because they treat you well and are really lovely with us. They never raise their voice at me and treat you well and I understand the classes. And well, many places [in my life] you don't have this. So that is why I like school.

Even for eleven-year-old Johan David, this sentiment is evident:

HB: Do you like going to school?
JOHAN DAVID: Yes! Because they teach well and all my friends are here and it is a good place to be for a child.

As well as teachers, strong friendship groups can be seen as a strength of the space of school also. There is also a tension with 'other places' where the positive treatment and support does not exist. The space of the school can be conceptualised as a space-of-resistance amongst everyday violence.

This vision of the school as a site of refuge was challenged in late 2011, ten months after I had left. Someone entered the premise of *Colegio Minutos de Dios* and killed one of the cleaning staff with two gunshots at the entrance as she opened the locked gate in preparation for the students to leave from morning classes. I heard the news from teacher Ana Martinez who noted that the death was not reported by any media. More importantly to her was that the children had not been in the classroom nearby at the time and so thankfully had not witnessed the violence. Ana Martinez described her response to the event with the following: '[T]he young people here are strong, but the violence seeps into every part of their lives, how can we help as teachers when even this secure space is violated?' (personal communication, September 11 2011). The security and sense of refuge of such places is, as evidenced, highly contingent, and potentially transgressed. I had been absent from the community for almost a year when this event occurred. Resultantly, I do not wish to appropriate the trauma or distress that the killing undoubtedly caused in order to provide a simplistic 'illustrative' anecdote of the violence facing these young people. Nevertheless, when I heard the news, I was profoundly shocked for several days, thinking of the children I knew at that school and the support staff with whom I often ate lunch while there. I realised part of the depth of my shock was due to the fact I had begun to conceptualise the space of the school as an inviolable space. Realising this made me aware how I had simplified the daily environment in my own mind, despite my awareness of the complexities of the situation. Thus, I include this story here to problematise

140 *Resilience and Resistance*

the notion of absolute refuge, and to contextualise the sense in which any space can ameliorate but not negate the multiple violences that characterise the social fabric of the community.

Community Organisations

In addition to the school, which underlies the daily routines of young people, and constitutes a significant location where young people can meaningfully engage, young people participate in a variety of other formal and informal spheres of connectivity. The *fundación* had concluded its work in the community when I returned in 2016, however, during the initial, substantial fieldwork in 2010 *Fundación Pies Descalzos* played a large role in many young people's lives, partly due to its support and connection to the school. In addition to helping provide funding for hot lunch meals at the school as part of their nutrition programs, young people were also welcome to drop past and spend time in the *casita* (little house) where there was a small library, several computers, and various other activities (as well as a small office for the *fundación*'s workers). Additionally, the *fundación* ran homework workshops, supported various parents to run after-school homework centres in their houses, provided community forums to assist parents and guardians with issues that arise in their relationships with young people, and assisted in the provision of supplies to grow community gardens of vegetables within the community. While many of these activities were aimed at parents and guardians, many others required direct relationships with young people who take ownership over the projects that the *fundación* run.

Alba Lucy Guerrero's work in Cazucá with the program Shooting Cameras for Peace (SCP) also located in Cazucá, a photography-based educational program that builds spaces of support for marginalised children, demonstrates the value ascribed to such programs by the young people themselves. Guerrero notes that 'children had created alternative visions of themselves where they felt empowered through their participation within SCP' (2008, 171), and further argues that the space of SCP allowed children who were marginalised a chance to find a voice and functions to mediate a break down in isolation (2008, 181). In Cazucá, youth-driven projects, including hip-hop collectives and independent photography projects, provide space for a 'symbolic voice that identifies the problems facing young people' (Duque 2009, 48) and foster support and relationships to build community and a sense of collective identity.

The *fundación* was often mentioned in discussions as one of the things that are 'good' about the community. Fifteen-year-old Paola notes the reason why the *fundación* is considered 'good':

> Well, what the foundation does is good. Also, the activities of the foundation and that, it is good for us, for us young people, if we want to grow and move ahead. It is very good …

Resilience and Resistance 141

Ana Milena, the field-coordinator in Cazucá for the *fundación*, sees their role as supportive of the important role of education. She noted that the education in Colombia is generally of 'very bad quality' and while the teachers work incredibly hard to improve that in Cazucá, the foundation can support those efforts through nutritional programs, the provision of access to technology, and psychological support through other activities that 'show young people that they matter and can make a difference'. *Fundación Pies Descalzos* was not the only organisation working in the community, or even the only one working with a focus on young people. Among a range of others, *Tiempo de Juego* (Time to Play) fosters positive relationships between young people through soccer and associated activities, while *Fundación Batuta* provides group music classes as well as individual instrument practice to disadvantaged communities around Colombia, and also worked within the two school sites. In addition, there are a range of other organisations working in the community focused on social justice, employment, and assistance to IDPs. All these organisations work to strengthen the community's resilience and support them in their efforts. These sites, including school, where violence is ameliorated are all governed by adults; however, as Villamizar and Zamora note, they provide an opportunity for more horizontal relationships between adults and children, and a more secure location for self development (2005, 71). Those focused on young people provide varying forms of refuge from the violences of the community and opportunities for young people to engage in different forms of community building, skill-sharing, and strengthening individual capacity as well as collaborative resilience.

Planning for the Future and Belief in Change

The ability of young people to articulate their desires for the future is often overlooked, but in seeking sites of resistance and forms of building resilience, these articulations are profoundly important both individually and in creating a collective vision of everyday-peace. Boyden and Mann (2000) and Burgess (2008) recognise that positive outlook and ability to articulate ideas for the future are underrecognised aspects of resilience. Individual aspirations, and the invocation of relationships with peers or adults, highlight how temporal notions – in this case, a belief in change – contribute to the way in which young people conceive of their everyday lives. The future is conceptualised as a site of potentiality and resilience by many young people, grounded in experiences of the present. An example is in fifteen-year-old Susana's description of the future. She describes the future as a time when things could be better for the community. This description is not passive; it includes actions she wants to take, and recognises the context of her life also:

> For me, the future is as we've been discussing already, that things change. Not so much for me, but for everyone; say, that one day the *barrio* will be fixed, the streets will be fixed, they will given houses to the very poor

142 *Resilience and Resistance*

people ... My future then is to study, finish my high school degree (*bachilerato*), have a job, further that career, help my mother forward, help my siblings because they've been left alone, or if one day my mother can't do it, well, I would have to because I'm the eldest. But yes, for me, my future is study now, work so that nothing can interrupt my dreams. Because for me, my dream is to help poor people to create many places so they'll not go hungry, so they can study, so they have many opportunities. This is my future.

While idealistic, this vision outlined by Susana is fundamentally grounded in the complex realities of violence and social exclusion which characterise her life. She identifies problems with the *barrio*, familial obligations exacerbated by poverty, and recognises generalised problems of poverty, hunger, and lack of opportunity that exist in the community around her. Her responses to these problems locate herself as a proactive agent for that change – but one who has thought about the steps that would be required to achieve it. There is a rational logic behind her emotive purpose, and these two things together connects a resilience that is practiced and supported in the present with an aspirational resistance, built on her ability to envision a future.

The challenges of Cazucá's environment form the context in which both individual and collective efforts are located. Acute consciousness of the way Cazucá is seen 'outside', coupled with the daily experiences of violence and conflict, make young people both highly motivated and defensive of their ability to achieve things in the future. In a conversation with sixteen-year-old Christian, fifteen-year-old Luz Milena and sixteen-year-old Daniela the tension and challenges are evident:

CHRISTIAN: ...[But] of course there are good things about Cazucá also, because here we also learn how to be very just people. Everything isn't violent. Here we learn how to be a person and that. Well, in Bogotá, the opinion of Cazucá is shit. But that is because they do not try and speak with us. But we do try to find other ways of being good people.

LUZ MILENA: Yes, there are also many people who want to get ahead and so they look for various paths that lead them here [interrupted]

DANIELA: Yeah, there are many people who have talent who want to succeed; and well, for me there are many people who truly have those talents here.

Similarly sixteen-year-old Felipe highlights the way violence can result in collective resilience building:

[after describing different forms of violence that 'never leave'] in part it is bad because it affects us and it does damage to us ... but it is in part good, I guess, because it has taught us to support each other, to pull yourself forward and don't give up ...

Resilience and Resistance   143

The self-described aspirations of these young people are not without context. Sixteen-year-old Juan Carlos repeatedly notes that there could, and probably would, be problems and challenges in achieving success in his life. However he notes that when he has 'difficult moments', he remembers there are paths he does not want to take, and so continues to find the 'good path, which is also the difficult path', and just 'fight and fight'.

Young people also detailed what they wanted to study or do later in life. Sixteen-year-old Christian wants to 'get a scholarship to study medicine', but notes that if that was not possible he would consider a career in the army. More than a few young people mentioned joining either the army or the police during our conversations. This initially seemed at odds with many of the stories of the dislike of government forces present in the community and the conflict more generally. However, Ana Milena from the *fundación* notes that the army often offers scholarships, or simply reliable income to young people and recruiters often approach students from schools in places like Cazucá. This is not to say all young people who expressed an interest in this career had this motivation, but it helps explain the higher-than-expected number of responses received to this effect. Ana Milena notes that many young people see it simply as an 'opportunity to work', where they can be guaranteed an income and people 'have to respect them then'. It brings attention to the tension that exists between strategies for everyday resistance and existence, and the pressures and power of structures that shape these young people's lives and potential opportunities.

There is a diversity of aspirational careers that young people described. Fifteen-year-old Luz Milena wants to graduate from school and perhaps become a nurse. In another conversation seventeen-year-old Juliana keeps her options open:

> I would like to study communication, and journalism, and would like to be perhaps be a news presenter or something like that. But I also like the idea of studying law, but it is very difficult.

Fifteen-year-old Paola has wanted to study medicine since she was very young, and eleven-year-old Monica wants to run a business. Twelve-year-old Sebastian loves airplanes and wants to be a pilot, while his friend, eleven-year-old Andrea, wants to be a singer (and demonstrated her talents during the interview). Such observations may seem trite when presented in this way; however, young people's articulation of such desires demonstrates an aspirational resilience. They respond to violence and the foreclosing of opportunities in their present with optimism about the future. The fact that many had not only vague ideas but also specific goals, for example Susana's plans for the future discussed above, demonstrates a conviction in moving forward and finding responses and paths beyond the difficulties of their present everyday lives. It also underscores the way in which young people's lives are not defined entirely by their social exclusion or the violence characteristic of their daily encounters. Desires and dreams are expressed in a way that recognises the

144   *Resilience and Resistance*

difficulty of the objective – both for structural reasons, and their inherent difficulty (such as pursuing law as a career) – but which further demonstrate their resistance to narratives that foreclose opportunities.

The emancipatory potential of such ambitions is important to recognise. The structural realities of life in Cazucá often preclude young people from pursuing professional careers. In research conducted on education programs in Comuna 4 (which includes Cazucá), Burgess discusses the aspirations of young people interviewed, which echo conversations I had. He notes that

> although the children noticed that young people in the community were unemployed, worked in the informal sector or worked in seasonal jobs or in stores, they all maintained their ideas of working as professionals in fields requiring, in most cases, a college education, except for those interested in joining the military.
>
> (2008, 273)

Such an observation is important, and the reality of the limited opportunities to pursue higher education or further qualification is significant. Nevertheless, in terms of recognising young people's articulations of their future – both to legitimate their experiences in the present, and support their resilience and coping mechanisms with aspirational desires – simply by being expressed their future plans have merit that affect their present organisation and under-standing of their lives.

The difficulties of Cazucá are seen as the context in which the successes are measured. The efforts to affect change, located in everyday practices and supported from physical sites that assist in the amelioration or abeyance of violence, allow the potential for young people's day-to-day routines to con-tribute to positive visions of the future, and to constructively locate them-selves within those imaginings. It is the challenges of environments that are violent, as well as attitudes that are dismissive of youth, that have the poten-tial to stifle these ambitions. The resilience that is fostered by spaces offered by sites such as the school and the *fundación*, strengthen the ability of young people's contributions to be recognised in building everyday notions of peace amidst multiple violences.

Conclusions

To recognise the individuals that continue to live amongst violences and who make meaning of their lives day to day in ways that resist or ameliorate those violences grounds an everyday-peace-amidst-violence as an embodied prac-tice. Such an understanding of everyday peace is fraught and difficult but holds potential for reconfiguring the way in which Cazucá and similarly marginalised places are discussed, how explanations for causes of violence are articulated and how young people are actively engaged in ongoing processes of building peace. Antonius Robben and Carolyn Nordstrom (1996, 6–7) draw attention to the fact that 'the lives of those who suffer under violence or are engaged in warfare are not defined exclusively in global political, economic, social, or military terms but also in the small, often creative acts of the everyday'. It is in the securing practices of everyday resilience and in ideas of resistance driven by exclusionary practices and expectations upon the state, that understandings of everyday peace gain resonance and applicability in contexts of ongoing violence.

Particular sites hold potential for resistant and transformative action, providing young people with more secure spaces that foster their individual potential and encourages creative engagement. The community itself, as well as sites such as the school and the *fundación*, provide spaces that mitigate the effects of pervasive violence and support resilience in young people. Such locations can function as spaces of opportunity. While they do not inherently bestow resilience or foster peacebuilding, their structure and affordances of engagement provide increased opportunities for agential young people to seek change and find support. The future, too, functions as a site in which young people invest hope and optimism to counter challenges and dangers in their present everyday lives. Such spaces exist *amidst* violence and while they are not inviolable or always ideal they hold the potential for more peaceable understandings and engagements with the everyday.

While narratives around young people often highlight their vulnerability in replicating existing 'cultures of violence', adults who work with and for young people are well aware of the ways in which young people contradict and subvert such narratives. Young people themselves argue compellingly for their inclusion and the validity of their observations. Young people articulate ways in which together they can strengthen community and build resilience by resisting the violence that surrounds them.

Understandings of resilience, rooted in collective understandings of what it means to endure, engage with constructions of peace that provide the space to ameliorate violence and enable opportunities. Resistance, not as a dichotomising practice against the liberal peace but as a response to the conditions of marginalisation and violence, acknowledges the expected role of the state while criticising its failings. Conceiving of resistance in this way, embedded in the narratives of young people who believe in the value of many of the promises of liberal peacebuilding, but who are aware of how they are excluded and disenfranchised by its discourses, build everyday resilience and strengthens relationships within peer groups and inter-generationally within the community.

It is disingenuous to suggest such practices of resistance are sufficient to cancel out the violences and insecurities of daily life. Rather, by identifying and validating the sites and relationships that strengthen resilience, young people in communities such as Cazucá can be legitimised as actors playing an active role in fostering peacebuilding at the everyday level. Peace, thus becomes bound to legitimacy through the site of the everyday where it enables individuals to participate and make claims to ways of living. Bringing these observations together argues for the importance of everyday forms of

146 *Resilience and Resistance*

resilience, everyday spaces of resistance, everyday collaborations for community building, and the sense that in spite of the challenges of structural marginality, social exclusion, and multiple violences, young people are capable of articulately and clearly demonstrating their understandings of how more inclusive and emancipatory notions of peace can be built in the everyday.

Notes

1 This clarification and discussion is not meant to invalidate the large body of health-sciences and psychosocial work concerning resilience (Werner 1996 is foundational here), which explores notions of 'risk' and 'resilience' as they affect individual's responses to trauma, or to discount its contribution in particular ways. However, for many of the reasons outlined by Boyden and Mann (2000), as discussed, such conceptualisations are limited.
2 The use of the term 'tactical responses' here is a deliberate invocation of de Certeau and his concept of strategic versus tactical agency (1984, 34–40). While those who hold power can wield it strategically, planning into the future and maximising potential benefits, those who are marginalised or lack authority and power respond tactically, 'taking advantage of 'opportunities'', calculating actions that can be taken in the absence of control (1984, 37).
3 Violent or disruptive acts by young people can, and should, still be understood as expressions of agency. While they may not be sanctioned by structures, institutions, or collective norms, there are often reasons why young people engage in violence, participate in gangs, or in other forms resist and respond to structures and norms. It can be understood as problematic, or not-preferred, action, but cannot be dismissed if we are to meaningful recognise and engage with young people's participation.
4 As this research was conducted through a school, it is not surprising the school featured in many conversations. In this section I discuss the benefits young people ascribe to the site of the school and the experience of attending. However, other authors have conducted research on those unable to attend school. Garzón (2005, 58) notes lack of opportunity to attend school as well as complete technical or higher education is a major concern for many families and young people who see their opportunities for a better future denied. See also Burgess (2008) and Guerrero (2008), who both conducted research with young people in Cazucá (and Comuna 4 more generally) who are not in formal education programs. Zea (2010, 11–12) writes about the particular difficulties that face displaced families in securing education opportunities for their children, and the social stigma that is involved in the attendance of displaced young people in urban schools.

References

Apfel, Roberta, and Bennett Simon. 1996. "Psychosocial Interventions for Children of War: The Value of a Model of Resiliency." *Medicine and Global Survival* 3. www.ippnw.org/pdf/mgs/3-apfel-simon.pdf

Bentancourt, Theresa Stichick, and Kashif Tanveer Khan. 2008. "The Mental Health of Children Affected by Armed Conflict: Protective Processes and Pathways to Resilience." *International Review of Psychiatry* 20(3):317–328.

Berents, Helen. 2014. "'It's About Finding a Way': Children, Sites of Opportunity, and Building Everyday Peace in Colombia." *International Journal of Children's Rights* 22(2):362–384.

Resilience and Resistance   147

Berents, Helen, and Charlotte ten Have. 2017. "Navigating Violence: Fear and Everyday Life in Colombia and Mexico." *International Journal for Crime, Justice and Social Democracy* 6(1):103–117.

Boyden, Jo, and Gillian Mann. 2000. "Children's Risk, Resilience and Coping in Extreme Situations." In *Handbook for Working with Children and Youth: Pathways to Resilience Across Cultures and Contexts*, edited by M. Ungar. Thousand Oaks, CA: SAGE.

Burgess, Ryan. 2008. "Formal and Nonformal Education: Impacting the Psychosocial Well-being of Displaced, Violence-Affected Children in Colombia." Doctor of Education, Teachers College, Columbia University, New York.

de Certeau, Michel. 1984. *The Practice of Everyday Life*. Berkeley, CA: California University Press.

Duque, Luisa Fernanda. 2009. *Educacion y conflicto: Altos de Cazucá*. Bogotá, Colombia: Fundacion para la Educacion y el Desarrollo (FEDES).

Garzón, Clara Stella. 2005. *Diagnóstico de género de la población de Soacha, con énfasis en las mujeres desplazadas*. Bogotá, Colombia: UNIFEM–Colombia.

Guerrero, Alba Lucy. 2008. "Internally Displaced Children Constructing Identities Within and Against Cultural Worlds: The Case of 'Shooting Cameras for Peace' in Colombia." Doctor of Philosophy, Education, University of California, Santa Barbara.

Jackson, Michael. 2002. *The Politics of Storytelling: Violence, Transgression and Intersubjectivity*. Copenhagen, Denmark: Museum Tusculanum Press, University of Copenhagen.

Luthar, Suniya S. 1993. "Annotation: Methodological and Conceptual Issues in Research on Childhood Resilience." *Journal of Child Psychology and Psychiatry* 34 (4):441–453.

Luthar, Suniya S. 2005. "Resilience in Development: A Synthesis of Research Across Five Decades." In *Developmental Psychopathology: Risk, Disorder, and Adaptation (Vol. 3, 2nd ed.)*, edited by D Cicchetti and D. J Cohen. New York: Wiley.

Masten, Ann S., Karin M. Best, and Norman Garmezy. 1990. "Resilience and Development: Contributions to the Study of Children Who Overcome Adversity." *Development and Psychopathology* 2: 425–444.

Nguyen-Gillham, Viet, Rita Giacaman, Ghada Naser, and Will Boyce. 2008. "Normalising the Abnormal: Palestinian Youth and the Contradictions of Resilience in Protected Conflict." *Health and Social Care in the Community* 16(3):291–298.

Pat-Horenczyk, Ruth, Miriam Schiff, and Osnat Doppelt. 2006. "Maintaining Routine Despite Ongoing Exposure to Terrorism: A Healthy Strategy for Adolescents?" *Journal of Adolescent Health* 39: 199–205.

Picon, Yuri Romero, Liliana Arciniegas, and Javier Jimenez Becerra. 2006. "Desplazamiento y Reconstruccion de Tejido Social en el Barrio Altos de la Florida." *Revista Tendencia & Retos* 11: 11–23.

Restrepo, Luis Alberto. 2004. "Violence and Fear in Colombia: Fragmentation of Space, Contraction of Time and Forms of Evasion." In *Armed Actors: Organised Violence and State Failure in Latin America*, edited by Kees Koonings and Dirk Kruijt. London: Zed Books.

Richmond, Oliver. 2010. "Resistance and the Post-Liberal Peace." *Millennium: Journal of International Studies* 38(3):665–692.

Robben, Antonius C. G. M., and Carolyn Nordstrom. 1996. "The Anthropology and Ethnography of Violence and Sociopolitical Conflict." In *Fieldwork Under Fire:*

148 *Resilience and Resistance*

Contemporary Studies of Violence and Culture, edited by Carolyn Nordstrom and Antonius C. G. M. Robben. Berkeley, CA: University of California Press.

Summerfield, Derek. 2002. "Effects of War: Moral Knowledge, Revenge, Reconciliation, and Medicalised Concepts of 'Recovery.'" *British Medical Journal* 325: 1105–1106.

Ungar, Michael. 2004. "A Constructionist Discourse on Resilience: Multiple Contexts, Multiple Realities Among At-Risk Children and Youth." *Youth and Society* 35 (3):341–365.

Ungar, Michael. 2008. "Resilience Across Cultures." *British Journal of Social Work* 38 (2):218–235.

Villamizar Rojas, Rosa, and Sara Zamora Vasquez. 2005. "Vivir juvenil en medios de conflictos urbanos: Una aproximacion en la zona colindante entre Bogotá y Soacha." In *Jovenes, Conflictos Urbanos y Alternativas de Inclusion*, edited by Viviana Sabogal Ruiz. Bogotá, Colombia: Plataforma Conflicto Urbano y Jovenes, CIVIS Suecia & ASDI.

Wessells, Michael. 2006. "A Living Wage: The Importance of Livelihood in Reintegrating Former Child Soldiers." In *A World Turned Upside Down: Social Ecological Approaches to Children in War Zones*, edited by Neil Boothby, Alison Strang and Michael Wessells. Bloomfield, CT: Kumarian Press.

Werner, E. E. 1996. "Vulnerable but Invincible: High-Risk Children From Birth to Adulthood." *European Journal of Child and Adolescent Psychiatry* 5(1):47–51.

Zea, Juan Esteban. 2010. "Internal Displacement in Colombia: Violence, Resettlement, and Resistance." Master of Arts, Anthropology, Portland State University, Portland, OR.

6 Notions of Everyday Peace

> Peace begins in the front-line actions of rebuilding the possibility of self (which violence has sought to undermine) and society (which massacres and destruction have sought to undermine). Without the trade routes, schools, clinics, and family relocation programs, without the art and literature and media that set up belief systems of resolution over conflict, without a sense of future, peace cannot emerge. No peace accords brokered at the elite levels will work if these bases are not there to build upon.
>
> - Carolyn Nordstrom, *Shadows of War*, 2004, 184

My time with the community was coming to an end. Having spent several months sitting in classes, hanging out in the playground, walking through the community, meeting family and friends, my conversations with many of the young people were turning towards the future. I was sitting in the school's small cafeteria during one lunch break with fifteen-year-old Paola, and Juliana and Alejandro, both seventeen-years-old, who I was going to finally record an interview with after we'd eaten. As we finished eating, we talked about small things such as a popular song that everyone was crazy about, their plans for the weekend, and an upcoming test in class. Amongst this conversation, fifteen-year-old Paola commented, 'You're not like other adults, Helen'. I paused and asked her what she meant. 'Other adults wouldn't sit down and ask us our opinions, they don't think we're worth anything until we have grown up'. Her friends nod along with her. This opinion of the adults in their lives had come up in many of my conversations, often articulated with a mixture of resignation and frustration. Paola's friend Alejandro interrupted to point out that there are 'some good adults', and it was these kinds of adults that he hoped he would become.

As we finished eating and stood up to put our plates on the trays with the dirty crockery and cups, a teacher walked past and spoke to Juliana. 'How's your mother, I heard she wasn't well? Are you doing ok?'. Juliana spoke briefly to the teacher as we collected our things. As we walked out of the door Alejandro said of the teacher, 'She's one of the good ones, she cares about us as people now'. When adults don't listen to these young people it is disheartening, but when they do, it can validate their belief in themselves.

150 *Notions of Everyday Peace*

We got settled in an empty classroom and record an interview. Part way through, in a conversation about the future of the community and Colombia, I asked, 'And do you think you can affect the future?' The three responded:

PAOLA: … it depends on the path we choose …
JULIANA: Yes.
PAOLA: If we pick a bad path, well it'll be a bad future. Good path, well, it will go well.
ALEJANDRO: Yes. This.
PAOLA: For me, I think yes, I want to choose a good future, and I think more than one of us has painted little butterflies (*maripositas*) in our dreams [all laugh]. Well, it is better to have these lovely dreams.
ALEJANDRO: But dreaming doesn't count for anything.
PAOLA: Uh-huh. Dreams don't count for anything, yes, until you make them happen. We people are fighters, entrepreneurs, and that. Each of us makes those decisions when we continue to study, continue to grow.

For these three young people, their sense of self and their ability to imagine a different future are profoundly connected to their ideas for a peaceable future. While adults often ignore them, when particular adults do listen to their ideas it reinforces a sense of their capacity to make change. Peace for many of the young people I spoke with is not a passive act, but deeply connected to their lived experience, and consciously created in response to insecurities and violence. It is taking the 'little butterflies' and acting to make them eventuate within their daily life that underpins a sense of peace.

Forwarding a concept of embodied-everyday-peace-amidst-violence requires not only exploring the manifestations and negotiations of multiple violences as described in previous chapters but must also take into account how young people understand notions of peace both abstractly and as a functional concept in their everyday lives. With the previous chapter having explored notions of resilience and resistance and the spaces in which young people foster these skills, this final chapter turns to consideration of the interrelation between young people and peace and the articulations by young people themselves of how their conceive of peace. In doing this, I introduce the final piece for an outline an everyday peace, conceived of amongst conflict rather than discretely post-conflict; arguing for a reconceptualisation of the concept as a kind of everyday-peace-amidst-violence. This exploration argues that this kind of reconceptualisation may be more useful in contexts of protracted conflict and insecure nascent efforts at formal peacebuilding, such as Colombia. An 'everyday' cannot be conceived of as static, but rather as an ongoing, constantly mutable and negotiated embodied process. There are implications in the discussion of an everyday peace of improvement or an imagined endpoint of peace – which is undeniably an important viewpoint to retain – and yet the occupants of Cazucá are living within a continuing, complex, and invasive violence, and so in this everyday life is not lived in one state or the

Notions of Everyday Peace 151

other but rather a 'peace-amidst-violence'. To discuss an everyday peace, but to also recognise its existence within a system of violence, is to recognise and acknowledge the embodied beings in that environment who move through violent terrain, negotiate the possibility of violence, and live amidst violence *every* day.

Thus, this chapter explores how young people conceive their role in the community and their articulations of notions of peace. Young people's everyday lives are profoundly shaped by social exclusion and violence, and their voices are often marginalised in an already marginal space. Accordingly, when the margins are made a central concern a more meaningful, complex everyday peace is evident. In the initial section this chapter explores how young people themselves view their role and their perception of adults' understanding of them. Turning the lens specifically on both adults and young people and asking how these relationships are characterised and understood highlights the liminal and fraught space young people occupy. It also outlines the ways and spaces in which their contribution for collective resilience and peacebuilding is acknowledged. The second endeavour of this chapter is to examine what peace means to young people in Cazucá, and draws out the variable understandings of peace that emerge from the difficult environments they inhabit. These include recognition that the idea of peace can be a difficult one to articulate and conceive, that notions of peace are formed in resistance to violence, and explorations of peace as dialogic. Engaging directly with young people's understandings of their liminality and their complex engagements with ideas of peace, locates the exploration of an everyday-peace-amidst-violence at the site of young people's lived experience.

While primarily focused on interviews conducted in 2010, this chapter picks up in places conversations had with participants in 2016, which demonstrate the ongoing contingent and fraught nature of everyday peace facing these individuals. Even with the signing of a peace accord in 2016, the lived reality of life for the occupants of Cazucá has not significantly changed. The complexities and challenges of protracted conflict and marginalisation mean that the experiences of insecurity and violence continue. Everyday peace, truly within the daily lives of Colombians, may be closer with the signing of a peace agreement with the FARC, but continues to be a tenuous proposition in the minds and lives of many participants. Young people's articulations of peace are frequently grounded in the realities of their everyday lives. They centre themselves as dialogical and active agents in creating and building such ideas within their lives and communities.

Everyday-peace, constituted of routines and day-to-day practices, strengthens relationships and collaborative potential; however, its ability to affect change in communities cannot occur without individuals choosing to engage in it. Without recognition of the role of young people's own everyday efforts to find and sustain peace, in the face of the challenges of multiple violences, a notion of embodied-everyday-peace-amidst-violence in communities such as Cazucá, is incomplete.

152 *Notions of Everyday Peace*

Peace in an Insecure Everyday

This book argues that peace is not only dependent on a notion of the everyday in which the rhythms of relationships and practices of day-to-day life are perpetuated but also in which complex responses to institutional marginalisation that build individuals' capacities without reference to the disinterested state are strengthened. This concept of everyday peace, in which these activities are carried out despite ongoing violence and social exclusion, is a more complex notion; one I have termed an *embodied-everyday-peace-amidst-violence*. In previous chapters, it has allowed me to explore the violent and insecure consequences of social exclusion, and acknowledge those who are within the margins find ways of fostering resilience amidst violence. Here, I extend it further to conceptualise the everyday nature of peace that can be found in such environments drawing out the final element of the concept as a whole.

Violence is not an abstract concept but rather, as has been explored in the previous chapters, the result of structural forces and individual choices. There is a wide range of research interested in the connection between endemic socioeconomic marginalisation and the choices of young people to engage in behaviour that is seen as violent or criminal.[1] In these discussions there is an explicit connection made between structural forces that restrict the choices available, and the individual choices of young people faced with these structurally limited horizons. However, frequently if inadvertently, peace and the peaceable potential of young people are not seen in the same way. Peacefulness is often seen simply as the natural potential of young people, and rhetoric can become bounded in the dominant discourse of childhood, which sees young people as sites of an embodied futurity and investment, the desirable outcome of their youth. Such discourses prevent meaningful exploration of the praxis of young people within their present everyday lives.

Peace can, more usefully, be conceived as something actively worked towards, not just an absence of violence, or in response to violence. A notion of peace that, rather than seeing peace simply as an absence of and reaction to the causes of violence, sees peace as having causes also has been developed by Stuart Kent and Jon Barnett (2012, 3). This conceptualisation explores the structures that allow collaborative efforts towards peace, and the way that (young) people participate in them (Kent and Barnett 2012). Such a framing is premised on recognising the strength of Johan Galtung's work (including 1969, 1990, 1996) but also allows the way individuals contribute to the structures that build positive forms of peace to be more deeply interrogated. In a complex, conflict-affected environment, attention to the forms and types of participation is key in conceptualising the way individuals respond to institutional marginalisation and find forms of resistance and strength in everyday practices. In Kent and Barnett's research, this conceptualisation allows them to understand how youth from the so-called 'crisis generation' in Bougainville, Papua New Guinea, are able to engage with the structures responsible for education, employment, and livelihood practices in manners that contribute to the community, rather than resorting to acts or threats of violence and without the need for 'structures of disincentives', such as imprisonment or other threats of violence (2012, 3). This way of envisioning peace allows space to critically examine the physical structures as well as structurally embedded assumptions about young people's competencies and willingness to engage.

Individuals affected by conflict continue to explore ways of building peace despite ongoing violences. Often such efforts are 'small', and fundamentally located at an intimate level (see Nordstrom 2004; Boege 2011; Koopman 2011). At the site of the everyday, communication and presence can form the basis of what Elise Boulding (2000) calls 'cultures of peace'. Peace, for Boulding, is bound up in everyday practices of relating, problem solving, working, and collective 'creative life'. 'Peaceableness' is inherent in these everyday practices. Similarly, John Paul Lederach relies on notions of 'ordinary language' and 'everyday understandings' to affect the nature of conflict (1995, 27). There is a closeness of social distance where peace is created between people, through conversation (Lederach 2005, 56–57). His notion of 'elicitive' peace (1997), where local knowledge and expertise is prioritised in notions of peace, is similarly embodied, relational, and requires the richness and plurality offered by the everyday. Bringing such notions together with Sylvester's notion of empathetic cooperation (1994) – to confront the challenges of social exclusion and hierarchical and distant structural power relations – recognises the ways in which the everyday holds possibilities for ordinary lives to speak back against seemingly disinterested forces.

A recognition of the challenges imposed by the environment and daily experiences of violence coupled with the perpetuating of violent models of problem solving by government, draws out the contingent nature of spaces in which engagement can run counter to dominant beliefs of young people's (in)competencies and passivity. This environment cannot be dichotomised as either violent or 'safe', or young people as either rejecting or naively embracing the possibility of peace. Rather it recognises that the social fabric within which complex relationships are built is fraught and often frayed. Furthermore, to focus on the way adults recognise the challenges present for young people allows recognition by adults of the potential for young people and the opportunity to build stronger, more inclusive, relationships.

The Role of Young People

Discussions with young people explored so far demonstrate that young people are more than capable of discussing, envisioning, and planning for the future in positive and constructive ways. However, the persistence of the dominant discourse reinforces the passivity and vulnerability of children and young people, and closes off possibilities to successfully engage with these opinions and plans. The relationship between young people and the adults who surround them are central to the inclusion of young people. Recognising

154 *Notions of Everyday Peace*

and accounting for the way in which adults perceive young people, as well as the ways in which young people themselves articulate their roles and positionalities, points to ways in which resiliencies and resistances are perceived and supported. Recalling the importance of recognising young people as active agents the opinions of both adults and young people about each other highlights both challenges and potential opportunities for recognising young people as positive contributors to notions of everyday peace. Here, I explore ideas young people have about their role and a sense of collective responsibility that was evident in their responses, as well as discuss the complex context of Colombia's violence in which these relationships are shaped.

It is in fostering more horizontal and respectful engagements between adults and young people that adults recognise young people's competencies. However, structural challenges, and endemic violence frustrate these efforts, and enduring stereotypes of young people's (in)abilities are pervasive obstacles in more fully accounting for young people's engagement. Alan Feldman (1991, 13) argues that those affected by violence and marginalisation already figure as objects in political discourse – in this case, young people are talked *about* – and thus their speaking should be recognised as legitimate. In such an argument young people's claims for voice and participation can be seen as claiming a space to be heard. There are also links back to Jackson's observation that such actions must have repercussions (2002), and the need find a way of strengthening the web of relationships (following Arendt) such that young people are taken into account.

Young people are acutely aware of the marginality of their position, and expressed desires to be listened to by adults – both parents and other adults such as teachers – and argued that they had unique perspectives on issues affecting the community that should be considered. The broader environment presents obstacles to everyday relationships with their parents. Many young people told me that their parents did not have very much time for them because they were always working and very tired. Seventeen-year-old Laura notes that because 'their jobs take so many hours' they get home and 'arrive tired and say 'Hi, good?' 'Good' ... what does that do? That doesn't do anything'. Twelve-year-old Sebastian says his parents care about him a lot but often it is the lady who lives nearby who collects him from school and looks after him. As discussed in Chapter Four, fractious or fragmented family relationships create insecurity for young people. Often this is not intentional; parents are simply too busy with subsistence endeavours to spend much time with their children even if they care for them a great deal.

The other aspect of the adult–child relationship is more deliberative, and young people see many adults as dismissive of the capabilities and efforts of young people in everyday routines and in contributing to broader community projects. There is a frustration evident in these narratives, as several young people criticise adults in their life for preventing them from helping. For some young people, the question of young people's role is grounded in economic

Notions of Everyday Peace   155

uncertainty. Fifteen-year-old Susana argues that adults often don't think to ask young people about their capabilities:

> Well for me I think that adults think we don't have the ability to fix things, or be organised and many say 'How are you going to help fix this problem? You aren't old enough.' And many times we have the same mentality as adults, we have a good ability to think and plan. And look, if I look for work when I am underage it is because I want to get ahead, it is because we don't want to live our life struggling ... But adults often do not ask us about our abilities. ... For example, I want to work a little now because I want to help my mother ...

Sixteen-year-old Felipe echoes Susana's comments in a different conversation, also highlighting the role reversal where young people are engaged and adults are in fact 'useless':

> Well, for me, some adults think that a youth because they are small they can't do many things, but they are almost old enough, they are sixteen, seventeen and they can't look for work because adults say wait, wait. ... What should we do? Many adults aren't good for anything, they are useless, and many times it is these adults who say that young people aren't good for anything.

Later in our conversation Felipe added the following thought:

> I think that adults think that young people are lacking experience, that we can't do things. ... But we have to learn, because if we don't then what will happen? So they should take time to speak to us.

Both Susana and Felipe see their potential in helping provide for their families, but opinions about young people's capabilities frustrate those goals. Felipe argues for the need for intergenerational knowledge transfer and engagement. The young people I spoke with were unanimous in their responses that adults should pay more attention to young people.

In addition to the perceived need to foster stronger familial relations, and to respect their competencies, young people identified their unique perspective on problems, and the fact that they have a stake in the outcomes into the future as key reasons for engagement. In these discussions the adults were generally not immediate family or community members, but rather politicians or others in positions of power and privilege:

HB: What do you have to contribute to these conversations with adults, if they listened?

PAOLA (15): Well, about the insecurity and everything, to try and fix this a little, because this area [Cazucá] is of very little concern to the politicians.

156   *Notions of Everyday Peace*

It is like a tiny black dot on a sheet of paper ... and so, to listen about how they can help the people who need it, because really now we see politicians that are worthless.

ALEJANDRO (15): Yes.

JULIANA (17): Yes, things are getting worse, well. [It would be better] that they pay attention to us, that older adults pay attention to the young people.

PAOLA: We need attention, because we are the future civilisation of Colombia. We have much to add.

These young people were acutely aware that there was already limited attention on the community as a whole by those in power, and that they as young people they were even more marginal. Towards the end of that same interview I asked if they had anything else to add. After pausing for a moment, they reiterated their earlier comments about being included and recognised:

PAOLA: That they [adults] take us into account

JULIANA: Yes, that they pay attention to us, the young people. Ehh, because our opinion about what this country needs is important.

PAOLA: Yes, that our words count, and that we are listened to. That it is very important to listen to us, and that, if they listened perhaps we could find a way to work together, but they must listen!

While adults I spoke with frequently highlighted the difficulties and challenges impeding young people, young people seem to recognise these issues as enduring, but note the need for active participation and recognition by adults of their views and experiences.

Some of the adults who work with these young people are aware of the broader narratives and stereotypes that pervade general discussions. One teacher noted that while generally 'young people are seen as people who cannot make decisions and are indefensible; in Cazucá they are often seen as delinquents and drug addicts' (Profe Claudia, written survey response). Another teacher at *Garcia Marquez* responded by linking the image of children in Colombia to the violence and the narco-trafficking, saying they are 'stigmatised' and this is exacerbated in Cazucá because of their 'social status and geographic location' (Profe Diego, written survey response). Visible in these accounts are many elements previously discussed, including the consequences of social exclusion, geographical stigma, and recognition of the way that notions of violent spaces fold in on those who occupy them.

Similarly, problematic politics and broad generalisations at elite levels hamper the potential for engagement with young people, according to their teachers: 'In Colombia, there are organisations and politicians which support childhood, but many times, it is us adults who stigmatise children and do not believe in them' (Profe Angelica, written survey response). This stigmatisation and marginalisation of young people is, according to some teachers,

Notions of Everyday Peace 157

connected to the potential for change in the future. Such a view is exemplified by teacher Gloria:

> Colombia is a country rich in natural resources but there is much crime and the people ... live with corruption and live without a sense of the future ... Young people must become leaders, as they have the talent to demonstrate to the world, but there does not exist, at this moment, a space for them and no one cares for their opinions.

The onus is on the government and adults in positions that allow them to affect change, according to the *fundación*'s Ana Milena; but more than this, these organisations and adults must allow space for young people's inclusion and voice also. She spoke about the obligation of the government at various levels to ensure the rights and provisions for young people. For Ana Milena, 'the greatest responsibility of the state [is to] guarantee opportunities of education and of employment also; because if not, history will repeat itself'.

Peace Amidst Cultures of Violence: Capacity and Challenges

The conflict in Colombia has created what Natalia from Children's rights NGO *Fundación Restrepo Barco* calls a 'culture of violence', in which the very acts and commitments by the government reinforce violent solutions to problems. In such a context, the notion of peace is fraught and difficult. Luis Alberto Restrepo (no connection to the above NGO) argues that fear of violence not only fragments space but also 'undermine[s] hope and ... foreshorten[s] the horizons of individual and collective futures' (2004, 180). Because of the enduring violence, the past ceases to be a useful guide for working towards the future, as 'existence therefore, tends to contract into an anxious present'; repetitive violence experienced both first-hand and via continual media coverage constitutes an 'obsessive reiteration of tragedy', which infects the collective national memory and dims future prospects (Restrepo 2004, 180). When speaking about the future in collective terms, there is a requirement for an accumulated social capital, a reciprocal confidence between citizens and the state, and between citizens themselves. However, when the social fabric is stretched or torn, collective perception of the future can become victim to vicious swings of confidence and depression, often resulting in violences.

The lure of violent responses to experiences of violence is a real challenge for young people (and in fact, all people) in situations like Cazucá. The *fundación*'s Ana Milena argues that peace can't be 'outside', but rather 'it has to be within you'. For Ana Milena, the cyclical nature of violence is one of the most difficult obstacles to creating peace:

> For some time ... in Colombia many young men, many young women become part of armed groups. Because they don't have ... because they are recruited or brought in with promises of payment, yes? But there have

158 *Notions of Everyday Peace*

been a large amount who have entered to get revenge. That their father was killed, their sister was raped. And many others, a large amount, enter because having a weapon in your hand gives you prestige; and some young people like this. That was from stories they have told me.

This culture of violence is not only local but also instituted and reinforced from the highest levels according to Natalia from *Fudacion Restrepo Barco*, who argues that government policies means 'solutions using weapons are strengthened every day'. She goes on to argue:

> If you have a government, like in my country, that is teaching these children ... from when they are young the army puts them in uniforms and includes military activities with civil ones ... Colombia does have a culture of violence, I think, and I say this from a personal position. I think that the government has strengthened this dialogue of conflict through weapons and not through peace. And this doesn't pertain directly to children but in various ways it arrives, like a cascade. If the government promotes that children should be soldiers for a day[2], then from above, from the highest balconies they encourage Colombia to find a solution to the conflict via weapons and with pressure, well then we are generating a culture of violence.

Countering this is complex and difficult. As Kent and Barnett (2012) argue, to counter violence requires recognition of such challenges so that responses can be identified and fostered. Such an endeavour is a conscious reaction to the effects of violence that foreshorten the future and annul collective opportunities.

In a similar vein, teacher Ana Martinez echoed Ana Milena's sentiment above, arguing that being able to build peaceful communities is very dependent on an ability to build peace within each self, and find other responses than violence. For Ana Martinez, this challenge is exacerbated by a taught passivity in which individuals feel distant from the events of conflict. For those beyond communities such as Cazucá, for whom the conflict might not be experienced so dramatically, Ana Martinez thinks that

> above all it is because we are very indifferent. ... So there is war in other places it's 'Oh, that is over there, elsewhere, it doesn't affect me, it doesn't have anything to do with me'. So we are very indifferent when it comes to peace. So I believe humans should be a little more conscientious that war affects everyone ... in any way. We have been made too passive, that we don't have enough capacity to digest it, study it, look at it, and look at the consequences. If there hadn't been so much war there wouldn't have been so many massacres. In Colombia we still haven't learned the lessons of wars that we've had and so continue to make war against others. So because of this I think we still lack a lot.

Notions of Everyday Peace   159

However, she recognises this depends on where the individual is located socially and spatially; such distancing of the conflict is not possible in Cazucá as she notes, 'And as you've seen in Cazucá, it is also relative thinking, no? It's that it is very dependent on what you associate with your surroundings'.

More than individual recognition, in response to questions about their ability to effect change or engage with adults many young people recognised the need for collective action. This is particularly evident in my conversation with fifteen-year-old Susana. Previously in our conversation, Susana had said she wanted to study so she could help families that were struggling, not only her family but other people as well. These sentiments are apparent again in her response to a discussion about whether young people can make a difference in Cazucá itself:

> I think that everything can change, but that to do that we have to help everyone equally. Not just those who are rich or very poor, but that we are all equal and we all get opportunities and money, and so then there would be help for people here, but not just here, in many places. And I am not only thinking of my future, my family, but thinking of the rest of the people.

A sense of collective responsibility and belief in the need to strengthen community ties was evident not only in Susana's response, but in several other participants also, for example in this conversation between fifteen-year-old Brayan Alexander and sixteen-year-old Felipe:

BRAYAN ALEXANDER: Yes, its like, for this. … If we are going to be equal … we need to change for *everyone*, all of this needs to change. Mmmm, well … I don't know. It is difficult … it is difficult to think of a solution because you have to fight for all the poor people in your family and you can't help them all, but you try. If this changed, then it would be possible.

The difficulty of creating a collective sense of movement, belief or change, is evident in Brayan Alexander's comment, but is explicit in Felipe's response to Brayan Alexander, when he notes that he sees adults as often selfish and that they do not think of others around them:

FELIPE: I also think that in many situations people think only of themselves. They want to improve but the only one they want to improve is themselves. And their family, maybe. And they don't say, 'Aaaiii let's all help, let's work together like a community'. No. What they wants is to get themselves ahead and not help others and they wants to get a good job and become rich, and that is the most important thing for them, and not to help others. That's how it is in this country.

Susana's belief, above, that everything can change is frustrated, according to her friends seventeen-year-old Laura and fourteen-year-old Camila

160   *Notions of Everyday Peace*

Andrea, who were also in the discussion, by adults being selfish and not thinking of other people. For these three young people, thinking of collective responsibility is something that young people do much better, and that is crucial for things to improve from their current situation. For Laura and Camila Andrea there is a responsibility in temporal terms, in their desire to make changes for their children. Camila Andrea notes that they themselves 'have to improve the future. For our children, well, for everyone'. Laura, in agreeing, also adds if they do not try and change things 'they [their children] will repeat the problems'. The conflict is not distant to young people's lives, and there are challenges to building peace amongst violence. The surrounding violences of life in Cazucá make violence an attractive response at times:

> Violence is a factor which has changed our way of seeing reality. It affects children and young people and makes them vulnerable. In Cazucá this situation is even worse.[3]
>
> (Profe Claudia, written survey response)

This perception of violence as profoundly affecting is tempered by recognition of the way in which young people find responses to such violences and reject narratives that claim that exposure to violence results, undeniably, in more violence. Ana Milena feels it is adults' responsibility to assist young people to find these pathways, but notes ultimately it is the young people themselves who must choose what to do. For Ana Milena, such assistance can take unexpected forms including prompts for creativity and more space(s) to pursue individual goals:

> And so we have to rethink what peace means and where it is, teach young people if they love to sing or to make art, well conquer with songs, yes? Conquer with a guitar, and not with a weapon.

Such fabulous imagery captures the sentiments expressed by young people in the previous section who noted that spaces such as the school as well as places like the *fundación*'s *casita* or other programs provide a space where violence is ameliorated and in which adults respect young people's opinions and engage *with* them. The manner in which the challenges of the environment, the preconceived notions of young people's place and (in)capacity, and the sentiments of young people as being able contributors should be read together. It is against this complex negotiation of place and competency that this chapter now turns to an exploration of understandings of peace, and what significance ideas of peacebuilding have for these young people.

Conceiving of Peace

Forwarding a concept of everyday-peace-amidst-violence requires not only exploring the manifestations and negotiations of multiple violences but also

Notions of Everyday Peace 161

must take into account how young people understand the notion of peace both abstractly and as a functional (or dysfunctional) concept in their everyday lives. Having considered the violent and insecure context young people live within, their responses to violence through forms of resistance and resilience, and recognising their capacity in all these facets of their everyday life for meaning making, I turn to explicit considerations of the concept of peace. Discussions with young people in response to the initial question 'what does peace mean for you?' prompted a wide range of definitions and explorations of the concept of peace. Many of these were broad and generalised and peace was defined with generic nouns and adjectives. Several of these conversations, however, complicated these ideas by introducing discussions of the role and location of the family and home, the site of the school, and the importance of friends. Additionally, discussions could invoke 'local' experiences alongside a critique of the role of the government in frustrating peace. Some young people said they could not define peace, but often provided rich discussion of how its absence affected their lives. Over thirty years ago Johan Galtung noted that research on 'peace' should always be considered to be definitionally problematic (1985, 143) and that it is in these difficulties that more useful discussion of peace can emerge. Multifaceted and necessarily partial descriptions and definitions of peace demonstrate the complexities of living in situations of insecurity as well as the varied ways young people coped and expressed resilience. The question of what peace means during the interviews was left deliberately open in the initial discussion to allow the respondents to interpret it how they wished; as a consequence the data are rich and varied and the implications for notions of everyday peace are clearly apparent.

Generalised Notions and Inability to Define Peace

In 1969, Johan Galtung identified a distinction between a conception of 'negative' peace and one of 'positive' peace – recognising even in the act of description the problems inherent in binary definitions (1969, 183). To adopt Galtung's distinction here, the idea of negative peace, grounded in an absence of 'direct' (1985, 145), or 'personal' violence (1969, 183) is strongly articulated by many young people. The idea of positive peace is more complex as it requires an 'absence of structural violence' (Galtung 1969, 183) or possible efforts to critique or transform structures which inflict or perpetuate violence (Galtung 1985, 146). In a very general sense, many of the broad definitions given by the young people in Cazucá fit one or the other of these descriptions. While for many it was the cessation or absence of violence that defined peace, for others there was a requirement for social justice and a sense of positive collective construction before peace could be seen as achieved. For some young people peace is associated generally with positive emotions or experiences. For both eleven-year-old Javier and ten-year-old Natalia peace indicated friendship and love, while her classmate twelve-year-old Ingrid said simply 'tranquillity'. Such words were invoked in other descriptions attached to people or places also.

162   *Notions of Everyday Peace*

The most universal description of peace is in opposition to violence, a very straightforward demonstration of negative peace. Peace appears when violence is lessened; violence in these contexts could be general experiences or can reference specific actors or situations. For twelve-year-old Sebastian and eleven-year-old Andrea their initial definition was very straightforward:

SEBASTIAN: How does peace appear for me?
HB: Mmhmm … [affirmation of the question]
SEBASTIAN: No, it's that there is a lot of violence. Peace is like a symbol of there not being violence.
ANDREA: Well, yes, that there would be no more violence.

For eleven-year-old Johan David it was the absence of specific groups of people that allowed peace, particularly that there are 'no *guerrilla*, [mutters too low to hear], mmm, that there aren't displaced people' (Johan David was himself, displaced). Eleven-year-old Juan Camilo identified homeless people (and more generally those with perceived social issues) as a group that challenged or prevented peace formation, which points to the complexity of intersecting perceived social and economic issues within a broader rubric of armed violence.

The conflict broadly also featured, with particular focus on the practices of conflict and the tools of conflict:

DAVID (11): For me, peace means that there isn't war with everyone else …
LUIS FERNANDO (11): No weapons in our lives.

Fifteen-year-old Susana expanded in her response on many of these features evident in other young people's answers but also includes features more often associated with notions of positive peace:

> Well, for me it's that, that there are no more injustices. For me, peace would be that the war would end completely; that there is no more injustice for the people who are poor, the people with very little resources. For me peace would be that we talk and that things end there. That, yes, that opportunities are achievable for everyone. That one person doesn't have more than others or less than others. That everything is fixed, that we speak and can say what we want, yes? That everything is fixed and there is no more violence done, that no, that you do something peacefully, where if you are going to create justice you do it for real and you don't do it violently …

This response not only expands the generalised comments about a cessation of violence but points to other elements seen as necessary for peace; in particular, concepts of social justice, the attainment of equality, the responsibility of the government, and the ability to be able to speak freely.

Notions of Everyday Peace 163

Human rights, or simply 'rights', associated closely with notions of social justice and repudiation of corruption become tied to the more general notion of an end of violence. Fifteen-year-old Sofia notes that for her peace would be that 'there is no more violence' but expanded by saying,

> and that we have respect for all rights. That even those locked up [in jail], they have rights and respect. For me, this is how peace helps, so everyone has rights. Not giving them up or taking them away, but to help everyone be okay.

While for Sofia the issue of rights involved everyone in the community, not just those in power, for sixteen-year-old Juan Carlos, the government was specifically called to account. Juan Carlos, who was particularly concerned with what he perceived as significant injustice as connected to poverty and the experience of the occupants of Cazucá as explored in Chapter Three, invoked these ideas once more in his definition of peace, also drawing upon ideas of social justice and rights:

> For me peace is being just, let's say, when you have rights, and when the government comes through on its promises, you know, that is a country that is just. It's that many governments are stealing our money, let's say, we pay taxes and sometimes that money never arrives. And so, for me, it is being just and fair, that is peace.

Evidently, while a cessation of violence is the ideal, there are many facets, in young people's opinions, to achieving that goal. Amongst these are primarily concepts of justice, equality, and recognition. These concepts are active, and are bound in a critique of the structures which perpetuate violence and which reinforce social exclusion. The exact definitions of positive or negative peace are less important; more important is the attention to both and recognising multiple experiences (see Galtung 1969, 145).

Conversations in 2016, with the FARC peace process underway but not yet signed, echoed these earlier discussions. Many young people, now in their 20s, were preoccupied with the way that, in their opinion, the peace process was so focused on specific communities – particularly rural communities – that they felt communities such as theirs were being overlooked. Among some young people there was very low levels of trust in the Santos government's ability to carry out any of the agreed outcomes, even if the peace agreement was signed. Peace, once again, is caught up in suspicions of corruption and a state that is not concerned with these communities; speaking with young people in 2016 I was reminded of Juan Carlos' scepticism five years before, of the ability or desire of the government to deliver services and support, and how this raised questions of the validity of an idea of 'peace'.

While some young people highlighted different responses or actions, or described requirements for peace to be achieved, some responded to the initial

164 *Notions of Everyday Peace*

broad question, 'What is peace to you?' by saying they could not define it. However, contrary to simplistic readings that could see these responses as apathy or ignorance, these young people could not define peace because of the situation of their lives. However, that did not prevent them from following such observations by describing processes or steps that they believed would resolve the issues, for example fifteen-year-old Paola and her seventeen-year-old friend Juliana on defining peace:

PAOLA: What is peace? I don't know. That word is difficult … we almost do not know it because here we always live with discord.
JULIANA: It is difficult.
PAOLA: It is difficult to know how to define it …
JULIANA: [interrupts] to define it …
PAOLA: … because although we might know of it, we haven't lived it.

The rejection of a clear definition of peace is linked closely to lived experience. Paola suggested that they 'might know of it' and later conversation with these young women demonstrated they could articulate the problems of building peace, the lack of individual experience of peace makes this initial response both accurate and telling for the forms of engagement young people see as practical.

This sense of peace being an unattainable or unknowable experience is also linked to the culpability of the government for perpetuating situations of exclusion and nonresponse in Cazucá.

HB: What does peace mean for you?
ROSA (15): For me, peace doesn't exist. First because, they say peace is happiness, love, where is the love? And where is the peace that we should be guided by? Well, friends of course, but [interrupted]
LAURA (17): It's because of the government…
ROSA: The government, our families. … They say that peace is in a happy home…
LAURA: Cheerful, free, happy . . .
ROSA: Yes. But, if you come into my home. … I could tell you of fights about a plate of food, about the lights, about the telephone [mobile phone], about the water, about everything! I told you we fight a lot. And so, where is the peace? Where is the love that they say you feel with that peace?
LAURA: And peace has to start from above also, from the government. Because if we want peace, first, before everything, every life needs a better, like, a better …
 [Brief discussion about the word she is looking for]
LAURA: No. A better [pauses and thinks] way, a better job, a better country, better people, [thinks for a moment] that we have jobs that …
CAMILA ANDREA: … permanent (or 'fixed', [*fijos*])
ROSA: Mmmm …

Notions of Everyday Peace 165

LAURA: Permanent, not like now.

While the three young women were adamant there was no peace presently, their narratives about the reasons why this was the case, as well as their thoughts on how to improve that situation, demonstrate the same level of complexity visible in their narratives and discussions about experiences of violence. In this discussion the conversation moved smoothly and logically between the absence of peace – associated with familial love – in the site of the local (the house) to the implication of obligations of the government in creating the conditions to allow 'every life' to have better opportunities. The implication in this discussion is of awareness between material situation, resilience, and institutional support for individual efforts.

The situations described as contrary to, or impeding, peace are seen as obstacles to a concept of lived peacefulness that includes 'better' jobs, politics, and people, in a way that could be permanent. Such narratives, while superficially depressed and lacking belief, attest to how even in difficult circumstances young people critically engage with their lives and what is required to improve such situations. To pick up on Susana's inclusion of the ability to 'speak and ... say what we want' as significant, it is this recognition of speech as a key feature in notions of peace at a local level to which I turn now.

Dialogic and Interconnected Peace

There is an important dialogic element to the construction and fostering of peace. The absence of this is also seen to contribute to ongoing violence, as evidenced in Susana's discussion mentioned previously where violence is seen as the way to solve problems not 'by speaking ... well they think it has to be violent and things aren't like that'. Dialogue in this way draws on Lederach's idea of elicitive peace where understandings of peace are relational, located in the everyday, and draw on 'ordinary language' to affect the experience of conflict (1995, 27). Dialogue – conversation, experience and relationality – is fundamental in building an argument for the serious recognition of young people as competent and contributory. Ideas of this were present at the school's Human Rights Forum (discussed at the beginning of Chapter Five), and throughout my conversations young people articulated the significance of a two-way exchange of experiences, both speaking *and* listening, as a crucial component of a notion of peace.

Several young people associated dialogue, speech, and talking centrally within their definition or discussion of peace. Fifteen-year-old Brayan Alexander links this need for speech with a sense of outcome, in this case 'justice':

> For me peace is justice, yes? Because, well, fighting is not fair or just. It is fair to speak of things, its just to talk. [Peace] is talking of things that cause fighting, and talking of things to achieve solutions, yes, with dialogue and not with violence.

166 *Notions of Everyday Peace*

While sixteen-year-old Felipe, in a different conversations, links speech with listening also:

> Peace. Peace has so many meanings ... peace is dialogue, but not only speaking because you can speak but not listen, it is dialogue with listening, and that listening to others, between people, so that we don't return to making the mistakes of the past. This is peace for me.

This recognition of the importance of not only speaking but also engaged listening and reciprocity echoes previous discussions of the importance of being heard. It is both the ability to speak and the recognition of that speech that allows an individual to 'appear in the world' – to invoke Arendt – and to effect change. If violence is associated with negation of experience and enforced silencing, it follows that speech and dialogue can be the form in which notions of peace and resilience can be built in such fraught communities, building/rebuilding the 'webs of relationships' that hold individuals together and respond to the violent abnegation of experience. In this way, young people recognising the role of speaking and listening is key in forming everyday peace.

Many of these ideas came together in discussions of peace in the context of the local community. Ideas of a cessation of violence, of working together, of respecting rights and being able, as a young person, to contribute to these things were at the heart of several responses. This discussion with twelve-year-old Alicia highlights the interrelationship between these concepts in the creation of peace, particularly in the way peace and violence are related:

ALICIA: Well, I think that we could improve the environment, and that with peace and no murders and no violence we could do more in the community, to improve for a better world, and for Cazucá, no?

HB: And what do you think about creating peace in Colombia?

ALICIA: Well, I think that peace is very good because in that way we could live like siblings together, doing many things, we could, um, we could, um we wouldn't violate other people, we wouldn't ignore people's rights, and we wouldn't attack other people.

HB: And do you think you can help in creating this peace?

ALICIA: Yes miss. I could help in creating peace. To live peacefully with other people. Tell them not to throw away their rubbish, to not do other things [trails off] ...

HB: And what does peace mean for you personally?

ALICIA: For me, what peace means is beauty, that we all could live together ... that there isn't violence, that there isn't ... that there isn't violence, that the rights of children or adults aren't violated that, well, and I also think it would be good that there isn't family violence and child abuse, all that.

HB: Do you think you can affect the future?

Notes of *Everyday Peace* 167

ALICIA: Yes miss. I think I could do things to make peace, tolerance, respect ... An end to the violence here would be good. That parents don't abuse their children, that thieves don't attack us or kill people. ... I would like for violence not to exist for me anymore so I can reach peace.

In young people's articulations of the requirements of peace, it is unhelpful to differentiate what might be seen as individual or locally focused responses from those that focus attention on the nation or government. For Alicia, peace required individual efforts to build positive relations, but she also wanted forms of embodied violence prevented and the provision of an idealised concept of rights and security – ostensibly provided by the state. There is no contradiction by Alicia when she talks about cleaning up the local environment and also desiring an end to the abuse of rights of both children and adults. In its most straightforward reading, this is an example of the function of a concept of the everyday, as linked to broader notions of peace, violence, and belonging.

Alicia's conversation with me highlights many of the underlying themes and issues around notions of peace. In all discussions with young people, whether they could 'define' peace or not, or whether their understanding of peace was linked to general themes or specific experiences, peace was an active undertaking. The young people recognised peace as something of relevance to their life and to be aspired towards despite, or because of, ongoing violence.

Conclusions

An embodied-everyday-peace-amidst-violence takes into account how young people understand the notion of peace both as present or absent in their daily lives, as well as an abstract concept. Young people's articulations of the idea of peace are reflective of this contingent and fraught understanding of their engagement and space in the world; however, rarely do they have no sense of a future or no sense of a notion of peace. Their articulations of notions of peace are frequently grounded in the realities of their everyday lives and often centre themselves as dialogical and active agents in creating or building such ideas within their lives. When adults recognise young people's capacity it enables young people to feel as if their actions have meaning in the world. However, often young people feel marginalised by these relationships which limits their ability to imagine a future where they are included.

To conceive of and theorise an everyday-peace-amidst-violence, young people's understandings of the concept of peace must be recognised both within their daily lives and as an abstract notion. Conversation, experience, and relationality are fundamental in building an argument for the serious recognition of young people as competent and contributory and are evident in many of the young people's responses. If violence is associated with negation of experience and enforced silencing, it follows that speech and dialogue can be the form in which notions of peace and resilience can be built in such fraught

168 *Notions of Everyday Peace*

communities, building/rebuilding the 'webs of relationships' that hold individuals together and respond to the violent abnegation of experience. The idea of peace, for young people remains fraught and reflective of their everyday lives. However, it is rare they have no sense of a future or understanding of peace. Ideas of everyday peace cannot be static or reified, but rather have powerful potential to release young people from preconceived forms of engagement and allows for a recognition of the way that routine and radical forms of everyday peace exist and are maintained *amidst* the multiple violences of these young people's lives.

Notes

1 For examples see, Scheper-Hughes 2004; Jutersonke, Muggah, and Rogers 2009; Maclure and Sotelo 2004; McIllwaine and Moser 2007.
2 'Soldiers for a Day' is a program run by the Colombian military that invites high school students to participate in 'army' activities for one day; the first was held in 1994 (*El Tiempo* 1994). There has been vocal criticism of the practice, aimed at familiarizing children with the 'war dynamic'. Cited in the *Child Soldier Global Report 2008*, the UN Special Rapporteur on the Right to Freedom of Opinion and Expression noted that the program 'militarize[s] the countryside' and 'ultimately endanger[s] entire villages, exposing them to the retaliation of the guerrillas' (Coalition to Stop the Use of Child Soldiers 2008).
3 Names of teachers who completed a survey questionnaire are pseudonyms. 'Profe' is a shortened form of the address *professor/a* for teachers, used by the students and myself in the school. It is used here to indicate their role and distinguish them from other respondents, including the two teachers I conducted recorded interviews with, who are referenced by their actual names.

References

Boege, Volker. 2011. "Hybrid Forms of Peace and Order on a South Sea Island: Experiences from Bougainville (Papua New Guinea)." In *Hybrid Forms of Peace: From Everyday Agency to Post-Liberalism*, edited by Oliver Richmond and Audra Mitchell. Basingstoke: Palgrave Macmillan.
Boulding, Elise. 2000. *Cultures of Peace: The Hidden Side of History.* Syracuse, NY: Syracuse University Press.
Coalition to Stop the Use of Child Soldiers. 2008. *Child Soldier Global Report 2008: Colombia.* London: Coalition to Stop the Use of Child Soldiers.
El Tiempo. 1994. "Ser soldados por un día." *El Tiempo.* www.eltiempo.com/archivo/documento/MAM-232898.
Feldman, Allen. 1991. *Formations of Violence: The Narrative of the Body and Political Terror in Northern Ireland.* Chicago, IL: University of Chicago Press.
Galtung, Johan. 1969. "Violence, Peace, and Peace Research." *Journal of Peace Research* 6(3):167–191.
Galtung, Johan. 1985. "Twenty-Five Years of Peace Research: Ten Challenges and Some Responses." *Journal of Peace Research* 22(2):141–158.
Galtung, Johan. 1990. "Structural Violence." *Journal of Peace Research* 27(3):291–305.
Galtung, Johan. 1996. *Peace by Peaceful Means: Peace and Conflict, Development and Civilization.* London: SAGE.

Jackson, Michael. 2002. *The Politics of Storytelling: Violence, Transgression and Intersubjectivity.* Copenhagen: Museum Tusculanum Press, University of Copenhagen.

Jutersonke, O., R. Muggah, and D. Rogers. 2009. "Gangs, Urban Violence, and Security Interventions in Central America." *Security Dialogue* 40(4–5):373–397.

Kent, Stuart, and Jon Barnett. 2012. "Localising Peace: The Young Men of Bougainville's 'Crisis Generation.'" *Political Geography* 31(1):34–43.

Koopman, Sara. 2011. "Alter-Geopolitics: Other Securities Are Happening." *Geoforum* 42: 274–284.

Lederach, John Paul. 1995. *Preparing for Peace: Conflict Transformation Across Cultures.* Syracuse, NY: Syracuse University Press.

Lederach, John Paul. 1997. *Building Peace: Sustainable Reconciliation in Divided Societies.* Tokyo: United Nations University Press.

Lederach, John Paul. 2005. *The Moral Imagination: The Art and Soul of Building Peace.* Syracuse, NY: Syracuse University Press.

Maclure, Richard, and M. Sotelo. 2004. "Youth Gangs in Nicaragua: Gang Membership as Structured Individualization." *Journal of Youth Studies* 7, no. 4: 417–432.

McIlwaine, Cathy, and Caroline O. N. Moser. 2007. "Living in Fear: How the Urban Poor Perceive Violence, Fear and Insecurity." In *Fractured Cities: Social Exclusion, Urban Violence and Contested Spaces in Latin America*, edited by Kees Koonings and Dirk Kruijt. London: Zed Books.

Nordstrom, Carolyn. 2004. *Shadows of War: Violence, Power and International Profiteering in the Twenty-First Century.* Berkeley, CA: University of California Press.

Restrepo, Luis Alberto. 2004. "Violence and Fear in Colombia: Fragmentation of Space, Contraction of Time and Forms of Evasion." In *Armed Actors: Organised Violence and State Failure in Latin America*, edited by Kees Koonings and Dirk Kruijt. London: Zed Books.

Scheper-Hughes, Nancy. 2004. "Dangerous and Endangered Youth: Social Structures and Determinants of Violence." *Annals New York Academy of Sciences* 1036: 13–46.

Sylvester, Christine. 1994. "Empathetic Co-operation: A Feminist Method for IR." *Millennium: Journal of International Studies* 23(3):315–334.

Conclusion

> Margins are not simply peripheral spaces. ... To suggest that margins are spaces of creativity is not to say that forms of politics and economics on the margins, often fashioned out of the need to survive, are not fraught with terrible dangers. It is, however, to draw attention to the fact that though certain populations are pathologized through various kinds of power/knowledge practices, they do not submit to these conditions passively.
>
> - Veena Das and Deborah Pool, *Authropology in the Margins of the State*, 2004, 19

As I sat with various young people in the dusty concrete playground of los Altos de Cazucá in 2010 talking about their experiences of violence and aspirations for peace, none of us could know that tentative, secret meetings were being planned between President Santos' government and the FARC leadership to discuss the possibility of negotiating an end to over half a century of conflict. The announcement of peace talks in 2012, and their subsequent slow development has occurred alongside the process of writing this book. Among some of the young people I have maintained contact with, scepticism borne of a long history of failures and betrayals became tentative hope, and more recently as steps of the agreement begin to be implemented, joy and concrete expressions of hope offered by a Colombia at peace. I watched with some disbelief when initial talks were announced but still followed the progress of the talks closely, reading every communique and summary. I woke early in the morning in Australia to watch with quiet excitement the live-stream of the August 2016 signing of the peace agreement in Cartagena, and exchanged long emotional messages with Colombian friends when the plebiscite to approve the peace deal failed in October 2016. I now watch with a cautiously optimistic but critical eye as aspects of the Final Accord are implemented and the FARC become an official political party.[1] This peace is a fragile thing. There are still many hurdles to overcome, and the formal signing and implementation is just a first step of a very fraught path.

Not all those I met in Cazucá are pleased at the process or outcome of the peace talks with the FARC. There is justifiably deep scepticism that a government who has so often been seen as absent, corrupt, and unable or unwilling to help, is now invested in issues facing marginal populations. There is justifiably deep distrust from some that a guerrilla force that for some were directly responsible for the deaths of family members and damage to their communities, is truly committed to this process or should have a role in political life in Colombia. One young friend told me in early 2017 that he still can't imagine what 'this peace everyone is talking about actually is'. He explains that 'we're still poor, there are still drug dealers on the corner, my father still can't find a good job, and the FARC are being given every opportunity. How is this peace?'. In contrast, another young friend joyfully posted on social media a photo of herself from Plaza Bolivar in Bogotá (where she had travelled up the highway to be part of the crowd celebrating the signing) posing with the Colombian flag and a peace dove painted on her cheeks, accompanied by the words 'this is the future I have waited for'.

The peace process with the FARC doesn't figure a great deal in these pages because it wasn't yet a reality for these young people and their community at the time the conversations that underpin this book took place. However, its presence now in the lives of Colombians will change conversations, prompt new possibilities, and offer potential for both positive actions and the chance to seek truth and justice. But it will also be confronted with and challenged by the complex interplay of everyday violences and resistances that have been the focus of this book, including continued violence and the rise of criminal gangs and new dangers, and the solidification of existing prejudices and animosities. These young people's lives are still lived at the interstices of possibility and insecurity, their bodies still caught up in the potential risks and possible resiliencies they have navigated their whole lives. From the mundane everyday to the national stage violence and peace remain entangled in the Colombian experience. The national attention on the peace process has allowed space for a human accounting of the costs of conflict to be heard: from regional forums, to the victims delegations, to the influence of NGOs and campaigners, and the thousands of feet on the street in towns and cities around the country marching for peace. These voices become part of the fabric of a story of everyday lives that are lived amidst violence, but with the capacity to build peace.

This book argues that an understanding of peace that is embodied, everyday, and located amidst ongoing violence can enhance both efforts to theorise peacebuilding and concrete efforts of peace making. It brings the margins to the centre of concern, legitimising the capacity and agency of young people and the resilience and collective action of social excluded, marginal communities. This book conceptualises a notion of *embodied-everyday-peace-amidst-violence* to consider the space, presence, and voice of young people as stakeholders in everyday efforts to respond to violence and insecurity, and build peace. Through this book, I have explored how young people affected by protracted conflict and living in situations of social exclusion actively understand and negotiate their everyday lives. I began with the claim that paying attention to those marginalised in understandings of peace and peacebuilding contributes to a more inclusive, representative notion of everyday peace. When young

172   *Conclusion*

people are absent from considerations of peacebuilding, we simply aren't getting a full picture of the capacity of communities to respond to violence and build peace; we aren't fully understanding peace. Respecting and engaging with young people who have been affected by protracted conflict and live in situations of social exclusion is crucial for building representative and constructive notions of peacebuilding. The challenges and opportunities for everyday resistances highlighted in my discussions with young people throughout this book demonstrate the significance of considering peace as an *embodied*, everyday encounter. In seeking the ongoing consequences of and the interconnected effects of living in situations of conflict, violence, and insecurity, it is crucial to explore the narratives of those individuals affected and who are frequently written out of the conversations.

By taking seriously the voices, experiences, and narratives of young people in los Altos de Cazucá, this book expands an emerging literature within international relations which recognises children and young people as competent actors of their lives and contributory agents to their communities. It also contributes to a growing body of evidence that discredits a notion of childhood as universal, protected, and innocent by demonstrating the ways in which young people navigate danger and foster spaces of resistance and resilience among themselves. By engaging with young people directly, by centring the margins and paying attention to the lived, everyday experiences that are often obscured by top-down, state-focused approaches to peacebuilding, this book has outlined a notion of an *embodied-everyday-peace-amidst-violence*. Through this book I have engaged with the stories shared with me by young Colombians and their community, but this attention to embodied everyday experiences of young people holds promise in considerations of conflicts and insecure environments in many other places around the world. I have sought to explore the place, presence, and experiences of young people, understood as stakeholders in a negotiation of what it means to live *cotidiano* (day-to-day) in the context of broader protracted conflict and everyday violences. An embodied-everyday-peace-amidst-violence recognises that peace is not simply an absolute absence of violence; peace is shaped through mundane and radical actions within the everyday lives of people subjected to multiple forms of violence.

In Chapter One, I situated the book within a growing body of literature that challenges statist, institutional, orthodox peacebuilding, and which seeks to pay greater attention to those excluded from these considerations. It took as its starting point the notion of an 'everyday peace'. However, it contends that these discussions, while critical of 'empty' liberal states, often do not endeavour (or fail in attempts) to 'repopulate' them in meaningful ways. This book's notion of an *embodied-everyday-peace-amidst-violence* thus centres the margins, paying attention to the embodied lived experiences that are so often written out of these accounts. This has required an engagement in theories offered by feminist international relations and embodiment theorists. These lenses allow a meaningful accounting of young people's lived experiences in

Conclusion 173

depth and complexity, and a more complete picture of what peacebuilding involves as a process at the everyday level.

In Chapter Two, I introduced the context of Colombia's history of violence and ongoing struggles for peace. This chapter allowed me to present a way of reading the conflict that outlines the broad events, institutions, and actors, but that also accounts for the everyday consequences of decades of insecurity, violence and exclusion, as well as profoundly everyday, radical efforts for peace. By paying attention to the broad historical overview, as well as various actors, and the particular history and consequences facing a specific community – that of los Altos de Cazucá – this chapter positioned the theoretical explorations from Chapter One in a specific geographic and temporal context. Together these first two chapters provided the theoretical and empirical context to unpack what an embodied-everyday-peace-amidst-violence might look like and contribute, articulated by young people in insecure marginal contexts.

In Chapters Three and Four, I explored the layers and intersections of violence that characterise the everyday life of Cazuca's young people. Bodies exist within and constitute spaces. The lifeworlds of young people – the tapestry of everyday experiences that form the foundations of being-in-the-world – are embodied and situated. When violence impinges and impedes, everyday life does not simply halt; instead, young people navigate these precarious terrains to continue living day to day.[2] In Chapter Three, I explored how insecurity is mapped within physical terrains, adopting Nordstrom's (2004) use of Auge's term non-place, a term that identifies the exclusion of the occupants of such places from broader recognition. More than this, the absence of the state in such places increases the insecurity and violence experienced by the inhabitants, circumscribing the spaces that they can occupy and move through. Such narrowing of these collective, public spaces of interaction frustrate attempts to build community and reinscribe patterns of insecurity. As well as profoundly affecting the everyday lives of the occupants of the barrio, practices of spatialised exclusion, the rendering of particular places as 'non-places' and unworthy of knowing, is a performance of influential power relations. Compounding the violent intervention by the state are the threats and violent acts of the armed gangs that control much of the territory of the community and enforce their authority by censoring movement and behaviour in the community. Young people do not simply stop, or passively receive these violences. Instead, they are able to identify these challenges and understand the impacts of such activity on their ability to move through the spaces of their neighbourhood. They respond to and challenge particular narratives about their community and the actions needed to change negative opinions about the security and safety of Cazucá. Young people actively negotiate both negative external narratives and localised spatial insecurities that constrain (but not halt) their everyday practices.

In Chapter Four, I built upon this recognition of insecure terrain to argue that the multiple violences experienced by young people in Cazucá are not

174   *Conclusion*

abstract but felt and experienced bodily. This exploration reinforces my argument for the visibility of the embodied consequences of violences in the everyday lives of such people. While the spatialised insecurity and exclusion detailed in the previous chapter highlighted the marginality of these young people, such structural issues exacerbate the violences experienced against and through the bodies of young people. The complex way radical violence intersects with mundane routines of everyday life is starkly visible in the experiences of young people in Cazucá. From the armed violence, threat, and extortion practiced by armed gangs; to the intimate violation of the bodies of women and girls through rape and sexual assault; to the insecurity and risk of teenage pregnancies and fraught personal relationships; to domestic violence and insecure family relationships, the threads of multiple violences run through all aspects of Cazucá's young people's lives.

These and other varied accounts of exclusion, spatialised insecurity, and violence that manifests at, on, and through the bodies of young people contribute to complicating dominant impressions in two ways. Firstly, young people's lives can be accounted for in more than passive voice and as more than just victims; and secondly, narratives of conflict and violence can be seen as complex and – especially in situations of protracted conflict such as Colombia's – requiring a nuanced engagement with everyday experience. While young people are not always able to avoid or prevent experiences of violence, they demonstrate a complex understanding of these multiple violences and the ways in which they affect and regulate their daily lives. Their everyday experiences are lived *amidst violence.*

Having established the fraught and difficult terrain and daily experiences of children and young people in Cazucá, in Chapters Five and Six I argue that there are ways of recognising and accounting for forms of *everyday peace*, which are conceived and practiced amidst these violences. To discuss violence in its multiple forms is not to claim such discussions as totalising. Instead exploring how young people themselves respond to and negotiate such violences challenges narratives that uncritically locate the cause of such problems solely within the spaces these young people occupy, and within and through *their* bodies, to the exclusion of more complex engagements with a broader context. Efforts to affect change, explored in Chapter Five, supported through the community and locations such as the school and the *fundacion* help ameliorate these multiple violences, allow the potential for young people to build collective understandings of resilience, and to locate their understandings of the future within day-to-day routines. Locations that foster resilience and function as spaces of opportunity strengthen young people's ability to articulate their contributions to building everyday notions of peace. While such spaces are not inviolable, they hold the potential for more peaceable engagements with the everyday.

Notions of everyday peace are informed by securing practices of *everyday resilience* against ongoing violence, and resistance in response to exclusionary practices by the state. To adequately account for the complex interplay of

Conclusion   175

violences and resilience in the lives of these young people, peace must be conceived of as not discrete from but existing amidst ongoing violence. The day-to-day activities of young people, when observed and treated as both serious and meaningful, often contradict, complicate, and subvert narratives that characterise them in simple binaries of innocent or delinquent and which exclude them from political participation. Both young people and the adults in their lives identify ways they can build resilience and foster community by resisting 'cultures of violence' that surround them. To conceive of and theorise an everyday-peace-amidst-violence, young people's understandings of the concept of peace both as an abstract concept and an everyday lived experience must be recognised. Conversation, experience, and relationality are fundamental to seriously recognise young people as competent, as is evident in many of the young people's responses throughout this book. The idea of peace, for the young people in this book, remains fraught and reflective of their everyday lives; however, it is rare for them to have no sense of what peace would mean for them or what is needed to obtain it. Thus in Chapter Six I argue that ideas of everyday peace cannot be static or reified, but rather have powerful potential to release young people (and other marginalised groups) from preconceived forms of engagement to instead recognise the way that routine and radical forms of everyday peace exist and are maintained *amidst* the multiple violences of these young people's lives.

While young people's lives are characterised by a dominant narrative of violence and insecurity, it is crucial to recognise this is not the only narrative, nor is it, at times, the most significant. Rather, the discussions that shape this book demonstrate that there is no simple way of characterising the experiences of those who live on *la loma* (the hillside). They demonstrate the problem with flattened or top-down readings of experiences of exclusion and marginalisation, particularly as they characterise young people and their lives. In paying attention to the lives and narratives of young people living at the margins, this project explores what is revealed and what is challenged when the assumed 'non-place' and the 'non-adult' are made the centre of the inquiry. Centring the margins, taking seriously the lived experience of those who live in liminal spaces, opens up a conceptual space that allows a rich, irreducible account of efforts to build peace within the everyday, amidst violence: an embodied, everyday peace amidst violence.

Margins and an Embodied Everyday Peace

This book has theorised an everyday peace that can be conceived of as embodied; recognising the physical presence of those who exist on the lived and theoretical margins of consideration. To do this, it pays attention to and builds from the narratives and lives of those in these marginalised, excluded situations. Conceiving of an *embodied* everyday peace in this way allows space for more than the orthodox peace's 'best suited' actors. Rather, it includes and recognises those on the margins and those within the shifting and fluid

176 *Conclusion*

borders who can contribute to a concept of an everyday peace. It explores how the discursive relationships between the complex everyday and the authority of the state are shaped by power, and how marginalised, local actors understand and respond to the regulatory impacts of violence and exclusion in their lives.

Understandings of young people so often fall into dichotomous categories: that of innocent victims or dangerous delinquents. Such categorisation misses the complexities of young people's *actual* lived experience in which this dichotomisation is not only insufficient but also potentially damaging. Young people are active meaning-makers and competent participants in their everyday lives and the everyday life of their community. Protracted conflict, social exclusion, violence, and insecurity profoundly affect young people, yet such narratives are not totalising. Rather, young people find ways of resisting violence, negotiating situations of insecurity and building collective resilience *amidst* the everyday violences of their lives.

The protracted conflict in Colombia has resulted in complex, difficult, and convoluted manifestations of violences in and through the lives of all Colombians, particularly young Colombians. The contribution of young people to their community and their navigation of challenges in their lives is rarely recognised but plays an important part in the life of communities, and in conceptualising the consequences of violence at an everyday level. Through building relationships with young people in Cazucá, and speaking with them about their lives and what they considered important to describe in relation to living in Cazucá, this book demonstrates the importance of consulting directly with young people and claims a space for their voices. Everyday forms of resilience and everyday sites of resistance are themselves significant. It is crucial to recognise that despite – and sometimes, because of – the violences that characterise their lives, young people have clear arguments for inclusive peace within the everyday.

In recognising young people as competent and contributory, an embodied everyday peace can be conceived of as more than abstract. Instead, it manifests as complex and counter to dichotomies of passivity and delinquency that characterises understandings of conflict-affected young people. An embodied everyday peace, articulated by young people themselves requires detailed negotiation of spatial boundaries of their daily lives, an understanding of the causes of multiple violences that they experience as violences against their bodily selves, and recognition of the validity of their aspirations for the future. The everyday, in this understanding, cannot be reduced merely to a notion of alterity to the liberal peace. Rather, an embodied everyday peace is partial, responsive, and collective. It draws on narratives and practices of resistance, resilience, collective notions of belonging, and aspirational planning for a different future. Ultimately this book argues for a more grounded approach to resolving protracted conflict and violences that make a sincere commitment to a notion of *embodied* everyday peace as its obligation and goal. This requires a recognition of the fact that everyday life manifests

Conclusion 177

not only in radical ways but in the resilience and routines of the everyday and, as a result, this book demonstrates the value of considering a notion of an everyday peace which exists *amidst* violence.

This project was driven by a commitment to the margins, emerging from feminist preoccupations, with its concomitant belief that those who occupy the margins have valid and significant contributions to make to discourses that concern their life. Such a claim is not only theoretical but also methodological. While attention to ethnographic fieldwork is emerging in international relations[3], there remains an urgent need within international relations to take seriously a commitment to ethnographic fieldwork and the voices of participants' sense-making as meaningful.

While this book has focused on Colombia, arguing its unique context can provide valuable lessons for thinking about everyday peace, the notion of an embodied, everyday peace amidst violence is instructive for other contexts affected by protracted conflict, insecurity, or post-conflict. Building on the claims made in this book that it is possible, and important, to speak of everyday peace as something that exists amidst violence, it would be useful to undertake comparative work in similar communities in other Colombian cities, as well as in other countries facing similar problems of displacement or protracted conflict. The concerns of this book also raise questions in relation to political belonging. Commenced here (see also Berents 2018), there is value in further exploration of how paying theoretical and empirical attention to the everyday lives of those relegated to 'non-places' can contribute to theorising political belonging in more inclusive ways. The strength of a notion of embodied-everyday-peace-amidst-violence is how it centres people's experiences of conflict and violence, and their capacity for building peace. In a global context of complex, protracted conflicts, lived through and between the everyday lives of individuals and communities, an analysis that starts within the everyday opens new possibilities for peacebuilding.

International relations has tended to see young people as of peripheral concern or a soft security issue. This is inadequate; young people must not be seen merely as an optional inclusion or in simplistic stereotypical ways, but rather as having capacity and political agency. If we are serious about building durable peace and strong institutions in conflict-affected contexts, we must pay attention to marginal violence and experiences, including young people, and recognise their knowledge as meaningful and legitimate. In exploring the margins, in endeavouring to centre two distinct foci of concern – young people, and what is often seen as the 'non-place' – this book has contributed a manner of rethinking the implications of young people's articulations of their everyday lives. In complicating the notion of 'everyday peace', this book has suggested new ways of expanding the boundaries of the fields of international relations and peacebuilding. It proposes and exemplifies a more tangible understanding of everyday peace and in doing so it complicates notions of violence and everyday peace as counter posed.

178 *Conclusion*

Theoretical accounts of peacebuilding, even those critical of orthodox liberal peacebuilding and which promote a notion of everyday peace, often fail to (re)populate the everyday landscape and engage in its complexities. Conceiving of peace as an embodied encounter among the complexities of the everyday – amidst multiple, interrelated violences, and through the narratives of frequently marginalised young people – is a necessarily partial endeavour. Taking young people's lives and narratives seriously recognises the difficulties of everyday violences and protracted conflict, but finds potential to build a notion of *embodied-everyday-peace-amidst-violence,* where a complex and fraught peace can be found. It is a potentially radical way of understanding peacebuilding that holds the possibility for a more inclusive, more constructive, and more responsive understanding of peace that begins in the routines and radical actions of everyday life.

Notes

1 Two valuable resources that have documented the detail of the politics and process throughout the peace talks: USIP's Virginia Bouvier's blog *Colombia Calls* as she accompanied the peace talks in Cuba and Colombia (https://vbouvier.wordpress.com), and the Washington Office on Latin America's (WOLA) *Colombia Peace* blog (http://colombiapeace.org/).
2 See also work I have undertaken with Charlotte ten Have on a theorisation of the 'skilled navigator' in communities affected by violence and insecurity in Latin America (Berents and ten Have 2017).
3 See Eckl (2008) and Vrasti (2008) for discussion on the absence of ethnography from international relations. See contributions to the volume edited by Schatz (2009) on political ethnography which compellingly argue for the value of ethnographic methods to addressing questions of power and politics (in particular Arias' [2009] piece on the potential of ethnography in Latin American contexts, and Wood's considerations of ethnography in relation to memory and politics in post civil war contexts [El Salvador in her work]).

References

Arias, Enrique Desmond. 2009. "Ethnography and the Study of Latin American Politics: An Agenda for Research." In *Political Ethnography: What Immersion Contributes to the Study of Power,* edited by Edward Schatz, 239–254. Chicago, IL: University of Chicago Press.
Berents, Helen. 2018. "Right(s) From the Ground Up: Internal Displacement, the Urban Periphery and Belonging to the City." In *The Politics of Identity: Place, Space, and Discourse,* edited by Chris and Dean Keep Agius. Manchester: Manchester University Press.
Berents, Helen, and Charlotte ten Have. 2017. "Navigating Violence: Fear and Everyday Life in Colombia and Mexico." *International Journal for Crime, Justice and Social Democracy* 6(1):103–117.
Bouvier, Viginia M. 2017. "Colombia Calls: Notes on a Nation's Struggle for Peace and Justice." https://vbouvier.wordpress.com.

Das, Veena, and Deborah Poole. 2004. "State and Its Margins: Comparative Ethnographies." In *Anthropology in the Margins of the State*, edited by Veena Das and Deborah Poole. Santa Fe, NM: School of American Research Press.

Eckl, Julian. 2008. "Responsible Scholarship After Leaving the Veranda." *International Political Sociology* 2: 187–190.

Nordstrom, Carolyn. 2004. *Shadows of War: Violence, Power and International Profiteering in the Twenty-First Century*. Berkeley, CA: University of California Press.

Schatz, Edward, ed. 2009. *Political Ethnography: What Immersion Contributes to the Study of Power*. Chicago, IL: The University of Chicago Press.

Vrasti, Wanda. 2008. "The Strange Case of Ethnography and International Relations." *Millennium: Journal of International Studies* 37(2):279–301.

Washington Office on Latin America (WOLA). "Colombia Peace: Monitoring Progress in Peace Dialogues." http://colombiapeace.org/.

Wood, Elisabeth Jean. 2009. "Ethnographic Research in the Shadow of Civil War." In *Political Ethnography: What Immersion Contributes to the Study of Power*, edited by Edward Schatz, 119–142. Chicago, IL: University of Chicago Press.

Index

adults: as knowing best for children 5; perception of young people 69, 121, 125, 145, 150, 154–157, 168; relationship with young people 121, 137, 141, 149, 154–157, 160–161; responsibility to assist young people 125, 160; *see also* young people; school, role of teachers; resilience, through intergenerational relationships

agency 4–6, 29, 30, 32, 42, 146n3; feminist approaches to 26, 40; tactical 33–34, 146n2; of young people 4–6, 12, 153–154, 177; *see also* young people; feminist IR

Altos de Cazucá, los *see* los Altos de Cazucá

armed gangs *see* gangs; los Altos de Cazucá

assassination 54, 56, 63, 110, 111; *see also* social cleansing

AUC 51, 55, 58, 68; demobilisation of 51–52, 58; *see also* Colombia conflict

Auge, Marc *see* 'non-place'

bacrim 52

bandas criminalesseebacrim

barrio 12, 63, 70n7, 83, 85, 92, 110, 111–112, 119–120; *see also* los Altos de Cazucá

Basta Ya! report 56 *see also* Colombia, consequences of conflict

belonging 9, 41, 85, 107, 133, 177; sense of as articulated by young people 96–97, 112, 133, 167; *see also* place

'best-suited' citizens 7, 27, 29, 30, 175–176; young people confounding notion of30; *see also* Richmond, Oliver

bodies: missing from accounts of peacebuilding 26–27, 33, 39; as

conceptual lenses 7–9, 12–13, 25, 39–41, 173; *see also* embodied, embodiment, embodied-everyday-peace-amidst-violence; feminist theories of bodily engagement with people

Boulding, Elise *see* cultures of peace

Bouvier, Virginia 60, 61, 178n1

Boyden, Jo and Gillian Mann 131, 141; *see also* resilience, young people's

Boyden, Jo and Joanna de Berry 6, 18n2

Burgess, Ryan 132, 141, 144

Burman, Erica 5, 25

Cazucá *see* los Altos de Cazucá

Centro Nacional de Memoria Historica 9, 56, 58

CESTRA-USIP 94, 101n3, 126n5

child: Convention on the Rights of the 5, 70n4; *see also* young people

child soldiers: "soldiers for a day" program 6n2, 158, 168n2; recruitment by armed groups of 51, 54–55, 62, 70n2, 90, 158; as used by Colombian army 54–55; *see also* Colombia, consequences of conflict

childhood 5–6; as lost 6, 12, 37; theories of 5–6, 18n2, 18n3, 153–154, 172; *see also* young people

children: inadequate support of IDP 57–59, 64, 67, 69n1, 146n4

Colegio Minutos de Dios 14, 115–116, 139; *see also* school

Coleman, Lara 87–88, 89; *see* uncivil spaces; spaces, constituted by power

Colombia: armed groups involved in the conflict 50–51, 52, 88–89; conflict 3, 9–11, 49–59, 82; consequences of conflict in 9–11, 18n8, 49–53, 54–60,

Index 181

66–69, 109, 111, 171; deaths in conflict 9, 51; forced displacement due to conflict in 10, 51, 53, 55–58, 63–64; history of violence in 9–10, 49–53, 82; illegal economies of drugs and arms in 51, 52–53, 55, 56–57; *La Violencia* in 49; legal moves to address conflict 58–60; murder of human rights activists in 10, 54, 61; *parapolitica* scandal 51–52, 56; peace efforts by indigenous communities in 61–62; peace efforts by women in 61; peace efforts by youth 6, 61, 62–63; peace process (2012–2016) 10, 59–60, 62, 151, 170–171; positive perceptions of 95, 96, 150–151, 157; US involvement in 52–53; young people's perception of 92–95, 113–116, 150, 156; *see also* AUC; Colombia 2012–2016 peace process; corruption; gangs; drugs; FARC; los Altos de Cazucá; peace; violence; young people, aspirations for the future

Colombia 2012–2016 peace process 11, 59–62, 170–171; implications for state control of land 60, 89; public opinion of 62, 96, 170–171, 163–164; referendum on 59, 61, 170; skepticism of 59, 164, 170–171; spoilers in 59, 170; *see also bacrim*; Colombia, conflict; peace; Santos, Juan Manuel; Uribe, Alvaro

community: notion of 1–2, 12, 36, 62, 86, 94, 102n4, 128–130, 133–136, 145, 159–160; *see also* los Altos de Cazucá

community organisations 140–141; *see also Fundación Pies Descalzos*

Comuna 4 11, 64–65; *see also* Soacha

conflict *see* Colombia; death; demobilisation; violence

Convention on the Rights of the Child 5

corruption 51–52, 53, 56, 93, 95, 96, 100, 163, 164

cultures of peace 36, 153

cultures of violence 145, 157

d'Costa, Bina 25, 43n3; *see also* feminist IR

Das, Veena 40–41

de Certeau, Michel 33–34, 36, 42, 146n2

death 68, 99; as a result of the conflict 9, 10, 49, 50–51, 61, 68; young people's experiences of 64, 68, 98, 105, 109, 110, 115, 120–121, 122, 139, 170–171; *see also* Colombia, conflict; violence

death threats 11–12, 54, 56, 67, 109, 110

demobilisation 10, 51–52, 54, 56, 58; *see also* AUC; Colombia 2012–2016 peace process

domestic violence *see* violence, domestic

drugs 1, 9, 53; impact on life in the community 68, 69, 91–92, 98, 100, 105, 109, 112, 156, 171; role in the conflict 51, 52, 53, 54, 55, 60; *see also* Colombia, conflict; los Altos de Cazucá; violence

Duffield, Mark 29, 34

education 136–139, 157; in los Altos de Cazucá 14, 65, 68, 136, 146n4; in Colombia 67, 132, 141; of IDPs 57–58, 146n4; *see also* school

elicitive peace *see* John Paul Lederach

ELN 9, 11, 50, 51, 55, 60; *see also* Colombia, conflict

embodied: experience as 3, 37, 39, 40, 90, 104–125, 134–136, 137, 144–145; understanding of peace 3, 8, 35–36, 40–42, 150–151, 153, 165–167, 171, 175–177; understanding the everyday as 26, 27, 32, 37–40, 104–124, 125, 149–150

embodied violence 104, 105–106, 108, 109, 110–116, 119–121, 123, 124

embodied-everyday-peace-amidst-violence 2–3, 6–9, 25, 26, 40–41, 42, 108, 144, 171–172, 175–178; *see also* everyday peace; peace, amidst violence

embodiment: feminist engagements with 8, 37–41. 172–173, 177; *see also* embodied; embodied violence; feminist IR; feminist embodiment theory; peace as embodied; Wilcox, Lauren

Enloe, Cynthia 12, 25, 38 *see also* feminist IR

ethnographic methods 6, 12–13, 18n2, 18n9, 177, 178n3

everyday (the) 4, 6–7, 15 30–34, 36, 37–41, 83, 88–89, 130, 150, 153, 154; as constantly negotiated 4, 90–101 150–151; as embodied 3, 7, 8, 37–41, 104–106, 107–108, 110–112, 171–172; as site of political engagement 7–8, 12, 25, 31, 33–35, 36, 48; as site of resilience 36–37, 128–130, 132–133, 149–151,153; as uncovering the margins 7, 8, 26, 27, 37–40, 88–89; routines of8, 15, 36–37, 99, 133–134, 135, 136–137, 154–156; *see also*

182 *Index*

resilience; peace; violence, as part of everyday life

everyday life 33–34, 37; *see also* de Certeau, Michel

everyday peace 2–3, 4, 6–8, 12, 26, 30–34, 35–36, 40–41, 42n1, 61–63, 84, 106–107, 130, 137, 141, 144, 145–146, 150–152, 161, 165–168, 171–172, 175–177; implications for peacebuilding 4, 7, 30–32, 34–35, 41–42; *see also* peace

everyday-peace-amidst-violence 37, 107–108, 144–146, 150, 152–153, 161, 167–168; *see also* embodied-everyday-peace-amidst-violence; peace, amidst violence

exclusion *see* social exclusion

family: as site of safety 67–68, 97, 119–120, 134; as site of violence 108, 115, 121–122; insecurity experienced by 54, 64, 97, 110, 111, 120–121, 158, 171; parents as positive role model 2, 121–122, 134, 140, 155; young people's contributions to 12, 67, 107, 134, 141–142, 155, 159–160; *see also* adults, relationships with young people; violence, domestic

FARC (*Fuerzas Armadas Revolucionarias de Colombia – Ejercito de Pueblo*) 9, 10, 50–51, 53–54, 59–60, 82, 89, 122, 163–164, 170–171

feminist embodiment theory: 8, 40

feminist IR 7–8, 25–26, 27, 37–39, 40–41

forced disappearances 9, 51, 54, 56, 97; *see also* Colombia, conflict

forced displacement 10, 48, 52, 55–58, 64, 67–68, 116; causes of 55–57; problems in arrival communities 11, 55–56, 64; *see also* Colombia, conflict; los Altos de Cazucá

Fundación Pies Descalzos 14, 140–143; positive perception of young people of 130, 140, 143; work in community 80–81, 140, 161

future, the: imagining change in 36, 128, 131, 141–144

Gaitán, Jorge Eliecer 49

gangs 90–92; as cause of violence 1, 12, 55, 61, 67–68, 88, 90, 98, 100, 106, 110–113, 123; belonging to 112, 146n3; presence as providing sense of security 111–112; *see also* Colombia, conflict; os Altos de Cazucá; violence

gender based violence 54, 60, 88, 113–116, 174; *see also* violence, against women's bodies; violence, against young men and boys; violence, sexual

Haraway, Donna *see* feminist embodiment theory

health care in Colombia 57, 65–67, 70n8, 118, 120–121

human rights 9–10, 32, 51, 86, 128–129, 132, 163

IDPs (Internally Displaced People) 10, 53, 57, 70n3; *see also* forced displacement

imaginative geographies 84, 87; as virulent 87–88; *see also* Springer, Simon

informal community *see* barrio

insecurity 33–37, 54–56, 171–174, 177; as connected to place 12, 35, 42, 69, 83–84, 87–88, 90, 97–98, 115–116; as lived experience 3, 4, 8, 34, 36–37, 84, 87, 90–94, 97, 107–109, 110–112, 123, 133–134, 156; of terrain 80–83, 99

Instituto Educativo Gabriel Garcia Marquez 14; *see also* school

invasiones 64, 85; *see also* barrio

IR: absence of people from mainstream theories of 7–8, 37–38, 39

Jabri, Vivienne 29

Jackson, Michael 107–108, 123–124, 135, 154

jovenes see young people

Jurisdicción Especial para la Paz see Colombia, legal moves to address conflicto

justice: formal mechanisms of 58–59; young people's sense of 93, 95, 96, 162–163, 166

Kent, Stuart and Jon Barnett 36, 152–153, 158

Koonings, Kees and Dirk Kruijt 35–36

la limpieza social 68, 111–112

la loma see los Altos de Cazucá

landslides *see* terrain, literally insecure

Lederach, John Paul 36, 153, 165; *see also* peace

Index 183

Ley de Justicia y Paz see Colombia, legal moves to address conflict
Ley de las Victimas see Colombia, legal moves to address conflict
liberal peace 7, 16, 25, 26, 27–29, 30–41, 132, 145, 176; and the non-liberal other 7, 29, 32; and the state 27–28, 34–35, 39, 132; critiques of 7, 16, 29–30, 30–41, 39, 48, 145–146; *see also* everyday peace; peace; peacebuilding; Richmond, Oliver
lifeworld 40, 106, 108, 116, 123, 125, 173; *see also* Jackson, Michael
listas negras 11, 68, 110; *see also* gangs
local peace 27, 32; *see also* everyday peace; peace
local turn 30, 42n1
los Altos de Cazucá 11–15, 63–68, 70n6, 70n7, 85–86; celebrations in the community 135–136; control contested by the state 1, 88, 90–92; efforts by occupants to respond to violence 1–2, 12, 89–90, 94–95, 97–99, 133, 134–135, 141–144; 'high risk' designation of 69; informality 1, 11, 63–65, 85; inhabitants constructed in opposition to citizens 85–87, 88, 100; insecure terrain 81–82, 99; life in 1–2, 11–14, 63–68, 90–93, 96, 97–99, 104–106, 110–120, 134–136, 141–144; negative external narratives of 1, 12, 83, 85–86, 87, 100, 142, 156, 157; presence of illegal armed groups in 67–68, 97–98, 110–112; provision of services by government 2, 66–67, 70n7, 94–96, 99, 118, 143; risks of violence in 1, 11–12, 65, 67–68, 107–109, 110–120, 160; security interventions in 1, 88; stigmatisation of 1, 12, 67–69, 83, 85–87, 90–96, 100–101, 156–167; strong sense of community in 96, 102n4, 128–130, 133, 135–136, 145, 166; *see also* community; everyday-peace-amidst-violence; non-place; peace; resilience; violence; young people

M-19 *see* Colombia, history of violence in
Mac Ginty, Roger 27, 30, 42n2
Meertens, Donny and Margarita Zambrano 54–55
Mitchell, Audra 27, 34, 43n2
motherhood 119–120, 137

Movimiento de los Niños por La Paz see Colombia, peace efforts by youth in

narratives: 2–3, 13, 17, 39; *see also* Wibben, Annick
non-adult *see* young people
'non-place' 2, 8, 16, 83, 85–87, 96, 100, 132
Nordstrom, Carolyn 35, 83, 85–86, 132, 144–145; *see also* non-place
'not-knowing' *see* non-place

pandillas see gangs
paramilitary violence 9, 50, 51–52, 56, 68, 89, 110, 112; *see also* Colombia, conflict
Parashar, Swati 38; *see also* feminist IR
Paris, Roland 27–28; and Timothy Sisk 28
passivity of children (assumed) 4–6, 101, 153–154; *see also* young people
Pastrana, Andrés 51, 53, 61, 82; *see also* Colombia, conflict
peace: amidst-violence 7, 37, 42, 151, 152, 160–161, 167–168; as absence of violence 104, 115, 161–163, 167; as action 104, 163, 165; as dialogue 163, 165–167; as embodied 3, 7, 8–9, 36, 40–42, 150–151, 153, 165–167, 171, 175–177; as end of conflict 162–163, 171; as everyday 2–3, 4, 6–8, 12, 26, 30–34, 35–36, 40–41, 42n1, 61–63, 84, 106–107, 130, 137, 141, 144, 145–146, 150–152, 161, 165–168, 171–172, 175–177; as having causes 152–153; as justice 93, 96, 163–164, 166; as unknowable 164–165; cultures of 36, 153; elicitive 36, 153, 165; emancipatory 30–31; from within 150–151, 158–159; hybrid 25, 30, 31, 32; inability to define 164–165; liberal 7, 16, 25, 26, 27–29, 30–41, 132, 145; movements for 60–63; negative 161, 163; positive 161–162, 163; *see also* Colombia 2012–2016 peace process; everyday peace, embodied-everyday-peace-amidst-violence; liberal peace; resilience; Richmond, Oliver
peace communities 61–62, 82–83
peacebuilding 3–4, 7, 11, 27–33, 34–38, 42n1, 132, 136–137, 145, 150–151, 160, 171–172
Pecaut, Daniel 69n1

184 *Index*

Pinzon Ochoa, Nelson M 68–69, 111–112

place: creation of familiar spaces 84–85; in opposition to non-place 2–3, 96, 100–101; los Altos de Cazucá as non-place 12, 83–87, 100, 173; *see also* Auge, Marc; los Altos de Cazucá; non-place; space

placing 86, 102n1

Plan Colombia 52–53; *see also* Colombia, conflict; Colombia, US involvement in

police 143; as corrupt 55–56, 91, 92; distrust of 84, 90–92, 111; physical presence in community 88, 89, 91, 100, 111; violent interventions of 1, 63, 68, 88–89, 90–92

politics of space 16, 83–84, 100

post-liberal peace 26–27; critiques of 32–33; *see also* everyday peace; liberal peace; Richmond, Oliver

poverty 10, 11–12, 35–36, 56, 63–64, 68, 106, 120–121, 136, 141–142, 163

pregnancy, teen 11, 113, 117–118, 138; as providing sense of purpose 119–120; impact on life 105, 117–119; lack of support services for 117–118, 120; *see also* sexual relationships

reparations *see* Colombia, legal moves to address conflict

resilience 2, 3, 8, 125, 130–132,133–136, 137, 141, 141–144, 152, 161; as everyday peace amidst violence 145–146; through intergenerational relationships 121–122, 137, 155–156

resistance 2, 3, 8, 40, 132–133, 135, 139, 141–142, 145, 161; as part of the everyday 30, 36–37, 130, 143, 145, 153; Oliver Richmond's conception of 31, 32–33, 61,132; *see also* Richmond, Oliver

Richani, Nazih 50, 53

Richmond, Oliver 3, 4, 26, 27–33, 34, 132; critiques of 32–33; everyday (empathetic and emancipatory) peace 7, 30–32, 34; limits of conceptualisation of the local 32, 132; on the liberal peace 7, 27–29, 31; *see also* everyday peace; post-liberal peace, critiques of

Ruta Pacifica de la Mujer 61 *see also* Colombia, peace efforts by women

Said, Edward *see* imaginative geographies

Santos, Boadventura de Sousa 87–88

Santos, Juan Manuel 53, 59–60, 67, 170

Scarry, Elaine 36, 123, 124

school 14, 67, 94, 128–129, 136–139, 141, 146n4; as affected by violence 98, 115–116, 136–137, 139; challenges in attending 57, 67, 105, 110–111 146n4; physical space of 94, 133, 136–137; role of teachers at 105, 137–138, 139; as site of lessened violence 133, 136–138, 160–161; space of opportunity 130, 137,145; positive perception of 102n4, 129, 136–139, 141, 161

security: notions of 28–29, 34–35

sex education 105, 117–118

sexual assault 51, 54, 106, 109, 113–115, 124, 125n2, 125n3, 125n4; against children 115–116

sexual relationships 106, 113–114, 117, 118–119, 125n4

skilled navigators *see* violence, navigation of

Soacha, municipality of 11, 63–64, 70n7, 86

Sobchack, Vivian *see* feminist embodiment theory

social cohesion 112, 122–124

social exclusion 12, 35–37, 83, 101, 152–153; consequences of 35–36, 120–121, 123–124, 141–142, 156–157; *see also* violence, symbolic; space

social suffering 107–108, 131–132; *see also* violence, as part of everyday life

sociology of youth 4–6, 18n2

space: as constituted by bodies 7–8, 12, 26, 38–41, 84, 105–106, 173, 175; as constituted by power relations 12, 39, 83, 84–85, 87–89, 90–92, 102n1; as policed by the state 88–89, 91–92; as rendered of little concern to the state 63, 83, 85–86, 90, 96, 173; as site of resilience 8, 16, 37, 130, 132–133, 133–134, 136–144; as supportive of youth participation 8, 128–129, 133–139, 142–143, 145, 154, 160–161; of the everyday 26, 33–34, 36–37, 83, 97–98, 100, 136–144, 154; *see also* non-place; place; social exclusion

spaces of violence 36, 37, 68, 84, 90, 97–99, 107–108, 110, 115–116, 124, 139

structural violence *see* violence, structural
Sylvester, Christine 25, 38–39, 40, 153; *see also* feminist IR
symbolic violence *see* violence, symbolic

tactical agency 33–34, 146n2
terrain: figuratively constructed as threat 84–90, 92–93, 96–97, 100–101; literal insecurity of 80–82, 99, 115–116; of everyday experiences of young people 39, 92–93, 96–98, 107–108, 149–151; of insecurity 34, 83, 106
the *fundación see Fundación Pies Descalzos*
Timochenko (Rodrigo Londoño) 59–60; *see also* Colombia 2012–2016 peace process

'uncivil' spaces 83–84, 87–88, 89–90
Uribe, Alvaro 51, 55, 60 *see also* Colombia
USA: involvement in Colombia conflict 53–55

Violence: against women's bodies 113–116, 118, 120–121, 125n2, 125n4; against young men and boys 115–116, 125n3; ameliorated by place and people 130, 133–138, 140–145; appropriation of land as 54, 55, 113; as attack on person's sense of self 100, 107–108, 154, 157, 158, 166; as banal 36; as breakdown of communal relations 35, 121, 122, 129, 157, 159, 166; as enacted on bodies 25, 109, 110–111, 112, 120–121; as exacerbating insecurity 12, 34, 88–89, 112–113; as normalized 36, 106, 108, 123; as part of everyday life 1–2, 3, 25–26, 34, 36, 37–38, 91–92, 95–98, 104–106, 108–109, 110–112, 113–118, 139–140 , 144–145, 150–151, 158–161, 170–171; as unpredictable 100–101; by gangs 1, 12, 55, 67–68, 88, 90, 98–100, 106, 110–111, 123; conflict related 9–11, 49–53, 113–115; consequences of protracted 12, 53–58, 63–67; culture of 145, 157–159; definitions of 8, 35, 36, 52–53, 107–108; domestic 91, 114–115, 121–122; embodied 7–8, 32, 39–40, 105–106, 107, 113–117, 120–121, 123, 124, 130; fear of 86, 97, 100; impact on lifeworlds 40, 108, 123,

124; intrafamilial 115 121–121; legitimizing state use of 88–89, 91–92; navigation of 37, 84, 99, 109, 171; recruitment by armed groups 146n3, 157–158; resilience in response to 131–132, 133–138, 140–145, 146, 150, 154; sexual 54, 109, 113–117, 125n2, 125n3, 125n4; stigmatisation of the community due to 35–36, 83, 85–90, 96–97, 105, 107, 152, 156–157; structural 42, 83–84, 88, 107–108, 121, 123, 152 162; symbolic 87–88, 96–97, 107, 108; threat of death/assassination 54, 56, 67; young people's perception of 1, 84, 91–92, 95–98, 100, 104–105, 113–118, 120–121, 122–123, 125, 146n3, 154–156, 161–164; *see also* Colombia, consequences of conflict; death; embodied-everyday-peace-amidst-violence; forced displacement; gangs; resilience; social suffering
voice of young people 3, 12–14, 26–27, 140, 154–155, 157, 172
vulnerability: structural 9, 34–36, 56, 108, 120

Weiss, Gail 8, 39 *see also* feminist embodiment theory
Wibben, Annick 13 *see also* feminist IR
Wilcox, Lauren 40–41 *see also* feminist embodiment theory; feminist IR
women: experience of violence 113–116, 118, 120–121, 125n2, 125n4
'womenandchildren' *see* Enloe, Cynthia

young people: agency of 4–6, 8, 12, 16, 41, 96–98, 123, 129, 133–145, 146n3, 149–150, 151, 152–157, 159–160, 167–168 , 171–172, 176; as becomings 4; as connected to community 134–136, 140; as inherently peaceable 152; as marginalized 4, 37–38, 83, 84, 100, 106, 108, 123, 130, 176–177; as resilient 130–132, 133–145; as vulnerable to violence 3, 10, 12, 53–58, 67–68, 97, 99, 100–101, 104–105, 110–113, 120–122, 158–159, 160–161; aspirations for the future 128–129, 141–144, 154–156, 164–165; definitions of 5; desired careers of 141–144, 156; everyday activities of 102n4, 133–134; friendships as important to 139, 162; in IR 5–6, 177; inclusion of 4–6, 41–42; legitimising

186 *Index*

the voices of 3, 5–6, 12–13, 26, 39, 132–133, 134, 171–172, 177; positive potential of 128–129; relationships with adults 4, 121–122, 125, 137–139, 149–150, 153–157, 165–166, 167–168; research in Colombia on 6, 61–63; research on agency of 4–6, 18n2; stigmatisation of 12, 68–69, 91–93, 96–98, 100 *see also* adults, perception of young people; child; childhood; Colombia, consequences of conflict; Colombia, peace efforts by youth; death, young people's experiences of; family; pregnancy, teen; school; sexual relationships; violence; voice of young people

youth, sociology of *see* sociology of youth